齊物
逍遙
2 0 2 5

ENLIGHTENED SOJOURN

Authored and Photographed by Wong How Man

黃效文——著

Wong How Man

Time Magazine honored Wong How Man among their 25 Asian Heroes in 2002, calling Wong "China's most accomplished living explorer". CNN has featured his work over a dozen times, including a half-hour profile by the network's anchor. Discovery Channel has made several documentaries about his work. The Wall Street Journal has also featured him on its front page. Wong began exploring China in 1974. He is Founder/President of the China Exploration & Research Society, a non-profit organization founded in 1986 specializing in exploration, research, conservation and education in remote China and neighboring countries. Wong has led six major expeditions for the National Geographic. He successfully defined the sources of the Yangtze, Mekong, Yellow River, Salween, Irrawaddy and the Brahmaputra rivers.

He conducts projects in Mainland China, India, Nepal, Bhutan, Laos, Myanmar, the Philippines, and also Taiwan. In these countries or regions, he has set up centers, theme exhibits, or permanent operation bases. Wong has authored over thirty books and has received many accolades, among them an honorary doctorate from his alma mater, the University of Wisconsin at River Falls, and the Lifetime Achievement Award from Monk Hsing Yun of Taiwan. He has been invited as keynote speaker at many international functions.

In 2023, the University of Hong Kong established the Wong How Man Centre for Exploration in order to perpetuate the legacy of his work into the future.

黃效文

《時代雜誌》在二〇〇二年曾選黃效文為亞洲二十五位英雄之一，稱他為「中國最有成就的在世探險家」。*CNN* 報導過黃效文的各項工作超過十二次之多，其中還包括主播 *Richard Quest* 的三十分鐘專訪。探索頻道也為他做的工作製作了好幾個紀錄片。《華爾街日報》也曾用頭版報導過他。

黃效文自一九七四年開始在中國探險。他是中國探險學會的創辦人和會長，這是個非營利組織，致力於在中國偏遠地區及鄰近國家的探險、研究、保育和教育工作。他曾經在美國《國家地理雜誌》帶領過六個重要的探險。他成功地定位的源頭包括長江、湄公河、黃河、薩爾溫江、伊洛瓦底江及雅魯藏布江。

他的學會主導的文化和自然保育項目橫跨中國和鄰近的國家，包括印度、尼泊爾、不丹、寮國、緬甸、菲律賓還有台灣。黃效文著作的書超過三十本並獲得過許多榮譽，他的母校威斯康辛大學頒發給他名譽博士學位，星雲大師也贈與他「華人世界終身成就獎」。他也是許多國際會議裡的專題演講人。

二〇二三年，香港大學成立了黃效文探險中心，以傳承他畢生的事業，並力圖讓他的精神與貢獻在未來繼續閃耀。

Preface

Yes, it is about time I go for an upgrade. It has taken me years to go from an Underwood typewriter to an IBM Selectric, then writing with WordStar on the Osborne 1, a 26-pounds portable computer, for over fifteen years to finally using Outlook on a Notebook. In-between there were tweets of sidetracked novice mechanical or electronic machines. Nonetheless, today I still use a fountain pen and a small pencil with eraser that I keep in my travelling bag, something almost sacred and essential like a security blanket for my writing. As the world spins faster, I tend to hold on to the past ever tighter, nostalgic it may be.

So for this book, the eighth in a series by the same title of "Enlightened Sojourn", I will experiment with an upgrade. But only in part as an exercise. It is January 2025 and the dawn of the new app DeepSeek rolling out in competition to ChatGPT. It posts such challenges that the top chipmaking company Nvidia lost almost US600 billion in valuation overnight, with many leading AI firms stock prices turning south. I never download apps, but asked my research assistant to help ask both

DeepSeek and ChatGPT to write a 50 words Foreword on modern exploration in China and Southeast Asia. While exploring the latest tech advances, I never forget legacy of our past. So I asked each app to pair up its respective Forewords with a short Chinese traditional poem, with English translation to match. Below are the results:

DeepSeek: Modern exploration in China and Southeast Asia blends cutting-edge technology with cultural curiosity, uncovering hidden ecosystems, ancient civilizations, and sustainable solutions. From mapping uncharted caves in Guangxi to studying biodiversity in Borneo, today's explorers tackle environmental challenges while preserving the region's rich heritage, revealing new insights into our interconnected World. (exactly 50 words, maximizing return)

ChatGPT: Modern exploration in China and Southeast Asia focuses on scientific research, environmental conservation, and cultural preservation. Expeditions uncover hidden ecosystems, ancient civilizations, and geological wonders. Urban exploration and technological advancements drive discoveries in deep-sea, underground, and remote landscapes. These efforts expand knowledge while balancing development with heritage protection. (48 words, two short of requested)

As with the Chinese traditional poems, below are the respective results:

DeepSeek:
遠山藏祕境，
碧海隱星晨。
步履尋無盡，
心隨天地真。

Distant mountains hide secret realms, Azure seas conceal the stars. Endless paths await the wanderer's steps, The heart follows the truth heaven and earth.

ChatGPT:
踏路雲深處，
星晨引夢行。
山高疑無盡，
心遠自通明。

Treading paths where clouds run deep, The stars guide dreams ahead. Mountains rise as if unending, Yet a distant heart sees clear.

Neither apps care about translating the poem in rhymes which is standard for Chinese poems. Incidentally, each respective poem uses two terms with four words total being the same. Thus I decided to create my own poem and its translation as below, also repeating those four words each used within their poem to have some conformity. It may or may not be better, yet certainly more personal to my own liking. This preface is written while sailing far at sea off Palawan in the South China Sea, or the West Philippines Sea, or even the West American Sea, if someone wants to stretch it.

萬里星晨路，
探尋天地間。
乾坤雖無盡，
神遊海與山。

Ten thousand miles of galaxy road, Exploring sky and earth from within. Cosmo though is boundless, Sea and mountain journey in between.

Smart as these apps, or programs, are, they can only produce generic answers using few to no adjectives, never personal or emotional, let alone replicate or replace my own first-hand experience in exploration. In fact, it won't even match second-hand information I personally collected from the mouth of people I came across during my exploration career. Yet, their respective Forewords are filled with politically and socially correct terms often used, and overused, by this generation.

Earlier this year, Bhutan's Queen Mother, her daughter and grandson visited Hong Kong. The 11-years-old grandson Vairochana Rinpoche, a reincarnated lama, is extremely wise and knowledgeable for his age. I thus asked this young Buddhist master to write yet another Foreword in fifty words. His writing is in the following pages, succinct and right to the point.

I am not bragging about past exploration achievements, but the here and now of our work. I always reminded myself that it is not what you have done that counts, but what you have done lately. Some such stories collected from others, as well as those of my own, are here in the following pages of this book. I hope you will enjoy reading them. As with the apps, capable as they are, cannot bring the story to life, or life to the story.

前言

舊鋼筆在稿紙上暈開最後一滴墨，電子鐘跳到了二〇二五年。

一切都是時候該更新了。

我的「寫作工具」演進史，始於安德伍德打字機沉重的機械按鍵，經歷了 IBM 電動打字機流暢的球形字模，又再重達二十六磅的奧斯本一號「可攜式」電腦上，與 WordStar 文書處理程序相伴十五載春秋，最終來到了如今筆記型電腦上的 Outlook。其間我還零星嘗試過各種機械或者電子設備，只是大多半途而廢。

然而，不管電子科技怎樣更新迭代，時至今日，我的包裡仍長年放著鋼筆和帶橡皮擦的短鉛筆，像某種帶著體溫的護身符，在數位洪流中成為我小小的「安全網」。世界轉得愈來愈快，我卻把過去的緩慢節奏抓得更緊，這或許是念舊使然。

不過在《齊物逍遙》系列的第八本裡，我決定「與時俱進」一點，嘗試些新玩意。時值二〇二五年一月，「DeepSeek 深度求索」問世，大大挑戰了 ChatGPT 的地位。其勢頭

之猛，竟讓半導體巨頭輝達市值一夜蒸發六千億美元，多家頂尖 AI 公司股價應聲下跌。

我請我的研究助理測試一下 DeepSeek 和 ChatGPT，分別交給他們「每人」兩個任務，一是以中國與東南亞現代探索為主題，寫一段五十字的序言體英文短文，二是就以探索為一個大主題，寫一首傳統的四句五言詩。

第一道測試的結果，DeepSeek 剛剛好給了我五十個英文字，ChatGPT 則「缺斤少兩」，只有四十八個字。熟悉英文的朋友可以自己對照一下兩個版本，給出你的評價。

第二個任務，兩首漢詩的原文如下：

遠山藏祕境，碧海隱星辰。步履尋無盡，心隨天地真。 作者：DeepSeek
踏路雲深處，星辰引夢行。山高疑無盡，心遠自通明。 作者：ChatGPT

兩位考生顯然都不在乎平仄押韻，這本是漢詩最基本的格律。不過有趣的是，它們生成的詩作竟不

約而同地使用了一些相同的字詞。於是，我決定自己寫一首詩，同樣用上這些詞，算是主動與兩位「詩人」呼應一下。可能未必更好，但一定更貼近我的本心。

此刻，我正乘船航行於巴拉望外海——這片水域，史上稱之為南中國海，有人堅持更新命名叫西菲律賓海，若真要抬槓，或許還能冠上西美利堅海的名號。波濤搖晃著筆身的投影，而詩句正從浪尖誕生：

萬里星晨路，探尋天地間。乾坤雖無盡，神遊海與山。

在我看來，這些人工智能再聰明，終究也只能產出公式的答案。貧瘠的形容詞，空洞的情感，更遑論模仿或取代我在探索途中親身經歷的點滴。那些從偶遇的旅人口中親耳聽來的故事，那些帶著呼吸與溫度的隻字片語，是冰冷的程序永遠無法做到的「真實」。

今年初，不丹四代國王的皇后，攜帶公主女兒與十一歲的外孫毗盧遮那仁波切造訪香

港。這位年幼的活佛，眉宇間流轉著超乎年齡的智慧。我於是也請他為本書撰寫一篇五十字的序文。其文字洗練，意蘊深遠，敬錄於後頁，以饗讀者。

我向來不願做探險勳章的陳列者，只願忠誠地紀錄此時此刻，每時每刻。多年來，我總是提醒著自己：昨日攀過的山峰皆成雲煙，此刻丈量的土地方見真章。本書中收錄著我從別人那兒聽到的故事，也有我的親身經歷和感悟，希望您讀到這些文字時，能體會到它們獨特的生命力。

探險家，求知若渴之人。
察世間之奇觀，裨益眾人理解並珍視萬物之美。
黃效文，終身探索不斷。
尋寰宇之奧妙，筆耕以共享其成。

因為再精密的演算法，也模擬不出篝火旁故事裡跳動的光，更複製不了講述者眼中，那片星空的倒影。

Foreword by Vairochana Rinpoche
Prince Ngawang Jigme Jigten Wangchuk of Bhutan (6.2013)

An explorer is one who is hungry for knowledge. To see the world and observe its curiosities, we begin to understand and value its beauty.

Wong How Man is a lifelong explorer. He is one with wisdom for he seeks to understand the world around us, and shares through his writings.

序
毗盧遮那仁波切

探險家,求知若渴之人。
察世間之奇觀,裨益眾人理解並珍視萬物之美。
黃效文,終身探索不斷。
尋寰宇之奧妙,筆耕以共享其成。

目次

YOUNG EXPLORER FIASCO 不走尋常路的少年探險家 —————— 020

CHINESE TRADITION SURIVAL & REVIVAL (Part 1) 故鄉之外的故鄉（上）—————— 034

CHINESE TRADITION SURIVAL & REVIVAL (Part 2) 故鄉之外的故鄉（下）—————— 050

SWAN SONG @ SWAN LAKE Curtain call of an indigenous Ainu lady
天鵝湖畔，餘音未散 與阿伊努人的不期而遇 —————— 070

RYUKYU ISLANDS Some provocative thinking on names
琉球群島 一名之思，萬邦之鏡 —————— 092

NEPALI STRANDED IN TIBET At long last citizens of China
被困在西藏的尼泊爾人 成為中國公民的他們 —————— 122

GYIRONG TO KATHMANDU Sojourn south of the Himalayas
從吉隆到加德滿都 喜馬拉雅南麓漫遊 —————— 142

ANNAPURNA Deadliest mountain in the world
安納布爾納 萬仞絕命處，世界第一巔 —————— 164

MUSTANG Guerilla hideout south of the Himalayas
木斯塘的暗哨 康人游擊隊的藏身之處 —————— 180

FIRST RESORT IN JAPAN circa 1878 Still leading in many ways
日本首家度假酒店 百年風華 典範猶存 —————————————————— 192

GIRL AT CENTER STAGE (Part 1) And the Hong Kong Connection
照片中央的女孩（上）她與來自香港的人們 ——————————————— 214

GIRL AT CENTER STAGE (Part 2) Friendship first Competition second
照片中央的女孩（下）友誼第一，比賽第二 ——————————————— 236

NATURE in future LESS RESERVE 大自然的未來 少一分保留，多一分自由 ———— 256

EXODUS OF TWO ISLAND COMMUNITIES IN 1955
18,000 civilian human shields saving Chiang Kai-shek's 10,000 troops (Part 1)
一九五五年大陳孤島的船與影 人肉盾，掩護撤離 ——————————————— 274

ABANDONED AND RESETTLED Two island communities of Mainland China (Part 2)
廢墟之上，潮聲歸來 被拋棄的大陳島和它重生的傳奇 ———————————— 294

不走尋常路的少年探險家

YOUNG EXPLORER FIASCO

Natuna, Indonesia – January 24, 2024

Natuna, Indonesia – January 24, 2024

YOUNG EXPLORER FIASCO

"It is great you are driving so slowly so that I can take in the street scene and absorb the spectacular view." I turned sideways and spoke to Dian who was behind the wheel of this nice Toyota van. "I don't have a driver's license so I must drive slowly," came his answer.

We had just stopped at the only traffic light in the town of Natuna, a far-off island in Southeast Asia, somewhere in the seas between Singapore and North Borneo. A third red light jumped up inside my heart beside the two others that faced me on the street with its many motorbikes. "What do you mean you don't have a license?" asked this fearless but inquisitive explorer.

I came from this island, and we never needed a license to drive a boat," Dian answered casually as if it was quite normal. "So, when I went to Jakarta in 2022, I rented a car. They didn't ask for my license, and I was driving first time with a stick shift, using only the first gear." Dian's story continued, "Soon the policeman stopped me, as I was going too slow and blocking up traffic. I had no license and told him the engine had some problem, so he simply gave me a ticket which I never paid. Gradually I learned to use the second gear and move faster. Now I can drive quite smoothly. It is so relaxing, just like playing a video game, and I am very good at that," he became more talkative, while I held even tighter to my seat.

Dian's last laugh / 迪安的微笑

"You know, I learned my English playing video games. Up till two years ago, I was ranked number three in Southeast Asia at the hot game of Black Desert. Our internet is real slow, as I was living in this very far-away island of Sedanau. My grandmother was Chinese and my grandfather was from Natuna." I sat up a bit as I listened to what seemed like a tall tale from a young man of 28. In some ways, I can relate to his story as I saw a Chinese temple sitting next to a Mosque at a waterfront community.

"Despite slow internet playing the game, I shot up in the rank and became known in this gaming community, and I had my own gang of admirers among gamers. They would not believe that I came from a small remote island. I was invited to visit these online friends I had made. One even invited me to Kyoto, and I stayed there for four days, then near Manila for another four days. Same with Singapore where I also visited. Playing the game is like a full time job of eight hours a day. Finally, I felt it was time to do something else more serious, so I sold my account to someone in Singapore for S$5,000."

YOUNG EXPLORER FIASCO   023

"My father started wondering how I suddenly gotten rich. But I gave some of it to my parents, bought my sisters new clothes and got myself a new phone and a second-hand motorcycle," Dian kept talking while driving. At one point the road was next to the edge of a cliff over the ocean. I wanted to ask him to concentrate on driving but the story got more and more incredible. I started forgetting about the long distance we were traveling, from one end of the island to the other end, a total of 65 kilometers. By then I had resigned myself to laying my life in the hands of this daredevil novice driver. Whenever it came to a bend, he would slow down to a crawl that was more reassuring, somewhat that is.

"Someone from Taiwan offered me a job there, but I feel attached to Natuna, in particular to my home island village, so I declined," continued Dian. I remember his name as the end of Celine Dione. I also joke to my team to call him Yoda, though his actual game persona I found out is "Family Name: Voltz, Character Name: Voltz, Class: Archer, Level: 63, Rank server SEA server before merge: #3 Archer, Period: 2020-2021."

My readers may mistake me as also a game expert. I admit to playing "Pong" while in college, and later "Space Invader", but that's all to it. I have never ever touched the subject in decades.

By now, Dian had demonstrated the truth of his driving story. After we pulled into a gas station, he stepped out of the car to fetch the service attendant. Suddenly Bill yelled out, "The car is rolling back!" Dian had forgotten to put on the parking emergency brake. I quickly leaned over to find the brake and pulled it up. Now I fully understood why his full name was Dian Riski Anugrah. His

Water edge Chinese temple / 岸邊的中式廟宇
Pagoda & Mosque neighbor / 毗鄰而立的寶塔與清真寺

One end of Natuna / 納土納的一角

middle name was most fitting.

The more I talked with Dian, the more I found out his knowledge base was so much broader than just that of a receptionist at the front desk of the posh Adiwana Resort hotel I checked into two days ago. I started pondering having Dian take me across the ocean to his village on Sedanau Island. (The spelling comes out underlined in red as "incorrect", but it is perfectly fitting in my dictionary.) Dian said there is a sizable community of Chinese descent there and a population of a rare monkey. But a visit will have to wait until I can find an excuse to convince my directors why I should explore so far, yet so close to the sensitive and controversial Nine Dash Line. And then I would ask to start a new project there, with Dian being our future project manager.

At the end of a three hours' drive, and adopting a laissez faire attitude of island style living, we reached our destination for lunch - a make-shift restaurant by a pristine ocean side with clear water. By then, I am totally convinced that my driver is not an explorer in the making, but a bona fide one worthy of a medal. He has delivered the four of us safely from one end of the island to the other end. Now the question is, will I make it back safely!

印尼 納土納 二〇二四年一月二十四日

不走尋常路的少年探險家

「你開車挺慢呀，這樣挺好，我能好好欣賞一下窗外的風景了！」我們正坐在一輛行進中的豐田麵包車上，我側過身，愜意地對駕駛席上的迪安說道。

「啊，我必須得開慢點，因為我沒有駕照。」

汽車在納土納這個小鎮唯一的紅綠燈前停下。這座東南亞的偏遠小島，坐落在新加坡與北婆羅洲之間的汪洋大海上。隨著紅燈亮起，我的心裡好像也響起了警笛，閒適感一掃而空。

「你說你沒有駕照，是什麼意思？」作為一個無所畏懼、好奇心旺盛的探險者，我此刻也不受控地愣愣問道。

「我從小就在島上長大，我們開船一直都不需要駕照。」迪安很隨意地回答，好像這是一件理所當然的事情。「二〇二二年我第一次去雅加達時租了一輛車，租車行也沒跟我要駕照，我就直接上路了。那是我第一次開手排檔的車，只會用一檔。」

「沒一會兒我就被警察攔下了，因為我開得太慢，導致交通堵塞。我告訴警察車子出

了點問題，他就給我開了張罰單，也沒查我駕照。不過，也正是因為沒駕照，所以我也不用交罰款啊。」

他語氣輕鬆得像是在聊一場電子遊戲。「後來我慢慢學會了用二檔，速度也快了起來。現在我開車已經很順手了！開車就像打遊戲機一樣輕鬆，我遊戲玩得特別好。」

他越聊越起勁，而我則抓緊了胸前的安全帶，心裡默念平安無事。

「其實我就是靠玩電子遊戲才學會英語的。兩年前，我還打到過《黑色沙漠》東南亞服排行榜的第三名。」《黑色沙漠》是一款韓國開發的網遊，在亞洲地區非常火爆，目前全球玩家總數已經超過五千萬。

迪安自豪地說：「不過我的網速太慢了，因為我家在一個很偏遠的小島上——塞達瑙島。我奶奶是華人，我爺爺是納土納本地人。」

聽到這兒，我不禁坐直了身子，開始認真聽起這個二十八歲的年輕人的「傳奇故事」。我對這裡的華人社區很感興趣，剛剛我們還在一個靠海的小村裡看到了一座緊挨著清真寺的華人廟宇。

Only red light in Natuna / 島上唯一的紅綠燈
End of drive / 路的盡頭

YOUNG EXPLORER FIASCO   029

「雖然網速慢，但我還是衝上了榜三，算是這個遊戲圈子裡的風雲人物，粉絲們都不敢相信我來自那麼偏僻的小島。」迪安繼續說。「幾個遊戲裡認識的網友還免費邀請過我去他們的國家玩。我去過京都，在那兒住了四天，還去過馬尼拉、新加坡。」

「當時玩遊戲就像是我的一份全職工作，每天要投入八小時。後來，我覺得該做點正經事了，我就把我的遊戲帳號賣給了一個新加坡人，賣了差不多五千新加坡元。」

「拿到錢以後，我先給了爸媽一部分，又給我妹妹們買了新衣服，還買了新手機和一輛二手摩托車。我爸當時特好奇，我怎麼突然變有錢了。」迪安繼續滔滔不絕地講著。此時，公路已經貼著懸崖邊蜿蜒，我很想提醒他專心開車，但他的故事實在太吸引人了，我聽得投入，甚至沒印象車程有多長。其實，我們已經從島的一頭到了另一頭，總共開了六十五公里。到後來，我已經放棄糾結，把生命安全完全交給了這個來自「敢死隊」的「老」司機。不過每當遇到彎道，他都會把車速降至爬行的程度，這倒讓我安心了點。

「有人從台灣給我介紹了一份工作，但我更想留在納土納，尤其是我家鄉的那個小島。所以我拒絕了。」迪安說。

迪安的名字的發音總是讓我聯想到歌手席琳・狄翁。又因為他聰明又幽默，所以開玩笑時我還給他起了個外號，《星際大戰》裡的角色「尤達」。不過後來我發現，他在《黑色沙漠》裡的網名更加有趣，是代表了力量與速度的「電壓」一詞的變體，聽起來科技感十足。遊戲資料顯示，他選的角色身分是弓箭手，等級六十三，二〇二至二〇

Natuna water edge homes / 納土納水上屋

Seaside restaurant / 海邊小餐廳

二一年期間在東南亞伺服器排名第三。

或許大家聽我說這些，會誤以為我也是個電子遊戲迷，但我得承認，我的電玩經歷僅限於大學時玩過美國雅達利推出的那款《乓》和日本太東的《太空侵略者》，此後幾十年我再沒碰過遊戲機了。

事實勝於雄辯，迪安的傳奇駕駛技術終於在我們去給車加油的時候得到了完美驗證。當時，「老司機」迪安把車開進加油站後，悠哉悠哉地下車去找服務員。就在這時，畢博士突然大喊：「車在往後滑！」

原來是迪安忘了拉手煞車！我趕緊探身過去，手忙腳亂地找到手煞車，一把拉了上去，才堪避免了「倒車事故」。就在那一刻，我終於徹底明白了迪安全名的深意。他的中間名的讀音，完完全全就是英語「風險」一詞的發音。這名字給他可謂是名副其實，命中註定。

這些天，隨著我對迪安更深入的了解，我發現他遠不止是一個豪華度假酒店前台的普通接待員。他的知識面廣得令人驚訝，超出了我的預期，頭腦也十分靈活。我開始認真考慮，是否該讓他帶我跨過大海，去他位於塞達瑙島的家鄉看看。迪安說，那裡有一個頗具規模的華人社區，還有一種非常稀有的猴子。

不過，這次探訪得先按下不表，我還需要找到一個合適的理由來說服我的董事會，去支持我探索一個既遙遠又靠近敏感且爭議不斷的「九段線」的地方。但其實，我已經開始在心裡盤算：「將來能否有機會在那兒啟動一個新項目，並讓迪安擔任項目經理呢？有這樣一位『風險』與『能力』並存的年輕人帶隊，想想就覺得會驚喜不斷。」

在經歷了三個小時「提心吊膽」的車程後，我們終於抵達了午餐目的地，一個簡陋卻別有風味的小餐館，餐桌旁邊就是一片清澈見底、毫無汙染的海岸線，整體風格就像這座島嶼的氛圍，隨遇而安。

此時此刻看著眼前的迪安，我深刻地意識到，我們的司機並不是什麼所謂的「探險家潛力股」，而是一個當之無愧的「完成式探險家」。他竟然成功地把我們四個人從島的一端安全送到了另一端，激動得我甚至想給他發一枚獎章。

不過，現在最重要的問題是：「回去的時候，我們還能一樣安全到達嗎？」

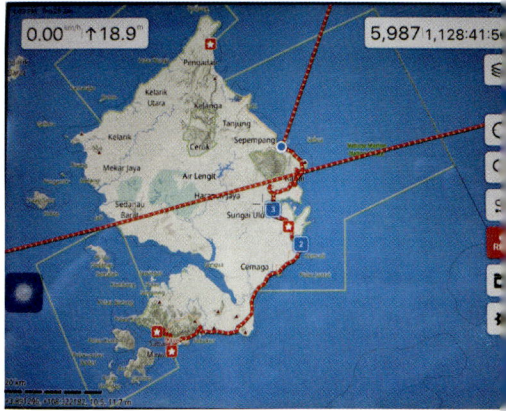

Natuna in middle of ocean / 納土納位置圖
Route driven by Dian / 迪安駕駛的路線

YOUNG EXPLORER FIASCO　　033

故鄉之外的故鄉（上）

CHINESE TRADITION SURIVAL & REVIVAL
(Part 1)

Singkawang, Indonesia – January 31, 2024

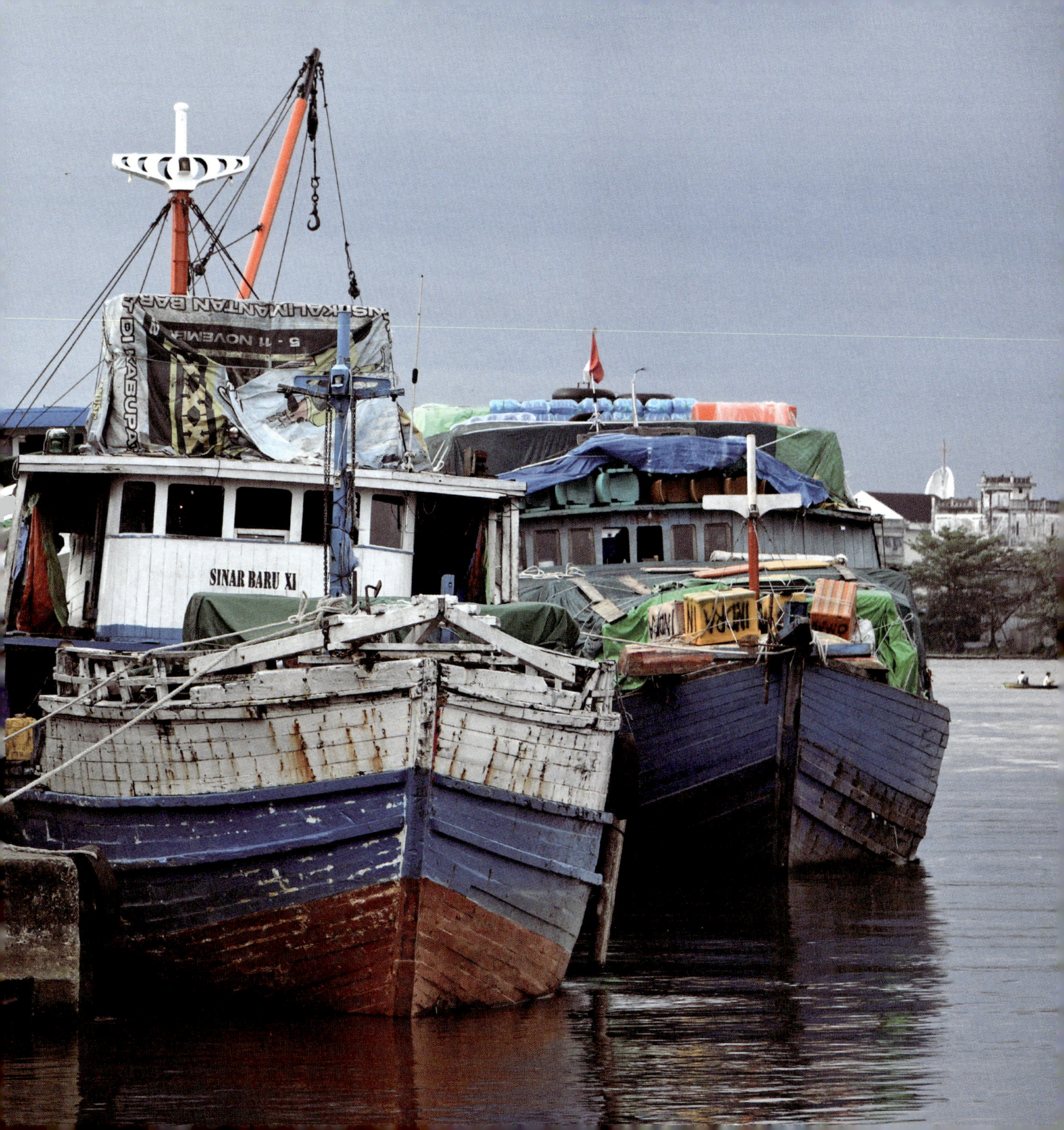
SINAR BARU XI

Singkawang, Indonesia – January 31, 2024

CHINESE TRADITION SURIVAL & REVIVAL (Part 1)

Singkawang, in Hakka Chinese meaning "Mountain Mouth Ocean", an area situated between mountains where a river estuary opens into the ocean, is hardly a name familiar to anyone. But Jiang Youcuo's six sisters, all living in Hong Kong now, are originally from this small town of around a quarter million people near the banks of the Sungai Sedau River in West Kalimantan of Borneo in Indonesia. Today, over half of the population there are Chinese with most being multi-generation descendants of early Chinese immigrants from Guangdong Province who came seeking a better life overseas. Thus, Singkawang is also known to locals as the New Gold Mountain, while the Old Gold Mountain refers to San Francisco. Chinese here figure that the proportion of Chinese in this town may actually exceeds 80%, defying the government census.

"My father married all my six sisters off to Hong Kong one after another," said Jiang. "One lives in Mongkok, one in Kwun Tong, one in Shatin and one in Ma An Shan," he rolled out these names in one breath as if he was totally familiar with all these places in Hong Kong.

"Why didn't your father also marry you off to Hong Kong?" I asked with some curiosity. "Are you kidding?" Jiang answered with a laugh. "Usually, a man in Hong Kong seeking a wife overseas is a working-class single immigrant from China, as no local woman would want to marry him. No one in his right mind in Hong Kong would want their daughter to be married to someone from such a remote place that no one has ever heard of," Jiang added in a matter-of-fact way. "There are special agents specializing in matchmaking and arranging such marriages of women to distant lands. For me, I can only stay home and make the best of it, making a living," Jiang exclaimed with a sigh. Jiang does not speak Chinese but crisp English, as he was educated in Bangalore in India. Today he is a restauranteur with two Chinese seafood restaurants in town.

City center Mosque / 市中心的清真寺

On his business card, Jiang's name is Abidin, a Hindi Indonesian name but phonetically sounding like Kepiting, meaning "crab" in Indonesian. Crab he does sell, and other seafood from the nearby coast and the river. I checked inside the kitchen and the chef was a young veiled Indonesian woman. We ordered steamed fish, tiger prawn and squid for our dinner just as the police chief and his underlings in uniform marched into the restaurant. They too ordered a sumptuous meal of seafood, clearing the remaining prawn and squid. In a town like this, the police chief holds sway, as he can be seen with his fully decorated uniform in many of public posters and murals throughout town. Having the police chief choose your place to have his meal is like having a Michelin star of recognition for your restaurant. Whether he pays or not is another matter.

CHINESE TRADITION SURIVAL & REVIVAL (Part 1)

Chinese temple & teahouse / 中式廟宇與茶館
Old style hotel / 傳統風格酒店

Joining us for our meal was another famous character of Singkawang. Dai Chijian was born in 1957, the year of the Scorpion Chicken. He recounted that he is the fourth generation living in Singkawang. His father was born in 1915 and was weak and sick, almost dying at a young age. So his father was sold to and adopted by the most worshipped God of Stone Temple. Thus father's name was changed to Dai Shi Cheng (Stone Love).

When eight years old, his father was sent to Shantou (Swatow) to study at a Jesuit American Missionary School. When the Japanese invaded Peiping (Beijing) in 1937, he was in college and tried to join Chiang Kai-shek's air force, but was rejected, as the minimum weight had to be 50 kg and his father was one kilogram short. He was smart and a great swimmer but had no chance to fight the Japanese. "He was good looking, and when Alain Delon met Brigitte Bardot, they got married," Dai recounted his family history with the drama of a storyteller.

As the story went, Dai Chijian, the last of two sons and four daughters turned out to be the favorite in the family, and naturally the favorite in town. He studied in the famed schools in Pontianak followed by attending two of the universities in Jakarta, eventually becoming a civil engineer. He worked at the Universitas Panca Bhakti of Pontianak and became Dean of Technology in 1987, quoting Dai in his own words, "the youngest and most

Singkawang city / 山口洋城

handsome Dean in Indonesia." In 1988 he joined the government, and... so on and so forth. I was given a long list of his titles until my head got dizzy. These included several martial arts and clan titles and recognitions.

Dai is known as the most knowledgeable historian/scholar of the town, as evidenced by his oral recounting of Singkawang's past once he sat down at our table. The rainy season had started and it had been pouring since we arrived. I took on an occasional drop, as there was a hole in the corrugated roof over my head. Dai's head, on the other hand, was revving on high rpm, and his speech seemed to be having difficulty keeping pace with his thoughts, starting a new sentence before the last one was finished. He had a huge vocabulary and spoke of man as "Homo sapiens", dropping names and dates better than yours truly, who is well known for connections and historical stories.

But one name stood out in particular, which Dai repeated many times. Luo Fongbo is mentioned in many historic records of the region. In the year 1777, Luo turned his Lan Fong Company, a clannish bodyguard mercenary type outfit, into the Lan Fong Republic, a country controlling a large tract of land in West Borneo. But when he paid tribute to the Qing Court in China, he retained the company's name in a humble manner. His country lasted until 1884, when the Dutch assimilated the Republic and installed a puppet government. The Republic was finally annihilated altogether in 1912 upon the fall of the Qing Empire. At that point, it was folded into the Dutch East India Company, a pseudo-commercial colonial operation.

Some legends of Chinese arrivals went much further back in history, to the Song and Ming

Café ready for Dragon Year / 換上新年裝扮的咖啡廳
Traditional tea making / 傳統茶藝

Motorcycle vender / 摩托小販

故鄉之外的故鄉（上）

Dynasties. While visiting a local wet market to check on marine fish, I stopped by a dry goods shop selling many varieties of dried marine food, like squid, shrimp and salted fish. One particular fish, a kind of Mackerel, drew my eyes. The skin was patterned in beautiful shades of silver and gray, and along the lateral line was a row of dark round dots. I took it in my hands and inspected it closely. Luo and Dai were with me at the market and said simultaneously, "This is also called the Cheng He fish, after the sea admiral of the Ming Dynasty."

Throughout Southeast Asia, among Chinese and even some of the locals, the seven voyages of Cheng He, who sailed the Seven Seas with his huge armada of over 300 ships, is famous. Often there are stories circulating, and even shrines built, in memory of him, such as in Malacca and distant Borneo. Some stories veer from fact to fiction, and here in Singkawang, there is one such circulating among the Chinese, even known in the marketplace.

"Everyone loves Cheng He, even the fish in the ocean," said Luo to me as Dai nodded his head in agreement. "One time, Cheng He's ship was leaking, and water was coming through the holes. The vessel was sinking," Lo continued. "These fish saw the danger and all of them swam next to the ship. Using their bodies, they blocked the leakage, and these round marks were thus left on their body." Luo ended the story with a smile. To pay my respect to this special fish, I bought half of a salted fish to take home. It costs a meager five dollars US. Later on, I would see at a seaside port a long row of these fish being dried at dockside to be preserved as more salted fish.

Though my visit to Singkawang was necessarily short, it brought me many great surviving stories of the past, with people that make the town's past very much alive today.

印尼 山口洋 二〇二四年一月三十一日

故鄉之外的故鄉（上）

「山口洋」是一個位於群山之間的小城，河流從群山之間蜿蜒而出，匯入汪洋大海，其地理位置恰如這個由客家移民帶給它的名字，有山，臨河，靠海。

即便名字如此形象，但是相信對大多數人來說它仍然非常陌生。有六個姊妹都嫁到香港的江有措先生的家，正是來自這個擁有約二十五萬人口的小城，位於印度尼西亞，婆羅洲西加里曼丹的松加伊瑟道河沿岸。

如今，這裡超過一半的居民為華人，絕大多數是早期來自中國廣東省的移民後代，他們為了追求更好的生活遠渡重洋，與美國的舊金山對應，稱山口洋為「新金山」。當地華人估計，該城的華人實際比例可能超過百分之八十，遠高於政府的普查數據。

「我父親把我六個姊妹一個接一個都嫁去了香港。」江有措說道。「有一個住在旺角、一個在觀塘、一個在沙田，還有一個在馬鞍山。」他一連串地說著，彷彿對香港的這些地方非常熟悉。「那你父親怎麼沒有把你也弄去香港？」我好奇地問。「你在開玩笑吧？」老江大笑著回答。「通常娶外地妻子的香港男人，大多是從中國大陸過去的單身工人，因為當地女人不願意嫁給他們。而在香港，沒人會願意把自己的女兒嫁給像我們這種來自偏遠又陌生地方的男人。」老江用一種理所當然的語氣說。「有一些

Chinese lion guarding city / 城市的守護者中式石獅　　　　　　　　New Year lanterns / 新年燈籠高高掛

專門從事這類婚姻介紹的中介，安排我們這種地方的女人嫁到遠處去。而我嘛，只能留在家裡，找個活計謀生囉。」老江說完長嘆一口氣。他不會說中文，但卻能流利地講英語，因為他曾在印度班加羅爾上過學，如今在當地經營著兩家中式海鮮餐廳。

江有揩名片上的名字是阿比丁，一個印度教名字，發音和印尼語中的「螃蟹」相似。他的餐廳也確實供應螃蟹，還有不少來自附近海域和河流的各式各樣的海鮮。我走進廚房，看到一位年輕的印尼穆斯林女廚師正在忙碌。我們點了清蒸魚、老虎蝦和魷魚作為晚餐。用餐時，當地的警察局長和幾位下屬穿著制服大搖大擺地走了進來。他們也點了一桌豐盛的海鮮，吃光了後廚今日所剩的蝦和魷魚。在這樣的小鎮，警察局長擁有極大的權勢，我們甚至能在許多鎮上的公共海報和壁畫中看到他的臉。若是警察局長選擇在你的餐廳用餐，簡直就像獲得了米其林星級的認可。至於他是否需要付錢，那又是另一回事了。

CHINESE TRADITION SURIVAL & REVIVAL (Part 1)　　045

Muslim lady chef / 穆斯林女廚師
Market venders / 市場小販

與我們一起用餐的,還有山口洋另一位頗有名氣的先生——出生於一九五七年的戴志堅。戴回憶說,他是家族在山口洋的第四代。他的父親出生於一九一五年,體弱多病,年幼時差點喪命,於是就被賣給當地最受敬奉的「石頭廟」裡的神明收養,就此改名為「戴石成」,意為石頭的愛結出來的成果。八歲時,戴石成被送往中國汕頭的一所耶穌會美國傳教學校求學,因為聰明伶俐,後來還成長為一名出色的游泳選手。一九三七年,日本侵略北平時,他正在大學就讀,一度想要加入蔣介石的空軍,然而由於空軍規定最低體重為五十公斤,他的父親僅差一公斤,最終被拒之門外,無緣參與抗日。戴志堅說起自己的父親,言語中總帶著些自豪,還有點他特有的誇張腔調:「我爸媽,就像亞蘭・德倫遇見碧姬・芭杜,那是金風玉露一相逢,勝卻人間無數啊!」聽戴志堅講他的家族史,好像在聽什麼戲劇段子一樣,他的感染力可不一般。

戴志堅是家中兩個兒子和四個女兒中最小的孩子,深受家人寵愛,也成為了小城裡小驕傲。他曾在坤甸的名校就讀,後來又去過雅加達的兩所大學深造,最終成為一名土木工程師。他曾在坤甸的一所綜合性私立大學任教,並於一九八七年成為該校的技術學院院長。戴自豪地說:「我可是印尼最年輕、最英俊的院長。」一九八八年後,他又進入政府工作。至於戴志堅的頭銜,那可是一長串,列舉得我頭昏腦脹。他滔滔不絕,從學術成就到武術段位,再到宗族榮譽,無所不包。

Market venders / 市場小販
Dry marine products / 晒乾的海產品

戴志堅被公認為是小城裡最博學的「歷史學家」，這一點從他甫一坐到我們餐桌旁便不曾停下的分享中展露無遺。適逢雨季，餐廳外雨聲嘈雜。我偶爾會被屋頂鐵皮上的漏水滴到，但戴先生可一點兒都不會被干擾，像正在高速運轉的引擎，語速快得幾乎跟不上他的思緒，往往一句話還沒說完，就開始了下一句。他的詞彙量驚人，經常引用「智人」之類的詞語，還能拋出比我這個以故事和歷史事件見長的人更豐富的名詞和準確的日期。

在戴的分享中，有一個名字尤為突出——羅芳伯，這個名字在婆羅洲的許多歷史記載中都有出現。一七七七年，羅芳伯將他的「蘭芳公司」，一個主要承接保鏢和傭兵業務的組織，發展為蘭芳共和國，成為一個控制印尼婆羅洲西部大面積土地的國家。但在向清朝朝廷進貢時，他仍謙卑地也聰明地保留了「公司」這個稱謂。這個國家存續至一八八四年，最終被荷蘭吞併並建立了傀儡政府。一九一二年清朝滅亡後，蘭芳共和國也便完全消失，併入荷蘭東印度公司，成為其殖民經濟的一部分。

當地華人的歷史甚至能追溯到宋朝和明朝。造訪當地的濕貨市場時，我發現了一家魚

Dai showing Cheng He fish / 鄭和魚

Drying Cheng He Mackerel / 晒乾的鄭和鯖魚

乾店，乾魷魚、鹵鹹蝦和鹹魚，多種海產品琳瑯滿目。但最吸引我的，是一種奇特的鯖魚，魚皮呈現出亮眼的銀灰色條紋，側線上則排列著一排黑色圓點。我拿起來仔細觀察，戴介紹說，這種魚叫「鄭和魚」，正是以明朝航海家鄭和命名的。

在整個東南亞，無論是華人還是土著，都對鄭和率領三百多艘船，七次下西洋的故事耳熟能詳。許多地方流傳著他的傳說，在馬六甲和遙遠的婆羅洲甚至還建有紀念他的神廟。山口洋的華人社群中，也流傳著一個與鄭和相關的奇聞。

「人人都愛鄭和，就連海中的魚都不例外。」江對我說，戴也點頭表示贊同。「有一次，鄭和的船漏水了，海水從破洞湧入，船眼看就要沉沒了，這些魚看到危險，紛紛游到船邊，用自己的身體堵住了漏水的洞，於是牠們的身上就留下了這些圓點。」

不得不說，這故事玄幻中又帶著些許合理。為了向這種特別的魚致敬，我買了一塊魚乾帶回家，只花了五美元。後來，我又在港口看了很多「鄭和魚」，一排排整齊地排列，晾晒，銀灰色的底色和黑色的圓形斑點在陽光下尤為特別。

雖然我們在山口洋只做了短暫的停留，但這座小城卻帶給了我無數動人的歷史傳說，也見證了這些讓小鎮歷史依然鮮活的人們。透過這些人的講述，過去好像並不遙遠，它變成了流動的河水，就這麼隨著每一條魚身上的斑點、每一個微笑、每一句話語，流轉了下來。

CHINESE TRADITION SURIVAL & REVIVAL (Part 1)

故鄉之外的故鄉（下）

CHINESE TRADITION SURIVAL & REVIVAL (Part 2)

Pontianak, Indonesia – February 2, 2024

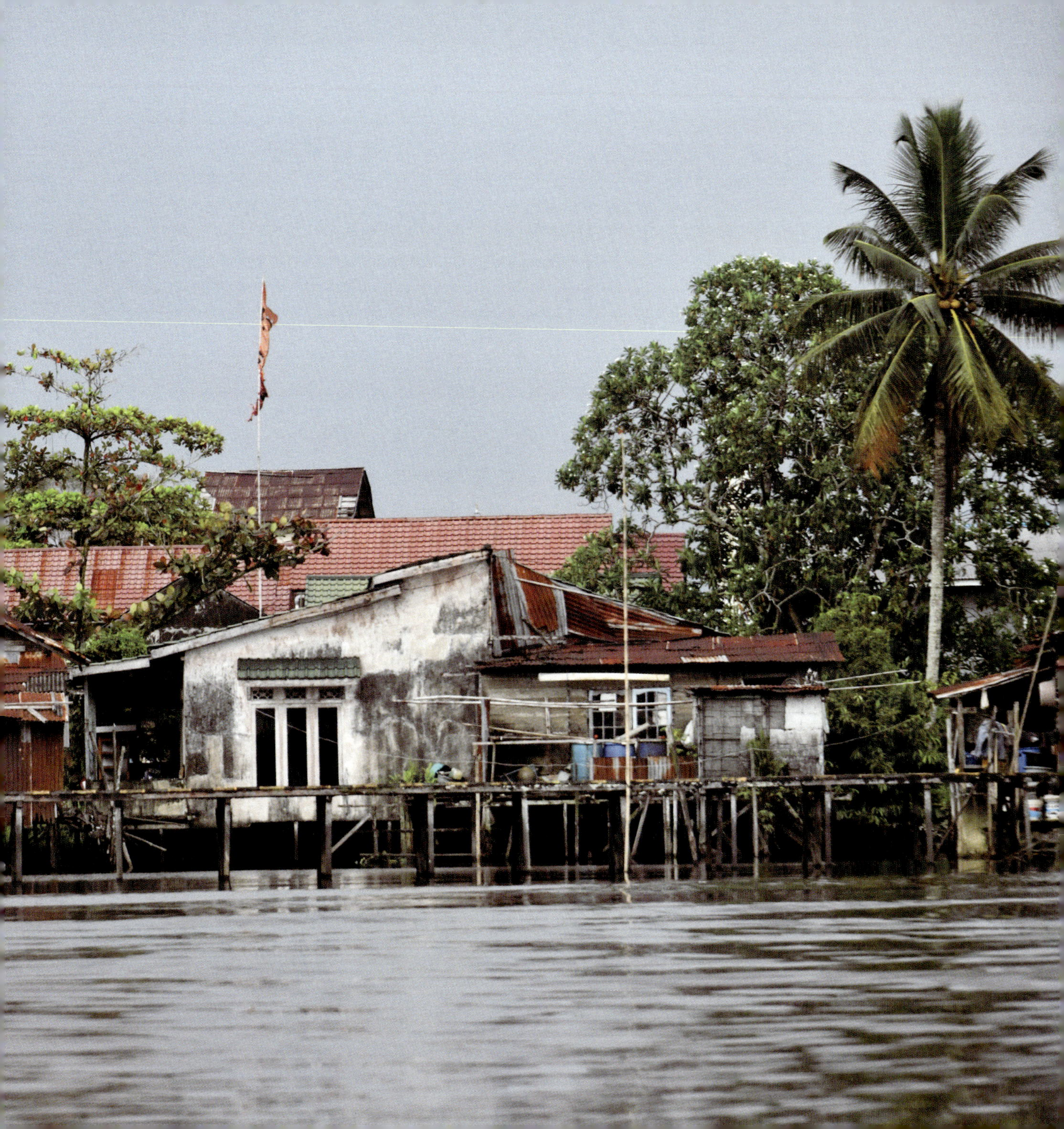

Pontianak, Indonesia – February 2, 2024

CHINESE TRADITION SURIVAL & REVIVAL (Part 2)

From Jakarta to Pontianak is a bit over an hour of flight time. Singkawang is around 150 kilometers to the north and took over three hours of driving, with a few long stretches along the west coast of Borneo. My intro to Mr. Lo and Mr. Dai was through a local contact, Mr. Henry Lai in Pontianak. Whereas my intro to Pontianak was through our project to preserve the last wooden sampan in Hong Kong. Historically, the best hard wood for making the most critical parts of a boat in southern China, like the center keel, the rib skeleton and the rear stern board must use "Kun Dian" wood from the jungle of Borneo, logged and taken down the Kapuas River to Pontianak. Even something as small as our wooden sampan relies on "Kun Dian" wood. And Kun Dian is the Chinese name for Pontianak. Thus my wish for years to visit Kun Dian, which is now finally realized.

Dr. Henry Lai is a writer, newspaper chief editor, lecturer, lawyer, business consultant and politician all rolled into one. He has multiple degrees from Indonesia and China, besides having resident and adjunct titles to various institutions including some from China. His breadth of knowledge and connections matches, or even surpasses, that of Mr. Dai whom I met in Singkawang. Thus in 1992, he accompanied Wahono, then Chairman of Indonesia's House of Representatives, to Beijing and acted as interpreter during the meeting between Jiang Zemin and the Indonesian head at the Great Hall of the People.

During traffic / 上班忙

National elections are coming up later this month on the 14th and everywhere there are flags and big billboards of candidates on the ballot. Henry is running for the post of representative for his Province of Pontianak, and his supporters and constituents are mainly within the Chinese communities. Nonetheless, he found time to entertain us in person and introduced us to many Chinese dignitaries of Pontianak.

He took us across the Kapuas River to the north bank where the Hakka Chinese live. The richer Chinese, many of whom are in business, especially those who were into timber and lumber trading before the government started restricting logging, are Shantouese, hailed from the China seacoast city of Shantou (Swatow). They tend to live on the south bank of the river. North bank of the river is closed to the equator so we took time to visit the monument where I stood on one foot in the northern hemisphere and one on the south as my iPad map displayed 0.0000° latitude. The thought crossed my mind briefly that it seems a good place to set up a project right around here, spanning both hemispheres.

Chen Zhenkun is known as a philanthropist not only among Chinese, but also a special friend for Indonesians of Pontianak. His most notable contributions are the many community-operated fire stations in Pontianak, now numbering into 62 stations for a population of just over half a million, one-third of whom are Chinese. We were taken to see the earliest one, started in 1949, the same year I was born, with a couple of the early push-cart pump machines sitting behind the newer ones. The firemen's outfits, equipment and helmets were all donated by Chen.

Whenever there is a fire in town, a volunteer firefighting force will be dispatched. There are some interesting protocols among such firemen. For example, if the house on fire belonged to relatives of one of the firemen and he wanted to brave the fire inside to save his kin, he would have to take off his uniform and helmet before leaving his troupe and entering the house. This would be to show that he was disassociating himself from the group and entered the burning house at his own risk.

Mr. Chen invited us to his garden home for a visit. Most impressive was an entire wall of framed pictures with all the local high officers and police chiefs. It is said that during Chinese New Year, the police chief would come pay respect to Chen, with a busload entourage of other police officers. Chen would never have to give out laisee or lucky money to the police, whereas in return the police must bring gifts to him. This must make Chen very proud of the reverse role compared to others who have to patronize the police. Among the pictures, one if with the former Police General Tito of Indonesia, now promoted to become Minister of Interior.

What was more impressive however was when Chen showed me a framed black and white old photo

One foot on each hemisphere / 雙腳橫跨兩半球
Equator pavilion / 赤道展示館

of his father when a young man, squatting with two baskets as a street vender. A much later photo shows him as an older gentleman with his much enlarged family while Chen a young man was standing among the last row of sons.

Later we were led into Chen's bedroom where he showed us next to his bed an entire set up of shortwave radio and walkie talkies. He demonstrated with pride how he could call up any of the fire stations and ask for a report on the current situation. Though some of the radio units were ancient and out of order, Chen kept them around as souvenirs to remember his long service to the community. Such service, now reaching totally 62 fire stations large and small, helps in reversing the expectation of Chinese among Indonesians, demonstrating they are not only here to make money, but are also key contributors to the community in civic activities. After the political turmoil of the mid 1960s, with riots against overseas Chinese in Indonesia, this kind of philanthropic work helps heal old wounds.

Owen Wong Yongron, now 71 years of age, is currently head of the Wong clan and took me, also a

Chen's father as vender / 陳的父親

Family Chen second left in back / 陳家大合照

Wong, to visit one of the Wong clan temples in Pontianak. In Pontianak, there are a total of 64 clan mausoleums or temples representing different surnames. He was proud to explain that Wong is one of the four largest family names in Pontianak. Some old drawings of the Wong ancestors and photographs of earlier heads of clan were hung on the walls. There was also a small stage where the local musical orchestra troupe would gather to play Swatowese and Chinese music. A room behind the stage houses many of the traditional Chinese string instruments.

Afterward, Owen showed me a local Chinese elementary school that he helped found which had over five hundred students with some forty teachers. Amazingly, two of the teachers of Mandarin were Indonesian. We visited two upper classes where around twenty students rose upon our arrival and bowed with their hands together. Some younger students were having judo lessons in the playground.

Owen, a wealthy rice merchant, said that for a long time after the 1960's anti-Chinese campaign, few Chinese were allowed to go to school until they organized themselves to build schools for their own kind. Behind the school is the huge Chinese cemetery where many of the deceased must have born witness to the excesses and atrocities of the past generations.

Yoseph Chen Setiawan is 73 years old and editor-in-chief of the Kun Dian Daily, a Chinese newspaper that has just passed twenty years since its founding. Of the eight-pages of this daily, front and second page are filled with local news, much of it related to local politics, as elections are coming up in two weeks. The international news looks like it is syndicated or translated from other international headline news. There is a fair bit of local advertising, and half a page is devoted to running an old serial martial arts fiction story by a famed Hong Kong author Leung Yu-seng who passed away fifteen years ago. Whether royalty is paid, I did not venture to ask Chen.

We were about to go to a nice seafood dinner when Henry took me to visit Mr. Wu YongWei, also known as Yohan Lin. It seems most Chinese have several names, a Chinese pinyin name, a Hakka or Swatowese version, and an Indonesian one. Anyhow, Wu's house is hidden behind some large dark buildings. As Lin, forty years old, walked me into his house, I could see a long row of lit aquariums each with a big fish inside. Just as I was going to ask, "Are they better steamed or grilled?" Lin said with some pride pointing at the first tank, "This one is worth a quarter million Renminbi Chinese money." My tongue jumped out just in time before it slipped out my query on the choice of recipe.

As we walked further, I could see that these fish, measuring around half a meter in length, had beautiful shiny large scales, some in silver, some in a tint of red, and a few dark golden red in color. Soon I found out from Lin that these are his pets and business fish, the highly endangered arowana fish. They are so rare that the pet fish market would value some at over half a million RMB each (USD60K). Indeed, Lin had just flown one for such an amount to China to a client who needed one of his Red Arowana before Chinese New Year.

"You know, I have been raising these arowana for thirteen years. There's a lot of regulations and restrictions in the cultivation of these fish. To sell

Old palace / 老皇宮
Lin & his priced Arowana / 林先生和他珍貴的龍魚

them, it must be raised, not from the wild, for at least over two generations, and each one must be implanted with an identification chip before shipping," Lin told me, introducing some of the intricacies of his pet fish farm. "I only raise arowana, and I can show you in the other room the baby ones," Lin offered. I learned later that it takes four years to raise a baby arowana to maturity.

"While they exist in a few Southeast Asian countries in remote freshwater rivers, those from the upper reaches of the Kapuas River here, the deep red golden ones, called in Chinese as Golden Dragon Fish, are the most rare and valuable," Lin added as he pointed to a few tanks each with an individual Red Arowana. I found out later that the Red Arowana is now considered to be a separate species, only found in the Kapuas River. "You will occasionally see such fish in aquariums or seafood tanks, on display only, certainly not for the dish, and in particular at Swatow restaurants or even high-end Chinese business offices as a symbol for good luck," Lin proclaimed with some noticeable pride. "There used to be one at the Lisboa Casino in Macau too," he did not forget to mention.

As Lin's father was hanging around with us near the fish tanks, I asked "Is your father also involved in raising these beautiful fish?" "No way! If one dies, he would have a heart attack to see so much money disappeared," answered Lin. As we walked out of his house, I finally understood why in a place like Pontianak where I have not seen one luxury car, there are two Mercedes sitting in the driveway, one a sports model, the other a sedan. No doubt Lin's business is prospering, even with a few arowana dying here and there. And in his tanks are several more Red Ferraris.

As I get into our crammed car and head for the seafood restaurant, I know that we'll be ordering some garoupa. Steamed or grilled won't make any difference at this point. It will just be a cheap old fish.

印尼 坤甸 二〇二四年二月二日

故鄉之外的故鄉（下）

從雅加達飛往坤甸只需一個多小時，而從坤甸再前往山口洋，卻是一段不短的旅程。向北一百五十公里，我們沿著婆羅洲西海岸開了三個多小時。不過還好，海岸線的美麗景色讓人感覺時間稍稍縮短了一些。

在坤甸，我透過當地的聯絡人賴民裕博士結識了山口洋的羅先生和戴志堅先生。冥冥之中，我對坤甸的第一印象，也與我們在香港保護最後一艘木製舢舨的項目連結了起來。

在歷史上，南中國製作船隻最重要的部位，比如龍骨、肋骨骨架和尾舵板，品種最優質的硬木就是婆羅洲叢林中的「坤甸木」。這些木材被砍伐後，會順著卡普阿斯河運到坤甸，再由坤甸出口至其他地方。小如我們的那艘木舢舨，也離不開「坤甸木」。「坤甸」的城市名便是由這「坤甸木」得來。多年來，我一直希望能親自來到這兒，看看傳說中的「坤甸木」，如今終於得償所願。

賴民裕博士擁有印尼和中國的多個學位，多才多藝，身兼多職。作家、報社總編輯、講師、律師、商業顧問和政治家都是他的頭銜。他目前在多家機構有常駐或兼職職務，其中還包括一些中國的組織。他的人脈和學識一樣廣，感覺上比山口洋的戴志堅先生

還要厲害。一九九二年，他還曾陪同時任印尼國會主席瓦霍諾前往北京。江澤民和瓦霍諾在人民大會堂會面的時候，他就坐在瓦霍諾背後充當翻譯。

本月十四日，印尼即將舉行全國大選。街頭巷尾，候選人的巨幅廣告牌和旗幟隨處可見，氛圍相當濃厚。賴博士正在競選坤甸的省代表，他的支持者和選民主要來自當地的華人社區。但即便在忙碌的競選時期，他仍抽出時間親自接待我們，熱情地向我們介紹了坤甸的許多華人名流。

賴博士帶我們穿過卡普阿斯河，來到了河的北岸，這裡是客家華人的聚居地。相較之下，較富裕的華人則通常居住在河的南岸，尤其是那些在政府開始限制伐木之前，從事木材和木料貿易的商人，他們大多是潮汕人，來自中國沿海城市汕頭。

卡普阿斯河的北岸靠近赤道，那裡有一座赤道紀念碑，我們特地前去參觀。我興奮地一腳踏在北半球，另一腳踩在南半球，好像身體成了連接兩個世界的橋梁。

抬頭環顧四周，再低頭看著平板上顯示的「零度」經緯，一種奇妙的感覺油然而生：「我正站在地球的『腰帶』上！」於是，一個有趣的念頭閃過腦海：「這個橫跨南北半球的特殊地點，看起

Kapuas River / 卡普阿斯河
Ocean & river ferry / 海河渡輪

來是個很適合展開跨半球項目的地方啊！」

陳鎮坤先生是華人社區知名的慈善家，坤甸當地的印尼人也視其為好友與恩人。他最為人熟知的貢獻，就是推動成立了坤甸的社區消防站。如今，這座只有五十多萬人口的小城，華人居然佔三分之一，而消防站竟然也多達六十二個。我們這次特地參觀了其中歷史最悠久的一座，建於一九四九年，和我同齡，內部仍存放著幾台早期的手推式水泵機，而這裡的消防員制服、裝備甚至頭盔，全都是陳鎮坤先生捐贈的。

每當城裡發生火災，志願消防隊便會出動。隊內有一個不成文的規定，如果火災現場有隊員的親友，並且在極度危險的情況下隊員仍選擇去救人的話，那麼這名隊員必須在前去營救前脫下自己的制服和頭盔。這樣做是為了表明他是以個人身分進入火場，與消防隊無關，並自願承擔所有風險。

我們受陳先生的邀請到他的花園別墅做客，剛進門，便被掛得滿滿當當的照片牆吸引，其中不少陳先生與當地高官和警察局長的合影。據說每逢農曆新年，警察局長都會帶著一車隨行的警官和禮物來向陳先生拜年，而陳先生從來不需要給警察派紅包。我想，陳先生肯定會感到自豪，畢竟大部分當地人都需要趕著巴結警察，而他卻手握著反轉這種傳統關係的實力。照片中還有一張合

Lai in back left / 左後方的賴博士在當翻譯
Crossing Kapuas Bridge / 跨越卡普阿斯大橋

Lai on left & Wong far right / 左一賴民裕，右三黃永榮

影引人注目，是陳先生與印尼前警察總長提托，提托如今已被升任為內政部部長。

不過真正令人動容的，是一張黑白老照片。那是陳先生的父親，年輕的他蹲在路邊，身旁擺著兩個籃子，以街頭小販的身分討生活。陳先生隨後又拿出一張合影，照片裡的父親已然年邁，身邊圍繞著他的大家庭，當時還是小伙子的陳先生站在最後一排。兩張照片放在一起，頗像一部濃縮的家族奮鬥史。

接著，陳先生帶我們參觀了他的臥室。他像個孩子炫耀自己的珍藏一樣，興致勃勃地向我們展示床邊那一整套短波無線電和對講機設備，還現場演示了如何與每一個消防站取得聯繫，隨時掌握最新情況。

雖然有些設備已經老舊失修，無法啟用，但陳先生仍然小心保存著這些他多年來為社區服務的見證。這六十二個大大小小的消防站，改變了印尼人對華人的刻板印象，向當地人證明了，華人不僅僅是來賺錢的，更是社區公益的重要參與者。

在二十世紀六〇年代中期，印尼曾爆發過針對海外華人的暴亂，許多人的生活被摧毀，傷痕難以癒合。而陳鎮坤先生這種無私的慈善事業，無疑成為了一股撫平舊傷的力量。他的行動不僅贏得了當地人的尊重，也讓華人社群在歷史的陰影中，重新站穩腳跟，展現出新的面貌與價值。

在坤甸的華人社群中，「黃」姓是四大姓氏之一，這是現年七十一歲的黃氏族長黃永榮先生跟我講的。他帶著我這位同姓訪客，前往參觀家族的一座江夏黃氏宗祠。在坤

甸，這樣的宗親祠堂共有六十四座。

祠堂內牆上掛滿了黃氏祖先的畫像和歷任族長的照片，內部還有一個小舞台，當地的樂團會在這裡演奏潮州音樂和中國傳統樂曲。舞台後方的儲物間裡，保存著許多中國傳統弦樂器。

那之後，黃永榮先生帶我去了一所受他資助創辦的華人小學。這所學校目前有五百多名學生和四十多名教師，其中有兩名教授普通話的教師竟然是印尼人，屬實有些令人意外。我們走進兩間高年級教室，約二十名學生在我們進門時立刻起身，雙手合十鞠躬行禮，恭敬和熱情讓人心生暖意。操場上，幾名低年級的學生正在上柔道課，歡笑聲此起彼伏，整個校園充滿了生機與活力。

黃永榮先生還是一名成功的米商，他一邊走一邊分享往事。他提到，二十世紀六〇年代的反華運動後，華人社群的孩子們長期無法進入正規學校讀書。為了不讓下一代失去教育的機會，當地華人自發組織，籌款建校，為自己的孩子開啟新的求學之路。而這所學校，就是他們努力的成果之一。

Fire machine No.1 circa 1949 / 一九四九年的消防機

Chen with police visitors / 陳鎮坤與警察合影

New firetruck with 1949 emblem / 帶有一九四九標誌的新型消防車

Chen & his radio gadget / 陳和他的無線電裝置
Pontianak Chinese school / 坤甸華校

學校的背後，是一片廣大的華人公墓，埋葬著無數曾經歷動盪歲月的逝者，他們親眼目睹了過去的暴力與苦難。每一座墓碑都不僅僅是先人的歸宿，更是那段歷史真實存在過的證明。

現年七十三歲的陳得時先生是《坤甸日報》的總編輯，這份華文報紙剛剛迎來創刊二十週年的里程碑。《坤甸日報》每日八版，頭版和第二版大多刊登本地新聞，近期尤以地方政治為主，因為兩週後即將舉行選舉。國際新聞看起來是翻譯或轉載自其他國際媒體的頭條。報紙上還有不少本地廣告，而其中半版則是用來連載一部經典的武俠小說，作者是已故香港名家梁羽生。至於報紙是否給梁羽生的家人付了版權費，我倒是沒冒昧地向陳先生提問。

原本我們正準備去享用一頓豐盛的海鮮晚餐，但賴博士先帶我去拜訪了一位名叫吳永威的先生，他還有個印尼名字，音譯過來叫林耀漢。似乎印尼的大多數華人都擁有好幾個名字，有漢語拼音的、客家或潮州發音的，還有一個印尼的版本。

吳先生的家隱藏在幾棟昏暗的大樓後面。進屋時，我看到一排排亮著燈的水族箱，每個箱裡都有一條大魚。正當我想開玩笑問一句「這些魚是清蒸好吃還是烤著好吃」的時候，吳先生用些許驕傲的語氣指著第一個水族箱說：「這條魚價值二十五萬人民幣。」

聽到這，我的舌頭繞著話在嘴裡轉了個圈，硬生生咽下了那句玩笑，不然可真就鬧笑話了。

再走近幾步，我細細打量這些魚。牠們大約半米長，鱗片大而閃亮，有些是銀色的、有些帶著紅色的光澤，還有幾條呈深金紅色，看起來極為華麗。吳先生告訴我，這些魚不僅是他的寵物，更是他的生意。

稀有的「亞洲龍魚」，尤其是「紅龍魚」，市場上能賣到超過六萬美元約五十多萬人民幣。吳先生說，年前，他剛剛把一條紅龍魚空運到中國，客人為了趕在農曆新年前擁有一條這樣的紅龍魚，毫不猶豫地支付了這筆天價。

「我養這些龍魚已經十三年了，培育這些魚有很多『說道』。龍魚是一種受保護的魚類，要出售，必須是人工養殖的魚，且至少要繁育到第二代以上。每條魚在運輸前都必須植入身分晶片。」吳先生一邊介紹，一邊分享這種觀賞魚飼養的門道。「我只專注於養殖龍魚，如果你有興趣，我可以帶你去另一個房間看看幼魚，從幼龍魚養到成熟需要整整四年的時間。」

「雖然這些魚在東南亞一些偏遠的淡水河中還能找到，但只有產自卡普阿斯河上游的，那種金色和深紅交雜的品種，才是最稀有、

HM at Wong clan mausoleum / HM 在黃氏祠堂
Wong clan mausoleum / 江夏黃氏祠堂

CHINESE TRADITION SURIVAL & REVIVAL (Part 2)　　067

最珍貴的品種，中國人稱他們為『金龍魚』。」我後來才了解到，紅龍魚已被認定為一個獨立的物種，僅存於卡普阿斯河流域。

「有時候你能在水族館或者海鮮餐廳的魚缸裡看到牠們，不過那只是展示用的，絕對不是拿來做菜的。尤其是在潮州餐廳，或者一些高端的華人企業辦公室，金龍魚通常被當作吉祥物一樣養著。據說以前澳門的葡京賭場裡也有一條。」

看到吳先生的父親正悠閒地站在魚缸旁，我隨口問了一句：「您父親也參與養殖嗎？」吳先生笑著搖頭：「他幹不了這個，心臟受不了！要是親眼見著死了一條，他想著這麼多錢打水漂，會犯心臟病的！」

走出吳先生的家，我終於明白，為什麼在坤甸這樣一個連豪車影子都看不到的地方，他家車道上卻能停著兩輛賓士：一輛跑車、一輛轎車。毫無疑問，吳先生的生意很興隆，儘管偶爾有幾條龍魚不幸「壯烈犧牲」，也絲毫不影響他的財運。畢竟他的魚缸裡，可是有幾條「紅色法拉利」呢。

坐進我們那擠得要命的小車，準備去吃晚餐時，我的心裡已經毫無波瀾了。我知道我們肯定要點石斑魚的，不過清蒸也好，烤著也罷，端上桌的，跟那「紅色法拉利」比，終究只是一條「平價代步魚」。從豪車展廳回頭，坐上了一輛共享單車，心裡實在是很難有滋有味啊。

Old palace / 老皇宮
Baby Arowana breeding / 培育中的龍魚幼苗

天鵝湖畔，餘音未散

SWAN SONG @ SWAN LAKE

Tsurui, Hokkaido – February 19, 2024

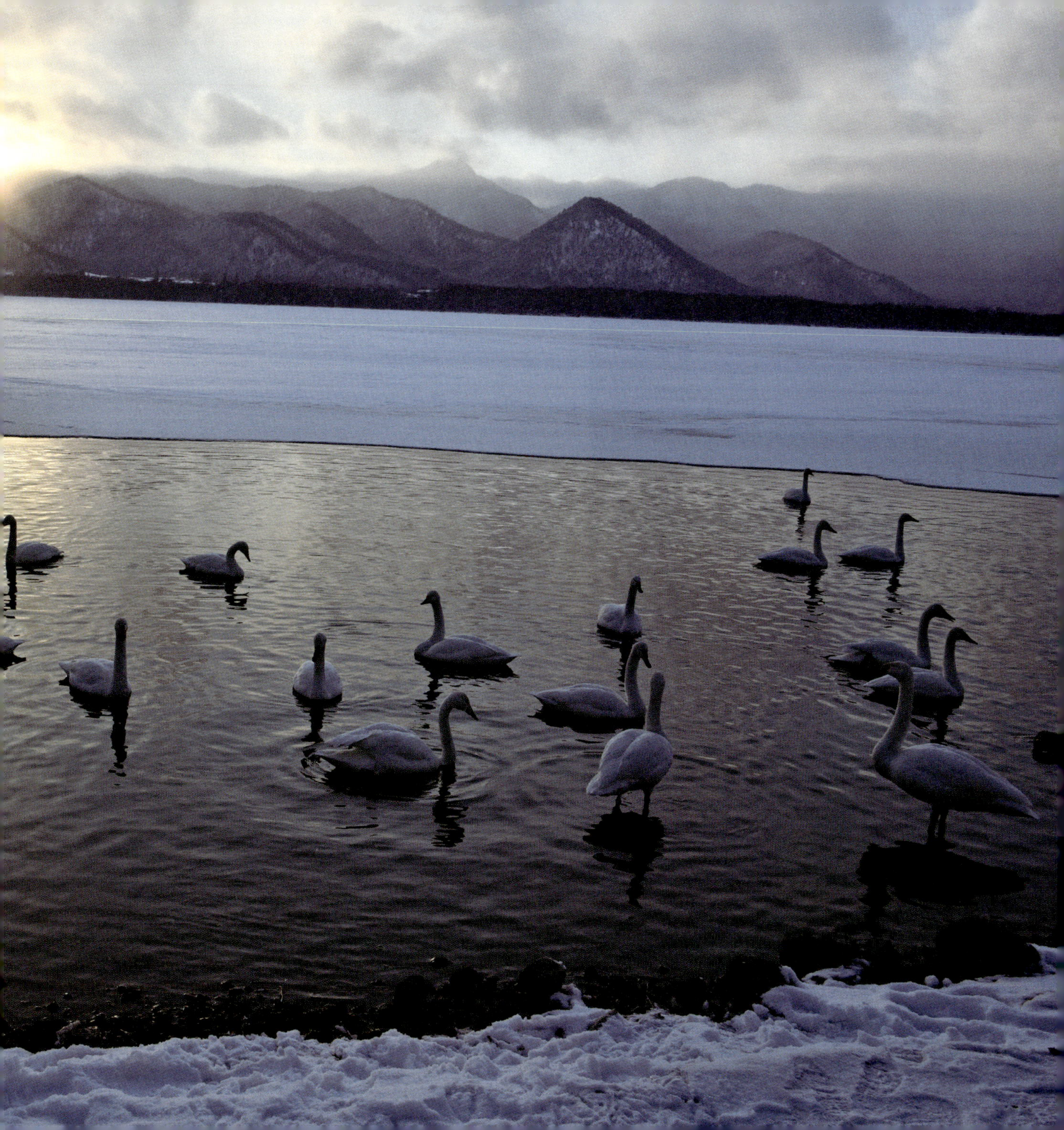

Tsurui, Hokkaido – February 19, 2024

SWAN SONG @ SWAN LAKE
Curtain call of an indigenous Ainu lady

For over four decades, I have been attracted, more by chance than by design, to some of the rarest indigenous people of Asia. First, in 1983, I spent time with the Ewenki reindeer herders, with less than 200 individuals remaining at the time. Later, we worked with the 300 Batak people deep inside Palawan's jungle in the Philippines, then the Tsou, former headhunters of Alishan, in Taiwan with around 2,000 people, followed by a visit to the Monpa of Bhutan with around 300. Even the Li nationality with around one million became a focus when their tradition disintegrated into tiny pockets of remnants of their former past.

I care little about big data except as contrast to highlight the importance of being small. Instead, I am always hooked into small groups, including endangered humans, not only wildlife. I have never been attracted by maximizing impact unlike what so many people today keep focusing on. Defying norms may run in an explorer's blood.

So it is not totally by chance, more by karma, that I should run into my first new friend of 2024, an indigenous Ainu person of Hokkaido. First, however, why are the Ainu special? Surviving in small numbers, only around 1,000 live in Sakhalin in the Russian Far East, I failed to meet any when visiting that island last December. I had read about and saw numerous pictures of the indigenous Ainu people of Hokkaido and Sakhalin Island, but I never thought I would have a totally chance encounter with one such interesting person. Let alone that it should happen in a most unlikely place, a spot where I had gone many times over the years to take a natural onsen bath with swans and ducks sharing the same spring.

Perhaps it is that same unconditional "sharing" of the Ainu tradition that brought us together. They have been, since time immemorial, traditional hunters/fishers/gatherers, and they would always share the spoils with relatives and neighbors. Such cooperative existence, natural communal behavior, seems to be a standard practice to ensure survival in more marginal areas of the world. Unfortunately, people living in more privileged areas with abundance have long lost, or been deprived of, such gratifying traits. Perhaps such traditions can be reintroduced through the now-popular experiential education curriculum - "emotionally-driven" rather than the dry "knowledge-based" teaching method common to schools and institutions today.

While in Hokkaido, I happened to come across a children's book on the Ainu written by an Ainu elder about his childhood and upbringing. It recounted some very interesting practices, such as their love of sharing; any prize from

Ewenki circa 1983 / 鄂溫克族，一九八三年
Batak circa 2019 / 巴塔克族，二〇一九年
Tsou circa 2016 / 鄒族，二〇一六年

hunting or fishing would be made into a stew to share with others in the community. They also practice cooperative house building, similar to what I had witnessed among the indigenous Batak of Palawan and Li nationality of Hainan Island.

When a new house is finished, Ainu people would offer sake and prayer sticks to the gods in a ceremony to thank them for the safe completion. Aromatic mugwart arrows were then fired into the thatch under-roof of the house to satisfy and quiet the spirits of the felled trees. Lastly, dumplings were scattered over the guests and the future inhabitants of the house with the wish that the members of this house should be blessed with food as abundantly as if it had fallen out of the sky.

Such ceremonial and communal house-building unfortunately became obsolete. Since the Meiji period, the dominant and dominating Japanese Yamato ethnic majority, advanced as they are in preserving their own culture, have adopted a totally opposite policy when it comes to that of the Ainu. While there are individual Ainu strongholds trying to resist the homogenizing attempt by the government to preserve their own culture and language, it was not until as late as August 2019 that Japan finally lifted their century-long policy of assimilating and integrating the Ainu into the larger Japanese race, and passed the legislation to recognize the

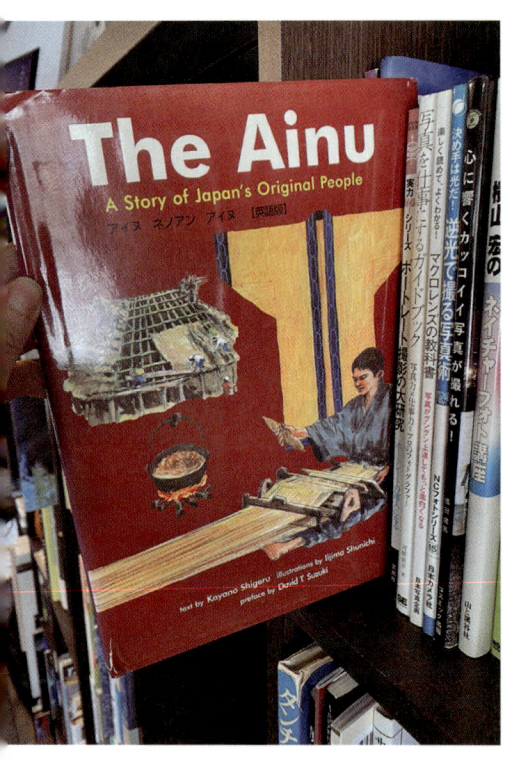

Ainu children book I came across / 阿伊努族童書

Ainu as indigenous to Hokkaido, having arrived there long before the Yamato people. One can only hope that this realization was not too little and too late.

The Ainu clothing was formerly made from bark taken from the outer layer of birch or elm, with the fiber treated and woven, then appliqued and embroidered meticulously with designs and motifs of the Ainu along the edges, like the ends of sleeves, the neck band and the hem. Evil spirits were said to be able to enter the body through such places, so the embroidery was to rope off evil spirits from entering the body. Bark cloth used for utensils carry similar motifs of the Ainu. I have also seen the use of bark to make clothing among the Batak of Palawan and Li of Hainan Island.

Other natural behaviors were also mentioned. For example, in winter, Ainu kids love going out to play, be it with a

Communal house building / 合作共建房

sled or building things from snow and ice, but their hands would get frozen. They would then run home to their mother, who would warm the little hands between her breasts, a simple and natural act.

Mountains, rivers, springs, trees, animals, fish, and all of nature were revered and respected as gods among the Ainu. Useful things were also considered to be gods, and each time, after the use of tools and materials, thanks was given to the gods with a prayer stick and sake offering.

Particular gods or spirits, however, could be scolded when bad things happened. For example, if an accident happened in the mountains or in a river, that particular god was severely scolded by saying : "you were negligent, god, and now look what has happened". When someone fell off a tree, a person might say : "Oh, god of the mountains, your lack of attention has caused a child to fall out of a tree in your garden! Be more careful, and don't let this happen again!" People could even threaten their gods : "If you desert me now and let me die, it is for sure that the awful stench arising from my corpse will rise up to heaven as a mist and trouble you forever!" The Ainu spoke to the gods in this manner because they believed they are on equal terms with the gods, and in exchange for taking good care of the gods, they expect the gods to reciprocate the favor.

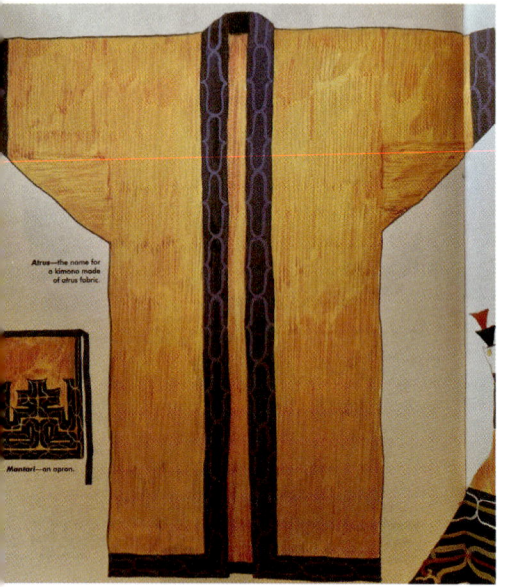

House warming ceremony / 喬遷儀式
Ainu design motifs / 阿伊努圖案

Official censuses show there are around 20,000 Ainu people in Japan and maybe 1,000 on Sakhalin in Russia. But many in the past hid their ethnic identity due to persecution, the assimilation policies, an inferiority complex, or other prejudices and biases. My encounter, short and sweet, with "The first ever Ainu" may well be a manifestation and reflection of the new-found identity of the Ainu.

I was alone soaking in the remote hot spring on the eastern lakefront of Kussharo Lake in Hokkaido when several Japanese arrived for their bath. It was near sunset, and I decided to leave the tiny pool to them. I managed to take a few nice photos of the swans before the sun set behind the distant hill on the other side of the lake. As I was walking toward my car, I ran into an old lady walking towards me. As with all rural Japanese in remote Hokkaido, she greeted me in Japanese. I drew a blank, smiled and bowed, as any person would do in this land. Nodding my head, I uttered that I was from Hong Kong. She smiled back and answered, "I am Ainu."

I was taken aback, as I had been hoping to meet an Ainu person for quite a long time. I did not know her name or how to address her, but she gestured for me to follow her. There were few houses in this remote community and within a minute, we ended up in front of her house, which was steps away from the hot spring.

Children play in snow / 孩子在雪地裡玩耍
Mother as hand warmer / 母親為孩子暖手

SWAN SONG @ SWAN LAKE

樺太アイヌノ家

I took off my snow boots and followed her into her house. It was a very modest old house and she invited me to sit down on her sofa. Soon, she brought out a cup of hot tea for me and then proceeded to show me a framed picture of her mother, saying "Ainu, Ainu." She gave me some leftover cooked pumpkin in a small bowl, and I ate it politely. Suddenly she noticed that I had no socks for my feet, and she took off her woolen socks and handed them to me. She gestured for me to put them on. I gestured back asking if she had knit these hand-made blue and white socks, and she nodded in the affirmative.

She took out a piece of paper and wrote down on it her name in Kanji which I can read - "Di Zi Gui Zi" (Teshi Keiko 弟子桂子) as it is pronounced in Mandarin, with the first two characters matching the nearby town

Sakhalin Ainu circa 1912 /
庫頁島的阿伊努人，一九一二年

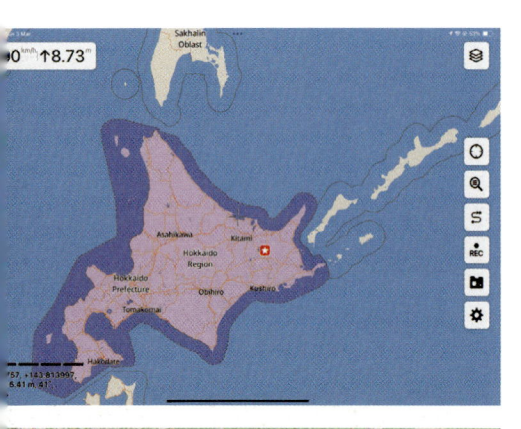

Lake Kushiro in Hokkaido / 北海道釧路湖
Swan onsen & Gui Zi home / 天鵝溫泉與桂子的家

of "Diziqu" (Teshikaga 弟子屈). Gui Zi in Chinese means Osmanthus, a plant with tiny yet very fragrant flowers celebrated by many poets and scholars. Then she proceeded to write down her address and telephone number in Japanese. Apparently, she expected me to look her up again.

Next to the sofa was a calendar on the wall. She pointed to the 23rd of the month and put out "eighty" with her fingers. That's when I figured out that she was turning 80 in a few short days. With my mobile phone, I called up my Japanese friend to talk to her and verified that indeed that was what she was trying to tell me. We had a short chat through my friend interpreting over the phone, but by then it is getting dark outside, and I rose to leave. I wanted to take off the socks she had lent to me, but she gestured for me to keep them on. It was such an impromptu meeting, and yet she was so graceful and generous. I thanked her profusely and walked to the door, asking her to please stay behind, but she escorted me all the way back to my car and waved goodbye.

It should have been an hour drive back to my friend's farmhouse where I stayed, but I was so filled with excitement at my first encounter with a true Ainu that I totally lost my direction on the way home. It took me an hour, including stopping at a gas station to ask for directions. Ultimately a passer-by pedestrian stopped to help me get back on the right road.

Gui Zi and her mother / 桂子與她的母親

That short but sweet rendezvous has now enticed me to continue to find out more about the indigenous Ainu people, and perhaps contribute in a small way by documenting and preserving their unique culture and heritage. Hopefully, Gui Zi's song at a beautiful swan lake will not be a last curtain call, but an ovation for more to come.

SWAN SONG @ SWAN LAKE

北海道 鶴居村 二〇二四年二月十九日

天鵝湖畔，餘音未散
與阿伊努人的不期而遇

四十餘載光陰裡，我總被亞洲最稀有的原住民部落所牽引。與其說是刻意追尋，不如說是命運的安排。

一九八三年，我初遇大興安嶺的鄂溫克族，彼時，馴鹿鈴聲搖曳的部落僅剩兩百人；接著，我又深入菲律賓巴拉望雨林，與三百巴塔克族人共居；再到發現台灣阿里山曾獵首的鄒族，只剩下兩千族人知曉各種祭典的故事；後來，我又輾轉不丹祕境，見證三百門巴族僧夾在經幡間守護古老的梵音。即便是還擁有百萬人口的黎族，其傳統文化在現代衝擊下也如碎星散落蒼穹。

我對大數據毫不關心，除非它能反襯「微小」的可貴。令我著迷的永遠是那些瀕危的少數，不僅是野生動植物，更包括即將消逝的人類族群。這種想法看起來與當今世人追逐的「影響力最大化」背道而馳，或許是因為叛逆的血液本就流淌在探險者的脈搏裡。

因此，當我在二〇二四年的開端與一位北海道的阿伊努族原住民相遇時，我相信這不是偶然，而是「命中注定的緣分」。為什麼阿伊努族於我而言如此特別呢？因為這個族群如今僅存少數，在俄羅斯遠東的薩哈林島上，只剩約一千人仍生活於此。去年

Monpa of Bhutan circa 2019 / 不丹門巴族，二〇一九年

十二月，我曾造訪該島，但遺憾未曾發現阿伊努人的足跡。

我讀過許多關於北海道與薩哈林島阿伊努人的文章，也看過他們的照片，卻從未想過，自己能親身邂逅這樣一位有趣的族人，更別提這命運般的相遇地點，竟然是一處我近年來多次造訪的溫泉池畔，在那裡，天鵝與野鴨悠然自得地與我共享溫暖的泉水，人與自然融為一體。

無獨有偶，在阿伊努族的傳統中，「共享精神」正是他們文化的核心。自遠古以來，他們便以狩獵、捕魚與採集為生，這些收穫並不僅屬於個人，而是屬於整個社群。他們總是毫不吝嗇地將自己所得與親朋鄰里共享。這種合作共存的生活方式，成為了他們在世界邊緣地帶生存的基石，也讓他們的文化充滿了溫暖與人性。

然而，這樣珍貴的品格在如今「富饒」的現代社會中早已被遺忘，或是被物質生活的洪流沖刷殆盡。機械式的知識灌輸型教學毫無意義，或許，當今流行的以情感為驅動力的「體驗式教育」，才能讓

Swan at swan lake / 天鵝湖
Lone swan / 天鵝

學生們從古老的智慧中有所感悟。

在北海道的時候,我偶然翻到了一本關於阿伊努族的童書,這本書由一位阿伊努族長者撰寫,記錄了他童年時代的生活與成長故事。書中描述了一些非常有趣的傳統習俗,例如他們對「分享」的熱愛:任何來自狩獵或捕魚的收穫,通常都會被燉成湯,與社群中的其他人一同分享。他們還有一種合作建房的傳統,這種傳統與菲律賓巴拉望的巴塔克族以及中國海南島的黎族十分相似。

當一座新房建成後,阿伊努人會舉行儀式,向神靈獻上清酒和祈禱棒,以感謝神靈保佑工程順利完成。接著,他們會將散發著香氣的艾草箭射進茅屋頂,用來撫慰那些棲身之處被砍伐的樹精,讓他們能夠安息。儀式的高潮是將一顆顆糯米團撒向賓客與新屋的住戶,寓意這個家庭將會如同天降甘霖般,永遠被庇佑,豐衣足食。

令人遺憾的是,這些充滿儀式感與社群精神的建房習俗,已經完全消失了。自明治時代以來,日本的主流民族——大和民族雖然在保存自身文化方面非常優秀,卻對阿伊努文化採取了完全相反的態度。他們推行嚴苛的同化政策,試圖將阿伊努人徹底融入主流社會,抹去他們的文化特徵與語言印記。儘管如此,阿伊努族中仍有一些堅韌的社群據點,努力對抗這種文化滅絕的洪流,守

Li hunter of Hainan circa 1984 / 海南島黎族獵人，一九八四年

護他們的傳統，只不過力量實在渺小。

直到二〇一九年八月，日本才終於正式廢除這項長達一個世紀的同化政策，透過立法承認阿伊努族為北海道的原住民族，這片土地在大和民族到來之前，早已是阿伊努人的家園。希望這分遲來的覺醒，能帶來更多的積極作用，而不會只是徒增諷刺罷了。

傳統的阿伊努族服飾以樺樹或榆樹的外皮為原料，將樹皮纖維精心處理後編織成布料，再在袖口、領口和下襬等邊緣處鑲嵌拼布，並以細緻的刺繡裝飾上獨特的阿伊努圖案。據說，邪靈會從這些容易敞開的部位侵入人體，因此刺繡的目的正是用來阻擋邪靈的入侵，同樣的紋樣也常見於用樹皮製作的日常用品上。巴塔克族和黎族也有類似的工藝，這兩個民族也慣用樹皮來製作服裝。

書中還提到了一些生活小細節。比如在冬天，孩子們喜歡在外頭玩雪、滑雪橇、捏雪人，總能玩得忘乎所以。當小手被凍得又紅又僵時，他們就會一邊吸著鼻涕，一邊飛奔回家，把冰涼的小手往媽媽懷裡一塞。媽媽們則總是會放下手邊的事，輕輕地把孩子的手夾在自己的胸口之間暖一暖。

對阿伊努人來說，大自然的一切都是神聖的。山川、河流、泉水、樹木、動物、魚類，每一樣都被視為神靈而受到尊敬。甚至連日常用的工具和物品，都被當作有靈的存在，每當用畢，他們總會拿起祈禱棒，舉起一杯清酒，向神靈輕聲道謝。

與大多數族群不同，阿伊努人對待神靈的特別之處是，他們不認為神靈總是高高在上

的存在。當不幸的事發生時，神靈可是會挨罵的。

比如，如果有人在山野間遇到意外，人們會毫不客氣地「責備」負責那片區域的神靈：「神明啊，你怎麼這麼馬虎！你看看，因為你的疏忽，出了多大的差錯！」如果有孩子從樹上摔下來，人們甚至會生氣地說：「山神，這棵樹可是你管的！怎麼能讓孩子摔下來呢？下次給我注意點，別讓這種事再發生了！」有時他們甚至會威脅神靈：「如果你現在敢拋棄我，讓我死掉，那我的屍體散發出的惡臭一定會化作霧氣，升到天上，永遠纏著你，讓你不得安寧！」

在阿伊努人的觀念中，人類和神靈並非主僕關係，而是平等的個體。他們認為，只要好好供奉、照顧神靈，那麼神靈就應該回報他們，這是一種互惠的默契。

根據官方統計，如今日本大約有兩萬名阿伊努人，俄羅斯的薩哈林島可能還有一千人左右。在過去漫長的歲月裡，許多阿伊努人因為同化政策遭受迫害，偏見和歧視帶來的自卑感使他們不得不隱藏自己的民族身分。

而在北海道屈斜路湖東岸這個偏僻的小溫泉畔，我竟無意中遇到了我生命中的「第一位阿伊努人」。

Lake Kussharo swan / 屈斜路湖的天鵝
Ainu Keiko / 阿伊努桂子

Onsen with swan / 跟天鵝一起泡溫泉

天鵝湖畔，餘音未散

那是一個傍晚，我獨自來到這方溫泉，水面被夕陽染成金紅色，四周靜謐得只剩下水聲風聲。不一會兒，眼見幾位日本人來了，我便打算起身離開，把小池讓給他們，趁著餘暉拍下幾張湖景。

走回停車場時，一位老婦人迎面走來。她穿著簡樸，步伐穩健，臉上帶著溫暖的微笑。她用日語向我打招呼，我學著這裡的人們禮貌地回以微笑和點頭，簡單說道：「我是從香港來的。」她停下腳步，輕聲說：「我是阿伊努人。」

我期待見到一位阿伊努人已經很久了，而當這個瞬間突然來臨，我一時沒反應過來，愣在那裡。我不知道她的名字，也不確定該如何稱呼她，但回過神來，發現她用手勢示意我跟她走。沒有猶豫，我跟了上去，在這個偏僻的小村落裡，房屋寥寥無幾，不到一分鐘，我們就走到了一個緊靠著溫泉的簡樸小屋，原來這裡是她的家。

我脫下雪靴，跟著她走進屋內。房子很舊，裝修簡單但溫馨，她微笑著請我坐在沙發上。不一會兒，她端來一杯熱茶，拿出一幅裱框的照片遞給我看，照片裡是她的母親。她指著照片說：「阿伊努，阿伊努。」隨後，她又端來一小碗自己做的南瓜請我品嚐，我禮貌地吃了幾口。她注意到我的腳上沒有穿襪子，於是脫下自己的藍白相間的羊毛襪遞給我，示意我穿上。我用手勢問她，這襪子是不是她親手織的，她點頭笑了。

接著，她拿出一張紙，用漢字寫下她的名字「弟子桂子」，前兩個字「弟子」正是附近小鎮「弟子屈」的名字。「桂子」在中文裡意為桂花，一種小巧卻芬芳的花。她又寫下了她的地址和電話，似乎希望我能再來拜訪她。

沙發旁的牆上掛著一個日曆，她指著本月的二十三日，用手指比劃著數字「八十」。我反應過來，原來她幾天後就要迎來八十歲的生日了。我拿出手機，打給一位日本朋友，讓他幫忙翻譯確認。透過朋友簡單聊了幾句後，天色漸暗，我不得不告辭。

臨走時，我想把襪子歸還，但她示意我穿著走。偶然的相遇雖然短暫，卻充滿了溫暖與慷慨。我向她深深鞠躬道謝，走向車時請她留在門口，但她堅持送我到車旁，微笑著揮手道別。

回到朋友農舍的車程本應只需一小時，但第一次與一位真正的阿伊努人相遇的激動讓我心神不寧，竟然迷失了方向。夜色漸深，路燈稀疏，我開過了一段又一段寂靜的鄉間小路，直到不得不停在一家加油站向人問路。最後，是一位路過的行人停下來，耐心地指引我，才讓我重新找到回家的方向。

這次偶然的相遇，不僅加深了我對阿伊努人文化的好奇，更讓我有了想要記錄下他們獨特傳統的渴望，也許這是我能為他們的文化傳承所做的一點微小貢獻。

桂子那句平靜但有力量的「我是阿伊努人」，讓我覺得這是這個族群正努力重新找回自我認同的一個縮影。我心中的念頭在不斷加深，有關桂子和阿伊努人的一切，不該止於這一場告別，希望桂子在這天鵝湖畔留下的足跡，不是謝幕，而是一曲序章，為更多未被講述的故事。

Pointing at 80th birthday / 桂子示意她八十歲的生日
My precious Ainu socks / 珍貴的阿伊努襪子

琉球群島

RYUKYU ISLANDS

Ryukyu – April 22, 2024

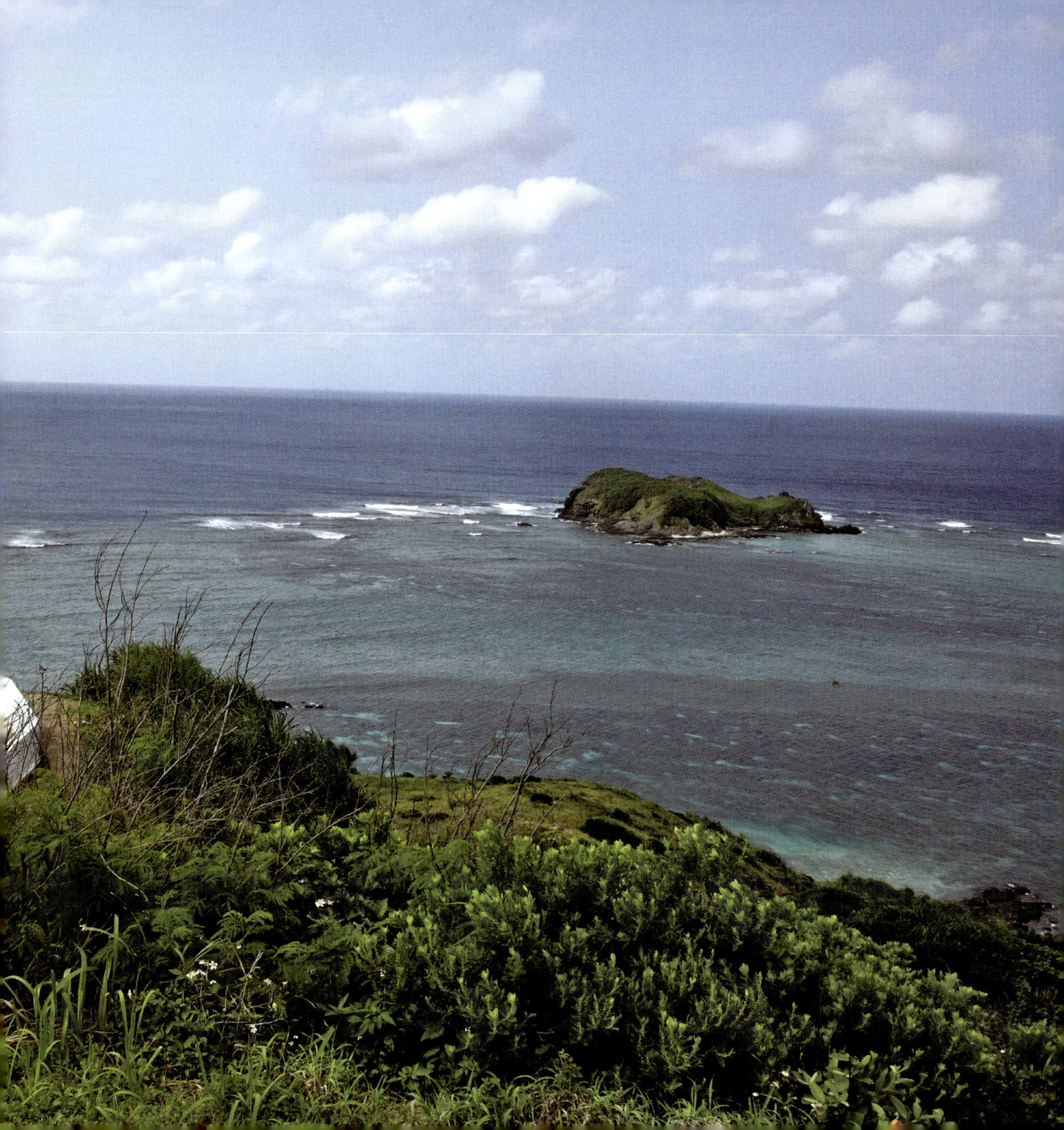

Ryukyu – April 22, 2024

RYUKYU ISLANDS
Some provocative thinking on names

Call it Ryukyu, Okinawa, or Yaeyama, if you like. However geographic name lasts longer than politically motivated names. Nearby to the Ryukyu is another example, Formosa, Taiwan, or the Republic of China. People choose what they prefer, sometimes according to current needs and reasons. When Chiang Kai-shek, a friend of America and a Christian, ruled over China, his Republic of China claimed Tibet was not an issue for others. But for the People's Republic of China? No way, that's another matter. It is a friend or foe issue, a principle related to the system of government, plus all the other rhetorics in-between. Claim also Mongolia if you will, which the map of China in Taiwan tends to do up till recently.

Exhibit A. Recently CERS acquired a 1908 atlas of China prepared by renowned British cartographer Edward Stanford whose eponymous maps store is still at Covent Garden of London. This atlas of China was compiled by Stanford for the UK-based China Inland Mission, a Christian missionary organization, during a time when the Qing Dynasty was about to collapse. Its map of China included, as expected, all of Tibet, even Outer Mongolia. Despite Taiwan was under Japanese occupation as a colony since 1895, Stanford obviously did not approve, and contained it inside the map page of Fukien (Fujian) Province.

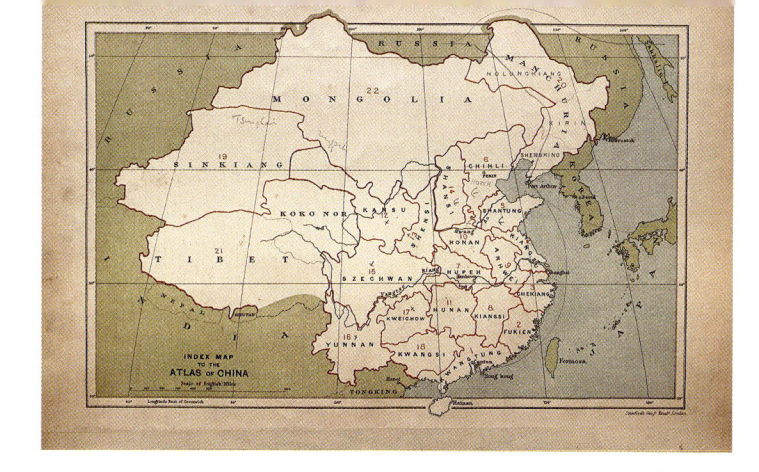

Stanford's Map of China / 中國地圖

Universal suffrage or democratic process as we call it in whatever high-sounding name, it is unlikely that Hawaii joining the USA as the 50th State in 1959, or Sikkim becoming part of India in 1975, can be reversed with a future round of the same procedure when sentiments and conditions should change. Unifying is considered a happy event, and the reverse of fortune to be divided will be labelled separatism.

Let's go back to names. Few people realize IBM represents International Business Machine, and 3M stands for Minnesota Mining and Manufacturing, let alone HSBC relates to Hong Kong and Shanghai. Where CERS (China Exploration & Research Society) has a major Center in the Tibetan area of Yunnan, within the last couple of centuries, the name has changed from Gyalthang to Zhongdian and now called Shangri-la, cashing in on James Hilton's book Lost Horizon.

Likewise, what contemporary maps all called the South China Sea suddenly for some and in part became the West Philippines Sea. But then the Philippines was a colony of Spain, then of the USA, up until 1946, when it was "granted" independence. The sale of Alaska was yet another case in point, a misfortune for Russia, and fortuitous for the US. Political sensitivity seems more acute these days when nationalism can become kingmaker, as well as diversifying of trouble at home, rallying for support that otherwise does not exist. The tensing up of the Spratly seems one such case.

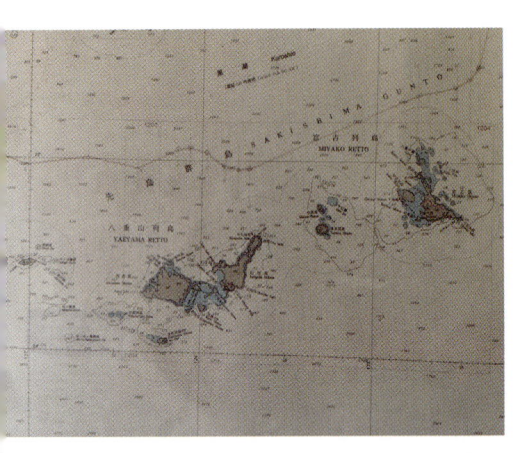

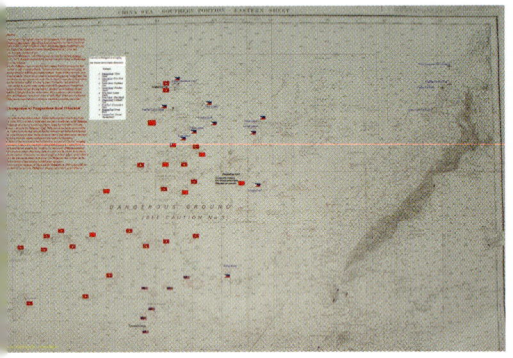

All the above rantings are just food for thought, be they convincing or not. But with such historical interpretations and a few questions in mind, I took a flight from Tokyo to Naha, then with a connecting flight to Ishigaki, hoping to visit the southernmost islands of the Ryukyu group of archipelagos. It seems interesting for a geographer to look at several of these long strings, at times overarching, of archipelagos in Asia. From the north there is the Aleutian, then the Kuril chain, here the Ryukyu, and further south the Paracel and Spratly group. They are all of present-day contention in one way or another, potential Hot Spots for a Cold War or a Hot War in the making.

I was told that it was farmers from Taiwan who were the intrepid pioneers and cultivators of the land in the larger islands in the south. So besides other interests in the geography of these islands, I wanted to talk to some original farmers from Taiwan.

Southern islands of Ryukyu Group /
琉球群島南部島嶼
Map of Spratly & Palawan /
南沙群島與巴拉望

Taking a circuit drive around the island, once out of the city center and along the coast is Tojinbaka, an archaeological site and now mausoleum dedicated to the Chinese. A sign in Chinese named it "Tomb of Tang", which was in reference to Chinese, a general term dating back to China's Dynasty Tang epoch era. The site was going through a major upgrade with new pavilions added. While the architectural style was quite common of that of southern China, the symbolic significance was not simple, representing the very early settlement of the Chinese community on the island.

In more contemporary times however, it was meant to remember an incident of Chinese laborer uprising, after a shipwreck with over 400 workers being stranded near here in 1852. These workers were on their way being shipped from coastal China to California, as part of the coolie trade. The rebellion was instigated by the slave-like condition these workers had to undergo, sold as laborers to America.

This incident happened at a time when Japan did not even claim these southern islands. Another old map CERS acquired, published in 1880 during the Meji period gave the evidence. It covered coastal China, the lower part of Japan, and all of the Ryukyu Islands and Taiwan. On this map, Japan is colored in pink, and the Ryukyu only has its upper section in pink, whereas the lower half, including Taiwan, is in white, as with coastal China. Before that time, Ryukyu was a kingdom, paying tribute annually to the Imperial Court of China.

Maps and history apart, I went on to look for the Taiwan connection as I traveled along the coast of Ishigaki. Passing an area with a wondrous waterfall, I arrived at the Sabichi Cave, a privately owned cave along the way to the northernmost tip of Ishigaki. It is a limestone tunnel leading to a beautiful part of the sea where the tidal wave hit a coast of karst. Many tourists make a stop here and pay for entry through the cave. Tsugumi Hirae lives here and manages the cave. Seventy years of age, she is a second-generation settler from Taiwan. She also operates a gift shop at the entrance to the Cave.

"My father came here from Taiwan 70 to 80 years ago when he was 32 years of age. He soon got married to my mother who was from here, and my grandmother was from Kabira. My father worked as a dentist. He passed away young at age 50 when I was only 11 years old. Without a license, he had to secretly conduct his dental practice behind our house. He also rode his motorcycle to various places to provide treatment, as well as traveled to remote islands to offer his service. He acquired his skills in Taiwan and brought along his dental tools here," Hirae was quite willing to tell us her family story as she continued.

"My family is mentioned in the book 'Taiwan in Yaeyama' by Yoshihiro Matsuda, a writer for the Yaeyama Daily Newspaper who is very interested in the Taiwanese settlers. He even went to Taiwan to collect research material. When the Taiwanese settled in Yaeyama, they experienced many hardships. As a child, my home was located midway between Nagura and the city center, an area frequently visited by Taiwanese. Therefore, I often hear Taiwanese being spoken and can understand it, though I am unable to speak it. Taiwanese people visited us often, even daily. At that time,

Tombs of Tang people / 唐人墓
Mausoleum temple / 唐陵廟

Beach of Ishigaki / 石垣島海灘

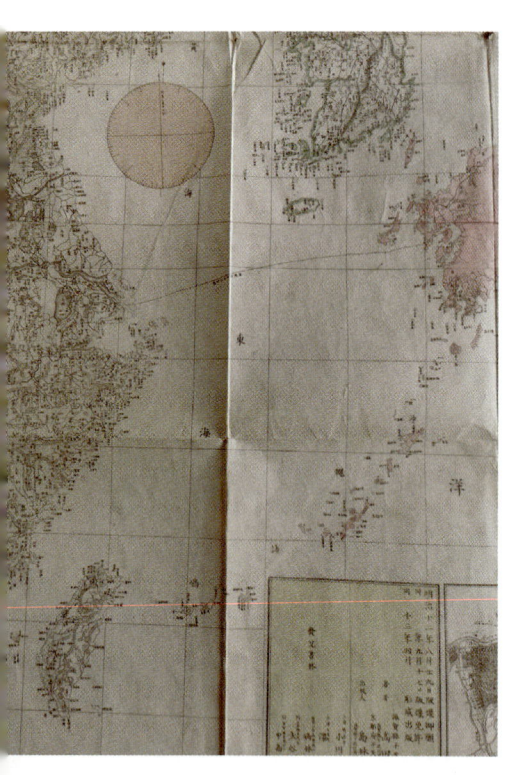

Ryukyu group island as half in red / 琉球群島地圖

the people from Taiwan were often bullied by the Japanese, so my mother told me to keep my Taiwanese heritage a secret," Hirae felt comfortable to reveal to us some of her inner feelings.

"It was us Taiwanese who brought the first pineapple plant to the island, and now it is known throughout Japan. The female members followed and came to help as farm workers," said Hirae. "At the time of my mother's generation, there was a ship in the southwestern islands connecting to Taiwan. My cousin is in Taiwan, but now no ships are going there. If I were to go, I would have to travel to Naha first and then fly to Taiwan. I really hope that they would re-establish a route for ships going to Taiwan," Hirae added her aspiring wishes as she thanked us for taking an interest in her.

With Hirae's information about pineapple, we went on to visit a pineapple farm, run by Dong Changdai, a 68-year-old lady of Taiwanese descent who has settled in Ishigaki for forty years. Her husband, though also of Taiwanese descent, was born in Japan and thus only speaks Japanese and Fukienese, but not Mandarin. As we arrived, Dong was packing her small van to get ready to go to market, delivering her farm vegetables, and above all some ripe pineapples from her farm. Dong is fluent in Mandarin Chinese, having grown up in Taipei. She apologized that she had to rush to market, nonetheless hurried to peel us a few small pineapples of her picking, apparently very proud of her product. They are most tasteful and sweet, being fresh from the field around us.

In fact, pineapples from the Ryukyus, in particular Ishigaki, are so famous that even its juice commands exorbitant prices. Online, a bottle of 500ml pure juice costs HK$148 or US$20. Another brand carried by HKTVmall of 900ml is on sale from HK$450 at a bargain of less than half price, yet still at HK$205. The juice, however, is as toxic to your wallet as to your palate, boasting that "each bottle uses three ripe pineapple juices, with a harmonious resonance of pineapple acid and sweetness in Ishigaki Island is memorable", perhaps even intoxicating if left alone to ferment.

We swung by to the northern tip of the island where a lighthouse marked Ishigaki's northernmost extremity. I always have an affinity for lighthouses wherever I go along the coast, as they are always situated at the most precipitous and strategic locations. This lighthouse on Ishigaki is no exception with a stone tablet depicting its position.

Our next stop is Miyako, one of the three bigger islands at the southernmost tip of the Ryukyu group. It is called by Taiwanese as Ba Chong Shan (eight layers of mountains). With its pristine white sand

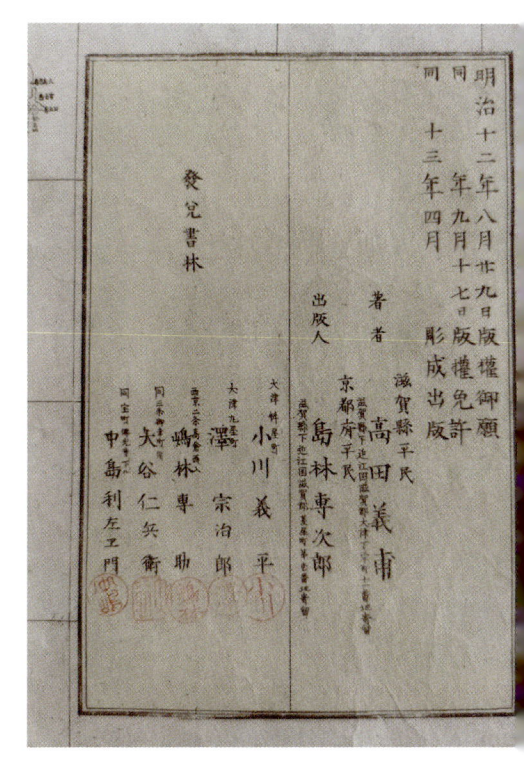

Map corner as endorsed by top retailers / 地圖邊頂級零售商認證的地圖

RYUKYU ISLANDS

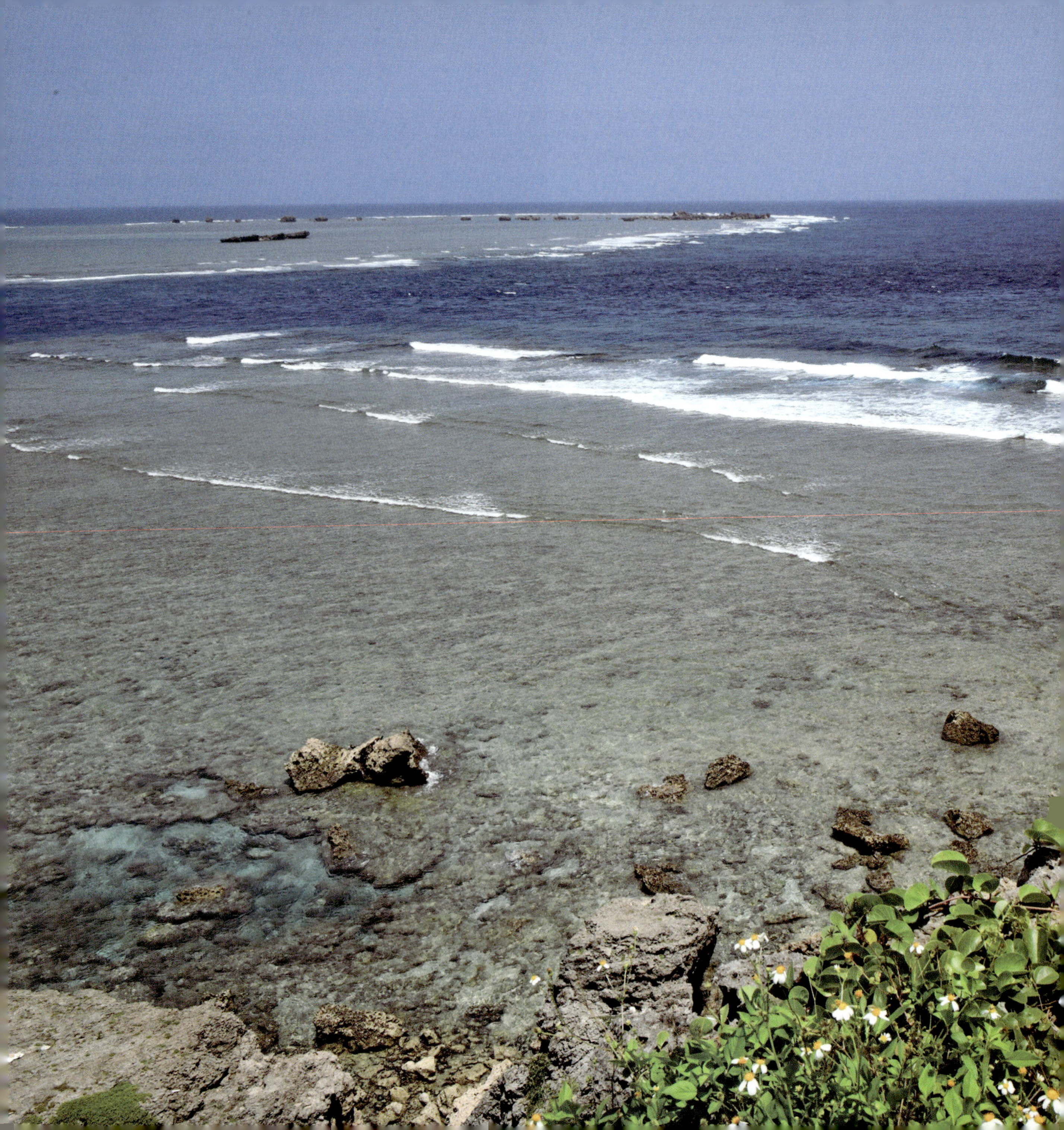

and turquoise-colored water around much of the island, it is a paradise for diving and snorkeling within Japan. I did not miss the chance to stop by one of the hot spots and took a break in snorkeling, looking at some of the near-coast coral and colorful fish.

At Miyakojima fishing port, we interviewed a local fisherman. Kuniyoshi is 70 years of age. All fish caught at sea here are auctioned off at Gyoren but it is not open to the public. The high-priced fish, such as Sujiara and Shirohamahaze are not sold to fishmongers, but only to luxury hotels. All fish caught here are consumed locally and not shipped to the mainland of Japan.

The most common fish sold at auction are the Onaga (Longtooth Grouper), Kannagi (Giant Grouper), tuna, Ise Ebi (Japanese Lobster), Nishikiebi (Ornate Shrimp) and Goshiki Ebi

Miyako coastline / 宮古島海岸

(Five-colored Shrimp). All these marine catches at Miyakjima are relatively inexpensive, at 3000 yens at most, compared to those in the Main Island of Japan. The catch is not very productive during the summer, though currently during our visit it is tuna season. Fishermen here use live bait, and with it has caught large fish sizing up to 13 kg. However, the Aochibiki (Bluefin Trevally) which used to be quite abundant has become more difficult to catch in recent years, perhaps due to over-catching.

We were hoping to buy some fresh catch for dinner. However, at the time of our visit, the boats were out at sea and wouldn't return until between 4 to 6pm. So we parted ways and drove around the island to visit another lighthouse, at the easternmost tip of Miyako. Here as I looked down at the pristine water during low tide, I could see a very large school of turquoise-colored fish. They looked like some giant grouper, floating in and out as the tide gushed in and out of the shore. It was a wondrous site as I left this point, being the last stop of my sojourn here in the southernmost part of Japan.

As I finished my short but interesting visit to the Ryukyu Islands, some earlier thoughts came into mind again, regarding the names used, both Ryukyu and Okinawa that I have seen in signages or shop names around the islands, at times right next to each other. So as name changes go in China: Canton has become Guangzhou, Peking is now Beijing, and Tibet is gradually spelled as Xi Zang. I would not be surprised that in time China may also become Zhong Guo. Such I cannot predict to come, though we have seen within my generation that Great Britain has kissed off its Greatness, and is now officially and popularly known as the United Kingdom. How long it will remain united

HM with Nemo / HM 與尼莫
School of coral fish / 珊瑚魚群
More coral fish / 五彩斑斕的珊瑚魚

is yet to be seen, let alone there are other countries with the prefix "United" as well. Provocative as it may sound, it may or may not become a reality in generations ahead. As an optimist, let's hope again for unity of all, rather than separation.

And as far as the people go, the Taiwanese settlers here in the Ryukus are fast being assimilated into the majority Japanese race. It gives me thoughts regarding the indigenous Ainu people living in Hokkaido to the north of Japan, one of its members I met just earlier this year. The century-long assimilation policy in Japan left such people with little dignity and identity, until only five years ago in 2019 when the Ainu were legally considered indigenous to Japan's northern region. Be it as it may, I would like to think that perhaps the Japanese have been for centuries being reverse assimilated by the Ainu, through their most popular and favorite diet choice of sashimi. After all, the Ainu are the original hunter fishermen of Japan, eating raw meat and fish before the dawn of fire is the most logical outcome, which the Japanese ultimately borrowed and adopted.

Unlike others who may come to the Ryukyu, or Okinawa, for its pristine ocean, fine seafood, or seaside hotels and resorts, it offers for me a chance to reflect on other matters beyond a few beautiful islands. As I look out over the horizon from the coast of Miyako on our last day in the Ryukyu Islands, the setting sun turns burning red over a graying sky. Suddenly I felt as if I was looking at the national flag of Japan. I hope in my mind that this is not a bad omen, as I know the sun will rise again tomorrow morning, for another brighter day ahead of us all. Of course, all meaning do not try to stop others in rising, even if they may surpass you someday!

Seacoast wave / 海岸的波浪

琉球 二〇二四年四月二十二日

琉球群島
―名之思，萬邦之鏡

「琉球」，你也可以稱它為「沖繩」或者「八重山」，隨你喜歡。歷史無數次證明，一片土地的地理名稱往往能比政治名稱存續得更為長久。環顧琉球附近，我們能找到另一個典型案例——「福爾摩沙」、「台灣」，當然你也可以叫它「中華民國」。人們基於當下的需求和特定的理由為一個地域賦予名稱，而這些選擇往往帶有明顯的時代烙印。

當美國的盟友，虔誠的基督徒——蔣介石先生執掌「中華民國」時，西藏是中國的一部分這個說法並不會引發外界的廣泛爭議。然而，當同樣的話出自「中華人民共和國」時，情況就完全不同了。這不僅僅是領土主權的問題，還涉及到敵友關係、意識形態原則，以及所有夾雜其間的政治修辭手段。至於外蒙古，若你願意，也可以把它畫進中國的一部分，之前台灣官方出版的中國地圖就蠻有這個傾向的。

不久前，香港中國探險學會收集了一本由英國著名製圖師愛德華・斯坦福於一九〇八年編製的《中國地圖集》，斯坦福大師的同名地圖商店至今仍坐落在倫敦的柯芬園。這本地圖集是他為英國基督傳教組織「中國內地會」編製的，當時，正值封建制舊中國風雨飄搖、瀕臨崩潰之際。

在這部地圖集中,中國的領土包括整個西藏地區,甚至還包括了外蒙古。而儘管自一八九五年起,台灣已被日本殖民統治,斯坦福依然將台灣劃歸在了福建省的地圖頁內。

「普選」或「民主程序」這些名詞,你把它解釋出花兒來,也沒辦法改變的事實是,一些歷史性決定一旦完成,幾乎不可能再被逆轉。比如一九五九年夏威夷加入美國成為第五十個州,又或者是一九七五年錫金併入印度,這些事,即使未來人們的想法或現實條件有所改變,也幾乎不可能透過相同的民主程序改變既定現實,畢竟單行道上總是沒有機會回頭。

歷史上,「統一」通常被認為是一件值得慶祝的事情,而與之相反的,「分裂」卻常常被視為不幸,「分裂主義」甚至是個人人喊打的負面標籤,這何嘗不是歷史敘事中的「雙重標準」。

話說回來,讓我們繼續來研究「命名」這件事。名字從來不只是簡單的符號,而是權力、歷史和文化的縮影,甚至能成為政治操控和經濟利益的工具。很多人可能不知道,IBM 其實是「國際商業機器公司」的縮寫,3M 指的是「明尼蘇達礦業製造公司」,而 HSBC 的全名是「香港上海匯豐銀行」。

中國探險研究學會在雲南藏區有一個重要中心,這個中心所在城

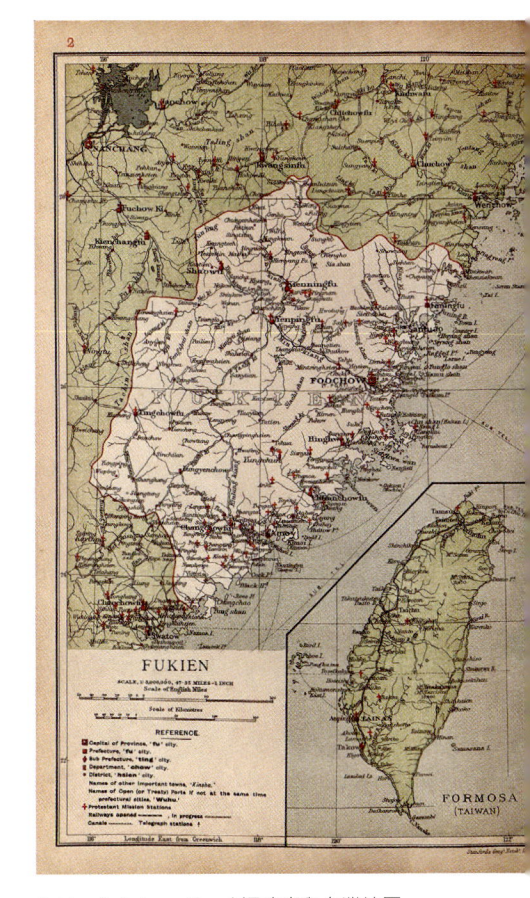

Fukien & Taiwan Map / 福建省與台灣地圖

Map of Kuril chain of islands / 千島群島

市的名字在過去兩百年裡一改再改,從「建塘」到「中甸」,如今又搖身一變成了「香格里拉」,顯然是為了迎合西方對詹姆斯·希爾頓小說《消失的地平線》中「烏托邦」的幻想,將文化炒作成旅遊資本。

類似的情況還發生在地圖上。長久以來被稱為「南海」的海域,突然在某些地方被改成「西菲律賓海」,菲律賓曾經是西班牙的殖民地,接著又被美國殖民,直到一九四六年才被「施捨」了獨立。而阿拉斯加的出售更是另一樁國際政治笑話,對俄羅斯來說是一次歷史性的失誤,對美國卻是撿了個大便宜。

今天,政治敏感性比以往任何時候都更加尖銳,民族主義成了操控輿論的利器,掩蓋內部矛盾的煙幕,煽動那些原本不存在的支持力量。「南沙群島」的緊張局勢就是一個活生生的例子,表面是國家主權的爭奪,背後卻是各國政治的角力。這一切,無非是人類歷史上不斷重演的劇本,只是換了個舞台罷了。

以上這些「牢騷」只是想分享一下我思考問題的角度,是否贊同,那就見仁見智了。懷著這些想法和幾分好奇,我從東京飛到那霸,再轉機到石垣島,計畫造訪琉球群島最南端的島嶼們。

對於地理學家來說,亞洲這些長鏈式的群島總是很有吸引力,像

一串串散落在海上的珍珠，有些相連，有些孤立。從北邊的阿留申群島，到千島群島，到琉球群島，再到更南邊的西沙和南沙群島，這些地方無一不背負著無休止的爭端，像是國際間的「火藥桶」，或者說是一場冷戰或熱戰的引信，隨時可能被點燃。

有人告訴我，南方那些較大島嶼上的土地，最早是由來自台灣的農民開墾和耕種的。他們是這片土地勇敢的開拓者。因此，除了對這些島嶼地理的興趣之外，我也特別希望能與一些來自台灣的農民聊聊他們的故事。

開車沿著環島公路兜了一圈，離開市中心後，沿著海岸線行駛，我來到了唐人墓。這裡是一處考古遺址，如今已成為紀念華人的陵墓。入口的中文標示牌上寫著「唐墓」，這裡的「唐」並非特指唐代，而是一種對中國人的泛稱，這種叫法最早可以追溯到唐朝。

整個遺址正在進行升級改造，新增了幾座涼亭，建築風格帶著濃濃的中國南方韻味。但這個地方的象徵意義並不僅停留於建築本身，它代表著華人社群在這座島嶼上極早期的定居歷史，承載著一段不容忽視的過去。

在更近代的歷史中，「唐人墓」更多是為了紀念一八五二年發生的一場華工起義。那一年，英國商船私運華工四百七十五人自廈門赴舊金山。這次運往美國的華工不肯賣身，於四月初發生暴動，殺死英船主，在琉球八重山島登岸逃亡。五月初，英船到琉球八重山島捕拿華工八十人，次年十一月，琉球將遇難華工一百七十五名送回中國福建，其餘均病死或自縊。

在這場起義發生的年代，日本甚至還沒有開始對這些南方島嶼聲索主權。探險學會收藏的一幅

一八八〇年明治時期出版的古地圖，提供了一個有力的佐證。這幅地圖涵蓋了中國沿海、日本南部、整個琉球群島以及台灣。在地圖上，日本被標示為粉紅色，而琉球群島只有北部被塗成粉紅色，南部包括台灣，都被標為與中國沿海地區相同的白色。這表明在此之前，琉球一直是一個獨立的王國，每年向中國朝廷進貢，維持著朝貢體系下的特殊地位。

暫時撇開地圖與歷史，我沿著石垣島的海岸線繼續尋找與台灣相關的蹤跡。在一處壯麗的瀑布後，是一個名為伊原間的石灰岩洞穴。這是個屬於私人的小景點，一條石灰岩隧道通向蔚藍的大海，海浪拍打著奇特的岩石地貌，許多遊客慕名而來，穿過洞穴，欣賞這片隱祕的美景。

這裡的主人是平江鶴美，一位七十歲的女性。她是來自台灣的二代移民，經營著這個洞穴景點和入口處的小禮品店。

「我的父親是大概七、八十年前從台灣來的，當時他三十二歲。」平江鶴美說。「他來這沒多久就和我母親結婚了，我母親是本地人，外祖母來自附近的川平村。父親去世得早，那年我才十一歲，他五十歲。他是一名牙醫，但因為沒有執照，只能偷偷在家後院看診。有時，他會騎著摩托車到偏遠的地方給人治牙，甚至跑到離島上去。他的技術是在台灣學的，來這裡時還帶著他的工具。」

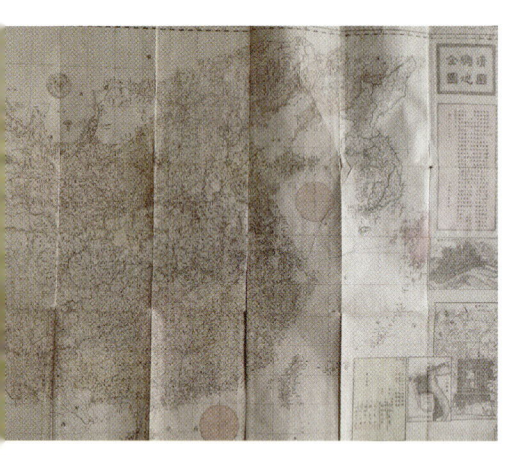

Japan's 1880 China coastal map /
日本一八八〇年出版的中國沿海地圖
Tsugumi Hirae / 平江鶴美

提到家人，她語氣輕和，繼續說：「松田良孝寫的《八重山的臺灣人》這本書提到了我們家族的故事。松田先生對台灣移民很感興趣，還特意去台灣蒐集資料。那時，台灣移民在八重山生活得很辛苦。我小時候，家住在名藏川和市中心之間，那裡是台灣人常聚集的地方。我聽著大人們講台灣話，聽得懂一些，但不太會說。」

說到這裡，她停頓了一下，語氣變得低沉：「那時台灣人常被日本人欺負。我母親總是叮囑我，不要讓別人知道我們有台灣血統，這是我們的祕密。」

「是我們台灣人把第一株鳳梨帶到這座島上的，現在這兒的鳳梨已經是全國聞名了。後來，還有許多台灣女性移民過來，幫忙在鳳梨農場打工。」平江鶴美說道。「在我母親那一代，這片西南群島還有船隻來往台灣。我堂兄弟住在台灣，可惜現在已經沒有船可以過去了。如果我要去台灣，得先到那霸，再搭飛機過去。我真的很希望能重新開通直達航線。」她說出了心願，並對我們關注她的故事表示感謝。

Ishigaki tobacco harvest / 菸葉收成

Ishigaki pineapple harvest / 剛摘下的鳳梨

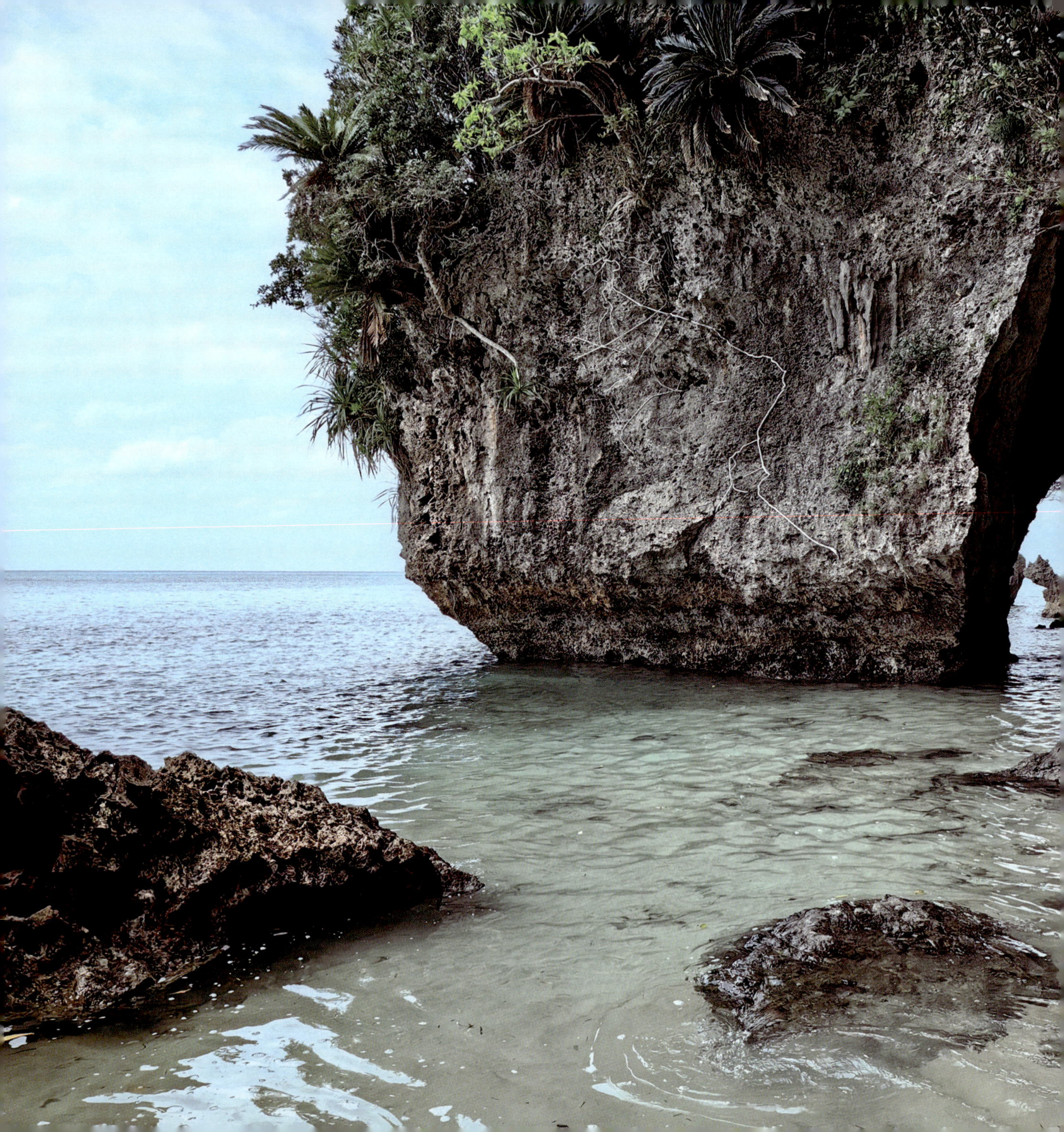

Sabichi Cave / 伊原間石灰岩洞穴
Sea coast beyond cave / 洞穴外的海岸

RYUKYU ISLANDS

根據平江鶴美提到的鳳梨的故事，我們找到了一家鳳梨農場。農場的主人叫東昌代，六十八歲的台灣裔女性，在石垣島已經生活了四十年。她的丈夫雖然也是台灣裔，但出生在日本，只會說日語和閩南話，不會講國語。

我們抵達時，東昌代正在忙著裝貨，準備開著她的小貨車去市場，出售農場的蔬菜和她最引以為傲的熟鳳梨。她成長於台北，國語流利。雖然她忙著出門，但仍熱情地為我們削了幾顆小鳳梨，這些剛從田裡摘下的水果，味道鮮甜濃郁，令人難忘。

石垣島的鳳梨名聲響亮，從鳳梨汁的價格就可見一斑。通常一瓶五百毫升的純鳳梨汁要價一百四十八港幣，約二十美元，在香港最火的網購平台上，一款九百毫升的品牌鳳梨汁，即使打折特價也要兩百零五港幣。這些鳳梨汁以每瓶使用三顆熟鳳梨榨成，口味酸甜交融為賣點，價格雖高，但味道確如其宣傳一樣令人印象深刻。如果放久一點，使其自然發酵，風味往往會變得更加「醇厚」。

在石垣島的最後一站，我們來到了最北端，一座燈塔矗立在懸崖之上，標誌著島嶼的極北點。我對燈塔有種與生俱來的喜愛——它們總是在最險峻、最重要的位置守望著大海。石垣島的這座燈塔也不例外，旁邊的石碑清楚地刻著它的地理坐標，彷彿在向來訪者訴說它的使命。

離開石垣島，我們前往宮古島，琉球群島南端的三大島嶼之一，台灣人稱它「八重山」。宮古島以環繞的白沙和碧藍的海水聞名，是浮潛愛好者的天堂。我當然不會錯過這樣的機會，選了一處熱門潛水點，戴上裝備跳入水中，看著五彩斑斕的魚兒在珊瑚間穿

梭，感受生機勃勃的海底世界。

在宮古島的漁港，我們採訪了一位當地漁夫，七十歲的國吉先生。他告訴我們，這裡所有的漁獲都會在漁聯進行拍賣，但這個拍賣市場並不對外開放。一些高價魚類，例如蘇子鯛和白濱鯊，只供應給高端酒店，並不出售給普通魚販。此外，這裡的所有漁獲都只供本地消費，並不外運。

在拍賣中最常見的魚類包括紅牙鯛（長牙石斑魚）、海神鯛（巨型石斑魚）、鮪魚，以及伊勢龍蝦、錦蝦和五色蝦。相比日本本土，宮古島的漁獲價格相對便宜，每公斤最高僅售三千日圓。夏季漁獲量通常較少，不過我們到訪時正值鮪魚的旺季。漁夫們使用活餌捕魚，有時能捕到重達十三公斤的大魚。不過，曾經數量豐富的藍笛鯛近年來卻越來越難捕到，可能是過度捕撈所致。

我們原本希望能買些新鮮的漁獲作晚餐，但當我們到訪時，漁船仍在海上作業，預計要等到下午四點到六點才能返港。於是，我們驅車繼續探索，前往宮古島最東端的燈塔。

站在燈塔下俯瞰退潮時的海水，視線穿透清澈的海洋，一大群湛藍色的魚在水中游動。牠們看起來像是巨型石斑，若隱若現地穿梭於岸邊與深海之間。這片如夢似幻的海景，成了我此行的壓軸畫面，為這次日本南端的旅程畫上了完美的句號。

結束了這次短暫但頗具趣味的琉球群島之旅，一些早先的思考再次浮現在腦海中。在旅途中，我頻繁地看到「琉球」和「沖繩」這兩個名稱交替出現在路邊的招牌上，有時甚至會並列出現。

這讓我想起中國地名在國際寫法上的變遷：廣州、北京等地曾經的國際寫法各有其特定的英文單詞，

Lighthouse on Miyako / 宮古島燈塔

Blue groupa at coast / 藍色石斑魚

並不是漢語拼音，而如今，西藏也越來越多以其拼音形式出現在世界各地的報導中。所以，我不會驚訝於未來的某一天，「中國」的英文單詞不再是大寫的「瓷器」，而是和它的城市一樣，變成中國人自己的漢字拼音。

我無法預測這樣的改變是否會發生，但我們這一代人已經見證了許多名稱的象徵被改寫──「大不列顛」早已放下了它的「大」，如今無論官方還是民間，都僅稱它為「聯合王國」。然而，這「聯合」的意義究竟又能維持多久？這個世界上冠以「聯合」之名的國家可不止一個，但名稱之下，團結又有幾分真實？

這樣的思考或許聽來有些挑釁，但歷史的規律從未寬恕過自滿的秩序。未來的某一天，我們可能會見證更多的崩解，也可能會看到新的聯合。不管怎樣，作為樂觀主義者的我，仍希望無論名稱如何變化，人心的連結能超越地理與政治的疆界，因為真正的團結並非來自名號，而是來自彼此的理解與尊重。

至於人群本身，琉球群島的台灣移民正在迅速被同化，融入日本主流社會。這讓我想起北海道的阿伊努族──一個我今年早些時候不期而遇的原住民群體。長達一個世紀的同化政策幾乎抹去了他們的身分與尊嚴，直至二〇一九年，日本政府才正式承認，阿伊努族為日本北部的原住民。

不過，換個方式思考，或許真正被同化的並非阿伊努族，而是日本人自己。刺身文化，這分如今被視為日本飲食精髓的傳統，很可能正是源自阿伊努族的飲食習慣。作為早期的獵人漁民，阿伊努族在掌握火的使用之前便以生肉與生魚為食，而這種樸素的飲

食方式,最終被日本人吸收並發揚光大。

他人奔赴琉球,或許為那琉璃海、雪浪盤,或是一枕潮聲的度假夢境,而於我,這片群島更像是一面澄明的鏡子,照見浮世之外的深闊。在宮古島的最後一個傍晚,天空灰濛濛的,落日卻紅得刺眼,像一面燒紅的鐵板懸在海天之間。那一刻我突然覺得,自己好像正凝視著日本的國旗。

這景象帶來了更多的思緒。世間潮汐起落,太陽每日如約而至,光耀如新。升升落落間,總有光亮,彼此包容便不會相互遮蔽,又何懼後人的光芒?

Japanese flag sunset / 日本國旗般的夕陽

被困在西藏的尼泊爾人

NEPALI STRANDED IN TIBET

Gyirong, Tibet – May, 2024

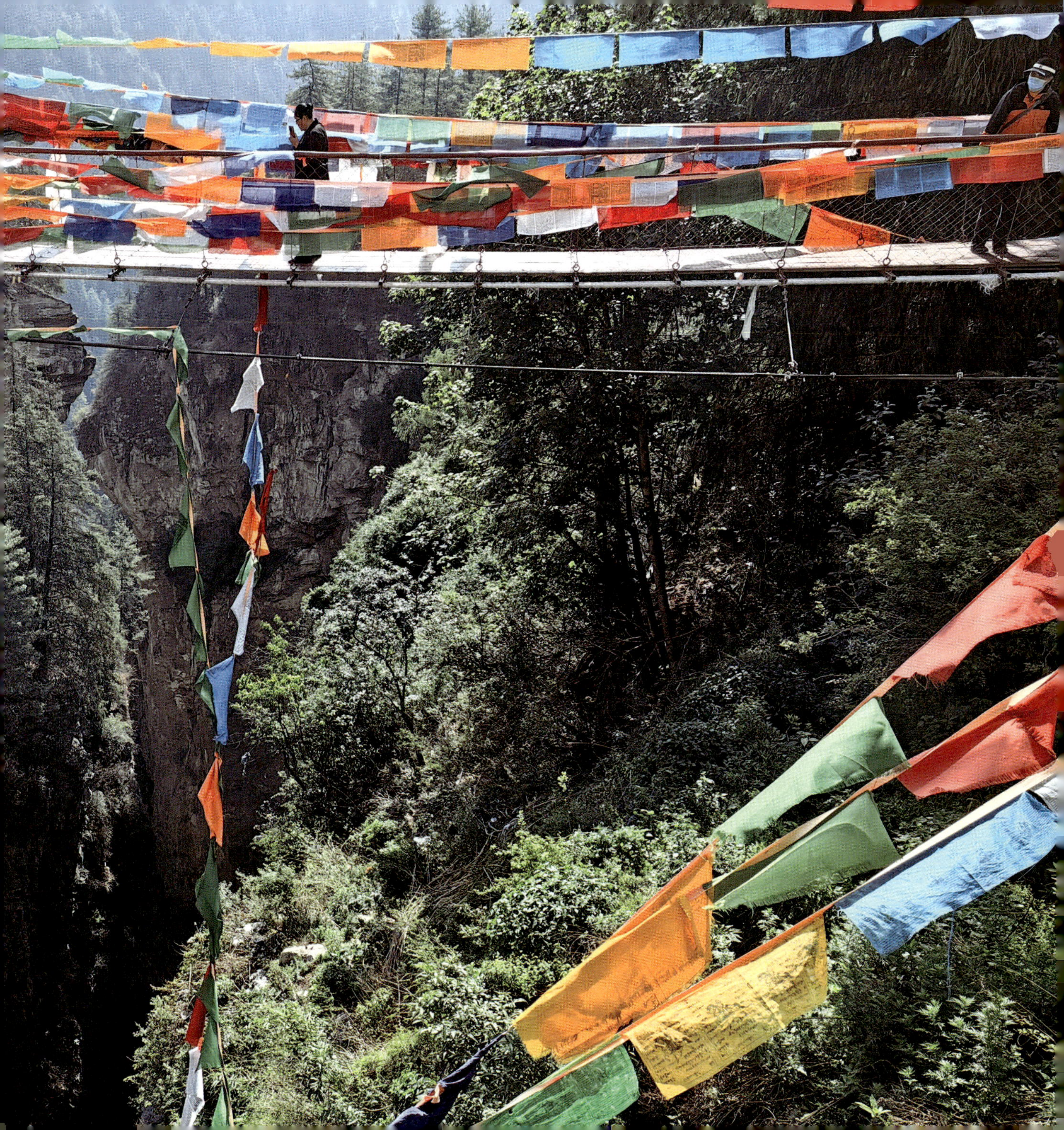

Gyirong, Tibet – May, 2024

NEPALI STRANDED IN TIBET
At long last citizens of China

Some two hundred years ago, a Nepali cavalry was dispatched to fight in Tibet during the Qing Dynasty. It was a time when Nepal as a Himalayan kingdom was at its zenith of power, led by a king who wanted to expand its influence into neighboring Tibet. The Tibetans lost the battle and requested the Qing court to intervene, sending in its reinforcement army. Ultimately the Nepali was defeated and retreated to south of the Himalayas. However, some of its army since then had been stranded in pockets of the border region inside Tibet. These are now known as the Daman people (meaning calvary), living much like refugees for over two hundred years. Over twenty years were these descendant Nepalis given Chinese citizenship, and thus finally can get around like a normal person. Before, they did not have any status, no identity cards, no schooling for their children. My team and I were on our way to explore northern Nepal, traveling from southern Tibet into the country, or former kingdom before its last king was abolished in 2008. I decided to pay a visit to the Daman people, few as they are now remaining in China. A recent survey put them at less than 300 individuals, 47 families in all, residing in one village the government has built for them.

Basong, 41 years of age, has been the village chief for many years, recently being elected again as

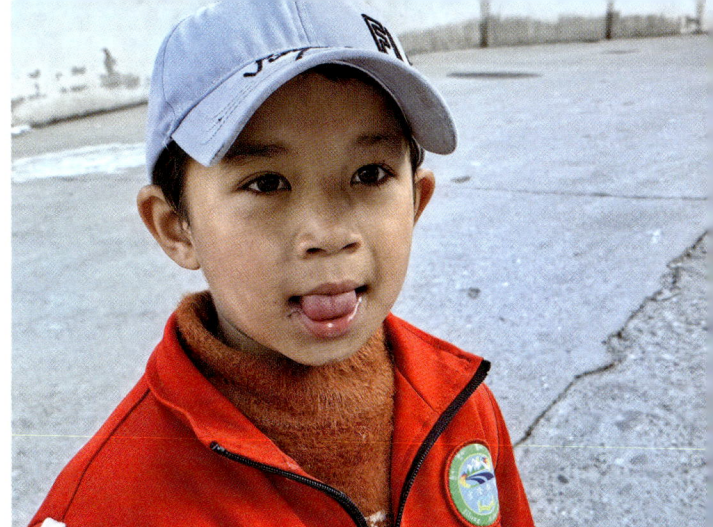

Daman woman & child / 達曼婦女與孩子

Daman boy / 達曼男孩

head. His father was also village chief before him, but was killed while trying to arbitrate between four of the villagers during a drunken brawl turned into a fighting bout. Basong was barely seven years old at the time. He is a bit shy and very humble, though obviously proud of being accepted as a member of the Communist Party. In fact, I found all Daman people I ran into quite modest and humble, due perhaps to their long generations of being stateless and looked down upon. But their lot is looking much brighter in the near future, as the government is caring more and more about minority nationalities' welfare and each of their unique identity. Many of the young men among the Daman are now being recruited into the local militia as border guards, at a pay of Rmb 300 per day.

After over two hundred years of being separated from their motherland of Nepal, today none of these Nepali Daman people speak Nepali, and Chinese and Tibetan have become their native tongue. For Basong's parents' and grandparents' generations before the founding of the PRC in 1949, the borderline was not very well defined and its control were not very strict. Thus they could cross the border, staying on the Nepal side in winter for warmer climates, and on Tibet's side during the summer. However, neither side would consider them its citizens, and thus stateless. Basong's wife is 45 years of age. Together they have two sons, one going to junior high, the other in primary at county town Gyirong. As for Basong, he has joined government study tour and visited Beijing, Hangzhou and Changsha.

In an ethnographic study by Chinese scholars ten years ago, it surveyed a total of 51 Daman families, with each household head listed. Unsurprisingly, all of them have Tibetan names, not one carries Nepali name. Today there are 47 Daman households in total. Now with full status to travel, some have moved to Lhasa or other provinces. Those remaining will soon be moving into a new and posh community that is built by the government for them, free of charge.

We went to have a look at these new houses and were amazed at how modern they are, each with a spacious living room, kitchen with facilities installed, and two or three bedrooms with modern bathrooms. Furthermore, there are six duplex villas with floor-to-ceiling windows, open kitchen,

Daman new villas / 達曼新村的別墅

Basong in front of new home / 巴桑的新家門前

bathtub outfacing, built to serve as their communal boutique hotel. A large dining area in a separate building serving also as a restaurant is included to help the Daman maintain a comprehensive coop business. The effort by the government to design a sustainable living model seems quite obvious.

In the past, the Daman people, without status and much skill, could only perform the most lowly and unwanted jobs in the area. Basong started doing odd jobs at the age of nine, like digging for potatoes and frying barley or other labor-intensive work. At that time the daily pay was RMB2 a day. Now life has improved beyond his imagination. Their work pay now is for men RMB220 and for women RMB210 per day, in rotation soon to begin with operating the new premises of tourist villas given to their community. In the past, as landless people, they are not allowed to collect cordyceps, or caterpillar fungus. Today, between May 20 to July 20, they can also go search for these high-value fungus in the mountains.

In the past, most Daman men engaged themselves in iron-smithing work. The locals called the Daman men as "Da Tie Jiang" which is considered a lowly job and somewhat a derogative term. We managed to locate two Daman artisans who are still maintaining their traditional occupation of iron-smithing. The main craftsman is Tashi Dengju, now 53 years of age. He started working in this profession at age 18. An elderly man sat and

Modern facilities / 非常現代化的設施

continued turning a hand-fan to blow air into the hearth of coal. When the piece of iron inside the burning coal is red hot, Tashi would take the axe-like metal out with a pair of plyers and hit the edge a dozen or so times, before putting the axe back to repeat the same process over again and again. Harnessing such metal into an axe would require a long time, but the finished piece can be sold for over RMB1000, not a small sum in this remote area, though ten years ago such axe commands only a quarter the price. Inflation has hit even remotest corners of China I assume.

Not far from the Daman new village and closer to the border with Nepal is a small temple on a hillock. The spartan temple Jipugurupu is where local Tibetans believe Guru Rinpoche, the highest monk of the Nyingma Sect of Tibetan Buddhism, has spent time meditating. The hike there takes about half an hour from the Tibetan Jipu Village situated next to a very deep gorge. The village is a clean community where the government has built and assigned houses to each household with many shops catering to local Tibetans coming here daily as pilgrims.

The main temple, though quite small, has an altar. There it has three seated statues. In the middle is Songtsen Gampo, the most revered Tibetan King of the 7th century. He famously had two wives, one a princess from China and the other a princess from Nepal, both sitting on his two sides in

Jipu Tibetan village / 吉普藏族村落
Tibetan weaver / 藏族婦女

Mountain between Nepal and Tibet / 尼泊爾和西藏邊境雪山

this shrine. In an adjacent smaller shrine also has two statues. Here only a statue of the King and his consort the Nepalese Princess are in it, without the Chinese Princess Wen Cheng. The fate of the Daman people seems to resonate that union in this temple and shrine, between China and Nepal, through a matchmaker in Tibet.

Much has been written about Princess Wen Cheng of China, and many shrines built. Even elaborate television series has been made. But little has been documented about the Nepalese Princess married to the Tibetan King before Princess Wen Cheng arrived in Lhasa. A booklet given to me by Her Majesty Kesang Choeden Wangchuck, the Royal Grandmother of Bhutan, recorded the Nepali King's final instructions to his daughter, Princess Bhrikuti Devi, before her departure to Lhasa. It may be of interest and for the record to quote below in whole:

O! Daughter, dear as my very eyes listen! In the extraordinary land called Tibet, with high mountains, pristine lands, and formidable snowy peaks, cool and cold, this palace of the gods. Whence four rivers fall and four seas are fair, where the five grains grow and various gems are found, where one finds ever so many joys and contentment and grain is eaten red. The subjects are not [ordinary]; their Lord King is a god. Not just the fourfold retinue, they're of the bodhisattva race. They lack the holy Dharma, yet the King's commands are Dharmic. They lack supreme Sangha friends, yet their true friend is the Nirmāṇakāya king. To such a land, my child you must go.

This statue of the Śākya Sage, object of my devotions, commissioned by Indra, Lord of Gods, *and of precious jewels made by Viśvakarman, bears Buddha's blessings. Consecrated by the Buddha himself, who said, "There is no difference between devotions to this holy object or to my physical remains." The Buddha's qualities are countless and limitless, and this image of the Victor, with qualities so limitless. Daughter of my heart, make it the object of your devotions. This Maitreya turning the Dharama wheel, sprung of itself up from the Victor's blessings, worship it and you will be born at Maitreya's feet and similar qualities without measure will arise. This Self-Arisen Sandalwood Tārā worship her and you are saved from eight fears and will awaken in your next life. Similar qualities without measure will arise. So, daughter of my heart, make it the support of your devotions.*

Ah! Child from who I cannot bear even a moment's separation, in the Tibetan land, where the language and race are different, make your comportment and disposition like this: Make your view loftier than the high sky, your behavior broader than the heavens; Make your dignity heavier than Meru, king of mountains, your smile more beautiful than a lotus; Make your dress tighter than knotted silk, your mind more obedient than white silk; Make your temperament softer than Chinese silk, keep [your belongings] better than a medicine pouch, in saving, be wiser than a honeybee. With the affection as of close kin, treat [others]

King & two Princesses / 藏王與兩位公主
King with Nepali Princess / 藏王與尼泊爾公主

NEPALI STRANDED IN TIBET 131

like a sister. Be profoundly accommodating like the ocean depths. Make your shoulders broad as the earth. Move your hands swift as lightning in the heavens. Make your hands clean as a lotus. Be kind to the wicked as to your own children. Respect the good as you do your masters. Love each sentient being as your mother. Strive in virtue like it is your occupation. Abandon sin like poison. Have great faith in the holy Dharma. Mind your tongue like a dead man's corpse. Keep moderation in food as in medicine. Work others' benefit like medicinal extracts. Be sure to be clear as the sun. If you do, benefit will come to Tibet, and you will awaken in your next life.

Ah, Cherished daughter, Thritsün, to you I grant a treasury of jewels- seven elephant loads. These implements of inexhaustible enjoyment I send, child, to carry you across the pass of poverty: artisans skilled with many tools and servants. I send, child, to accomplish your work, and this large group of servant girls. I send, child to attend and wait on you, the goods of marketplace and customs house, and all sundry delights wished for in Tibet. I send, beloved daughter, whatever you want. Of old, daughters have not ruled their fatherlands. Therefore, daughter, go to the center of Tibet, comfort the emanation-king and serve him. Propagate the good religion decreed [by the king]. Make the lord's palace secure. Erect holy images of the Three Jewels in Dharmic fashion. Build great monastic temples and statues. Make the Buddhadharma grow and

King Songtsen Gampo with his Chinese consort, Princess Wencheng and his Nepali consort, Bhrikuti Devi. (Ramoche Temple, Lhasa, Tibet)

King Songtsen Gampo with his two consorts, Princess Wencheng and Bhrikuti Devi.

The King of Nepal's Final Instructions To His Daughter Bhrikuti Devi / 尼泊爾國王對女兒的臨別囑託

offer to the Sangha. Delight the Tibetan king and ministers.

The happy ending of the Daman people is yet another positive, yet hidden, story for me who am optimistic and have spent half a century exploring China. It may only be a tiny story among the currently popular worldwide negative reporting of China from a media bent on discrediting the huge accomplishment of a rising China, be it because of paranoia or for whatever reason. Selective reporting, even fact-based, is not balanced reporting. I would not worry about declaring my own biases and prejudices, despite being Chinese and having seen China close up for fifty years. Claiming neutrality in this day and age in a highly politicized world is only for the naïve readers.

As reporting on China goes, the like of those I admired from an earlier generation, Theodore White for Time Magazine, Owen Lattimore for Pacific Affairs, and John Service for the Foreign Service, are all names of the past. All of them who wrote what they saw in real about China were sidelined, censored and ostracized. Today the internet in the hands of anyone has long blurred the line between fact and fiction. Long ago, the Chinese Yin and Yang circle with a curvy middle line is perhaps a good analogy, except that today even that line is becoming blurred as well. Dao can no longer explain our highly political and polarized world.

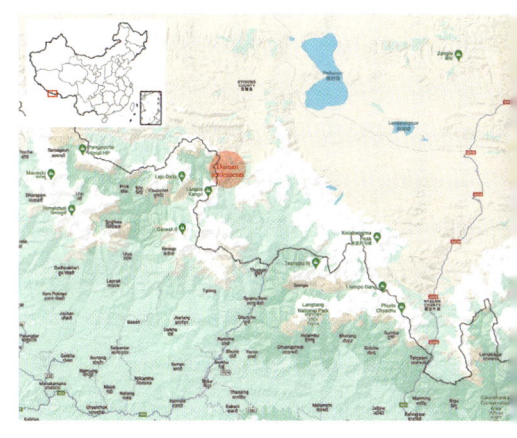

Border region of the Daman / 達曼人的邊境地區

西藏 吉隆 二〇二四年五月

被困在西藏的尼泊爾人 成為中國公民的他們

在約兩百年前的清朝，一場發生在西藏與尼泊爾邊境的戰爭，意外改變了一群人的命運。當時，尼泊爾作為喜馬拉雅山脈上的一個強盛王國，正處於它的權力巔峰。雄心勃勃的國王夢想著擴展王國的影響力，將觸角伸向鄰近的西藏。於是，一支精銳的尼泊爾騎兵部隊被派遣北上，跨越山脈，進攻這片土地。

然而，戰爭的結果並不如尼泊爾所願。藏軍受打擊後，向清廷求助，清朝隨即派出大批援軍，最終打敗了尼泊爾軍隊，迫使其撤回喜馬拉雅山以南。

不過，並非所有人都安全地撤回了自己的國家，一些尼泊爾士兵被困在西藏邊境的偏遠地區，無法返回故土。這些被困的士兵，逐漸定居於西藏，過著難民一樣的生活，成為了一個特殊的族群。他們，被稱為「達曼人」。

「達曼」一詞在藏語中，意為騎兵的後裔。時間推進到二十世紀末，二〇〇三年，中國政府終於決定給予達曼人中國公民身分，此前，他們沒有任何合法身分，沒有證件，無法接受教育，連最基本的社會保障都無從談起。

我和我的團隊從西藏南部出發，準備穿越邊境，進入尼泊爾北部——這個曾經的「喜

馬拉雅王國」。尼泊爾的最後一位國王已於二〇〇八年退位，古老的君主制國家如今成為了一個共和國。

我決定在這趟旅程中順路去探訪一下達曼這個族群。如今的達曼人只剩不到三百人，分散於四十七個家庭。他們絕大多數住在西藏日喀則市吉隆鎮的吉隆口岸附近，被政府安置在特意為他們建造的一個村莊裡。

現年四十一歲的巴桑已擔任村長多年，在剛結束的換屆中再次被推選為村長。他的父親也曾是村長，但在調解村民醉酒鬥毆時，不幸被誤傷並喪命。那時，巴桑才七歲。如今的巴桑性格略顯害羞，但十分謙虛。談吐中不時流露出他對自己共產黨員身分的自豪。

其實，我遇到的達曼人都十分謙遜，這或許跟他們的祖先在長達兩百多年的時間裡，因為無國籍身分而被鄙視的經歷有關。但現在，隨著政府越來越關注少數民族的福利和其獨特的文化身分，他們的生活正變得越來越光明。近些年，許多達曼年輕人被都招募進了「地方民兵隊」，擔任邊境守衛，每天的工資能有三百元人民幣。

經過兩百多年的分離，如今的達曼人已經完全與尼泊爾斷了聯

Daman militia / 達曼民兵

繫。他們不再說尼泊爾語，而是以藏語和漢語作為母語。在一九四九年中華人民共和國成立之前，也就是巴桑的父母和祖父母那代人的年代，邊境線並不清晰，管理也相對鬆散，他們可以自由穿越邊界，冬天到尼泊爾一側暖和一下，夏天則回到西藏避暑。然而，無論在哪一側，他們都不被視為合法公民，始終處於無國籍狀態。

巴桑的妻子今年四十五歲，兩人育有兩個兒子。大兒子正在吉隆縣城的初中就讀，小兒子則在當地的小學上學。作為村長的巴桑，曾參加過政府組織的學習考察團，去過北京、杭州和長沙等城市。

十年前，中國學者對達曼人進行了一次民族誌調查，記錄了當時五十一戶家庭的戶主名單。不出所料，這些戶主的名字全是藏語，沒有一個是尼泊爾名字。如今，達曼人總共只剩下四十七戶家庭。一些人獲得合法旅行的權利後，已經搬到了拉薩或其他省分生活。而那些留在村裡的達曼人，即將搬進政府為他們免費建造的新社區——一個設施完善、環境優美的現代化小區。

Iron smithing / 鐵匠打鐵　　Making an axe / 打造斧頭　　Finishing touches / 出爐前的最後修飾

我們參觀了一下這個即將竣工的新社區，其現代化程度實在是令人驚喜。每戶都配備了寬敞的客廳、設施齊全的廚房，以及兩到三間有獨立衛浴的臥室。此外，為支持達曼社群的經濟可持續發展，社區內還建有六棟帶有落地窗的雙層別墅，設計精美，配有開放式廚房和面向窗外的浴缸，這些別墅將作為精品酒店對外開放。社區內還有一棟大型餐廳，既可作為公共用餐區，也能運營為餐館。不難看出，政府在為達曼人設計可持續生活模式方面是花了心思的。

過去，達曼人因為沒有身分和技能，只能從事當地最卑微、最不受歡迎的工作。巴桑在九歲時便開始做零工，挖土豆、炒大麥等勞動力密集型工作沒少幹過。那時，他一天的工資僅有兩元人民幣。

如今，變化可謂是翻天覆地，達曼社群中男性的日薪能達到兩百二十元，女性兩百一十元，並且他們即將輪流參與經營社區新建的精品酒店，這將為他們帶來更多的收入機會。以前，這些沒有土地的達曼人甚至無法合法採集冬蟲夏草。但現在他們獲得了許可，每年五月二十日到七月二十日，可以按規定進山採集。

在過去沒有合法身分的時間裡，大多數達曼男性以當鐵匠為生，但這種職業並不被當地人尊重，他們會用「打鐵匠」直接指代達曼人，語氣間多少都摻雜著貶義。

我們找到了兩位仍然保有鐵匠技藝的達曼手藝人，其中一位是主匠塔希登居，今年五十三歲。他從十八歲開始打鐵，至今已有數十年經驗。在他的小作坊裡，一位年長的助手坐在一旁，用手搖風扇不斷向煤爐中送風，讓爐火保持旺盛。當鐵塊在煤火中燒得通紅，塔希便用鉗子將它夾出，快速地用錘子敲打十幾下，然後重新放回去加熱，反覆操作，最終將鐵塊打造成一把堅固的斧頭。

Tibetan home / 藏民家中
Tibetan pilgrims / 藏族香客

這樣一把斧頭需要耗費很長時間才能完成，所以在當地可以賣到超過一千元人民幣的價格，但是相比十年前，類似的斧頭只值四分之一的價錢。看來，即使是中國最偏遠的地區，通貨膨脹也一樣厲害。

在離達曼新村不遠處，靠近尼泊爾邊境的一個小山丘上，聳立著一座簡樸的寺廟——吉普古如普寺。當地藏人相信，這座寺廟曾是藏傳佛教寧瑪派的至高僧人蓮花生大士靜修冥想之地。從毗鄰深邃峽谷的吉普村步行到寺廟，大約需要半小時。吉普村的建設規規矩矩，非常整潔，政府為當地藏族每戶家庭都建了分配住房，還有許多商店為每日來此朝聖的藏人提供服務。

吉普寺的主殿雖然不大，但供奉著一座神聖的祭壇，祭壇上有三尊坐像：中間是七世紀最受尊敬的藏王松贊干布。這位藏王因娶了兩位公主而廣為人知——一位是來自中國的文成公主，另一位是來自尼泊爾的布里庫提公主，又名尺尊公主。兩位公主的坐像分別位於松贊干布的兩側，象徵著兩段歷史性的聯姻。

在寺廟另一旁的小殿裡，則僅供奉著兩尊雕像：松贊干布與他的尼泊爾妻子布里庫提公主，並沒有中國文成公主的身影。這種設置似乎在某種程度上反映了尼泊爾與西藏之間那段更早、更直接的聯繫，也無形中巧妙地折射出達曼人的命運——他們的歷史，

Guru Rinpoche sacred site / 蓮花生大士的靜修地

正是在尼泊爾與中國之間，經由西藏這片土地串聯起的一段故事。

中國文成公主的事蹟早已廣為人知，相關的寺廟、紀念碑甚至影視劇不勝枚舉。然而，尼泊爾公主布里庫提卻少有人提及。事實上，布里庫提是早於文成公主嫁給松贊干布的。

有幸的是，布里庫提的故事被一位尊貴的不丹王室成員記錄了下來——不丹太王太后格桑卻登曾贈予我一本小冊子，其中詳細記載了尼泊爾國王在布里庫提公主出嫁拉薩前，對她的臨別囑託。這段話雖然簡短，卻具有重要的歷史價值。我將全文引述如下，以供參考與記錄：

啊！吾女，如眸般珍貴的明珠，且聽父言！在那名為吐蕃的殊勝之地，
崇山巍峨，雪嶺皚皚；神宮淩空，清涼莊嚴；四河奔湧，四海澄明；五穀豐饒，珍寶遍野；眾生安樂，紅糧為食。其民非凡，其王如神；侍眾非俗，皆菩薩種。雖未廣聞佛法，王命即是法音；雖少僧伽聖友，化現君王為依；吾女啊，你須前往這般國土。

這尊釋迦牟尼像，由天神鑄造，匠神雕琢，佛陀親自加持，敬拜此像，如見我身。佛德無量，聖像莊嚴，吾女當誠心供奉，福澤綿長。彌勒轉法輪像，因佛力自然顯現，虔誠禮拜，來世必生其座下，無邊功德，自然增長。檀香自現度母像，虔心供奉，可免災厄，來世得解脫，福慧如海，無盡無量。

雪域異鄉，風俗不同，吾女當謹記：眼界高於天，胸懷廣如地；威儀重如山，微笑美

似蓮。衣著端莊，心思純淨；性情柔韌，持物謹慎。節儉如蜂，待親如己；包容似海，擔當若地。行事如閃電，雙手潔無瑕；待惡者如子，敬善者如師。視眾生如母，勤修善德；避惡如避毒，深信佛法。慎言如默，飲食有度；利他如藥，心明如日。如此，必能福澤雪域，來世得悟。

賜你珍寶七象載，無盡財富隨身行，巧匠僕從相隨，助你安度此生。愛女所願，皆可成就。自古女兒不治國，你當遠赴吐蕃，輔佐法王，弘揚佛法，穩固朝綱，興建寺廟，供奉三寶，廣施僧眾，使佛光普照，令王臣歡喜，來世得道。

我只能說，達曼人的幸福結局，對我這個懷著積極的態度在中國探索了半個世紀的人來說，又是一個美好卻註定鮮為人知的故事。當今的全球輿論對中國的崛起充滿偏見。我認為，即便是基於事實的「選擇性報導」，也絕非「公正的報導」。作為一名中國人，近距離觀察中國五十年，我毫不諱言自己的偏好。在這個高度政治化的時代，「中立」不過是天真讀者的幻想。

說到關於中國的報導，我敬重的上一代記者——《時代》週刊的白修德、《太平洋事務》的歐文‧拉鐵摩爾、美國外交官謝偉思——都已成為過去。這些如實記錄中國的人，最終都遭到排擠、審查和放逐，無數個例子向我們證明，真相從來不是討好的選擇。

今天，網際網路讓每個人都能發聲，但事實與虛構的界線早已模糊。一切都像一幅被打亂的「陰陽圖」：黑與白不再分明，象徵平衡的那條彎曲中線，早已被徹底撕裂。道家陰中有陽、陽中有陰的哲理，曾解釋世間萬物對立中的和諧，但如今，連對立都失去了邏輯，怕是剩下的只有一片無解的混沌。

從吉隆到加德滿都

GYIRONG TO KATHMANDU

Kathmandu, Nepal – May 25, 2024

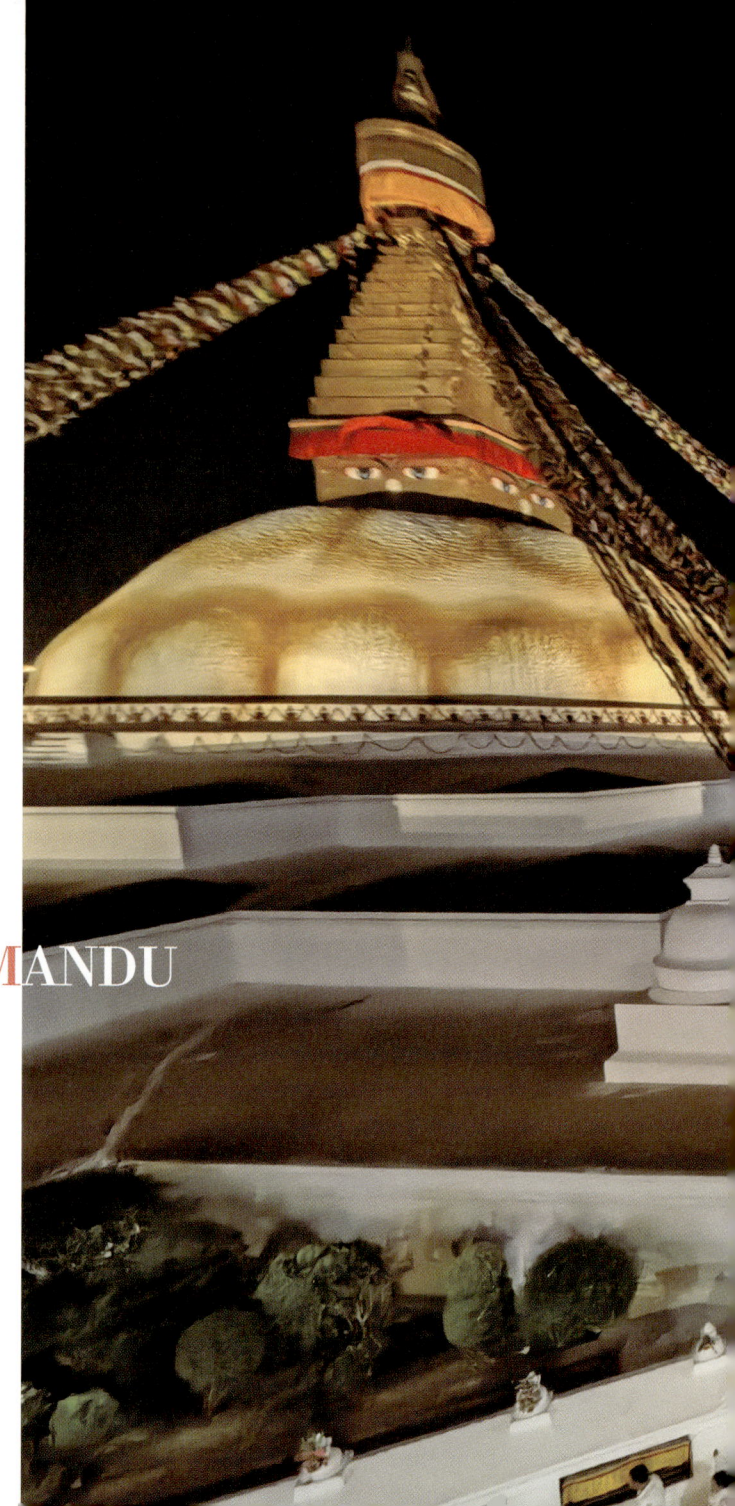

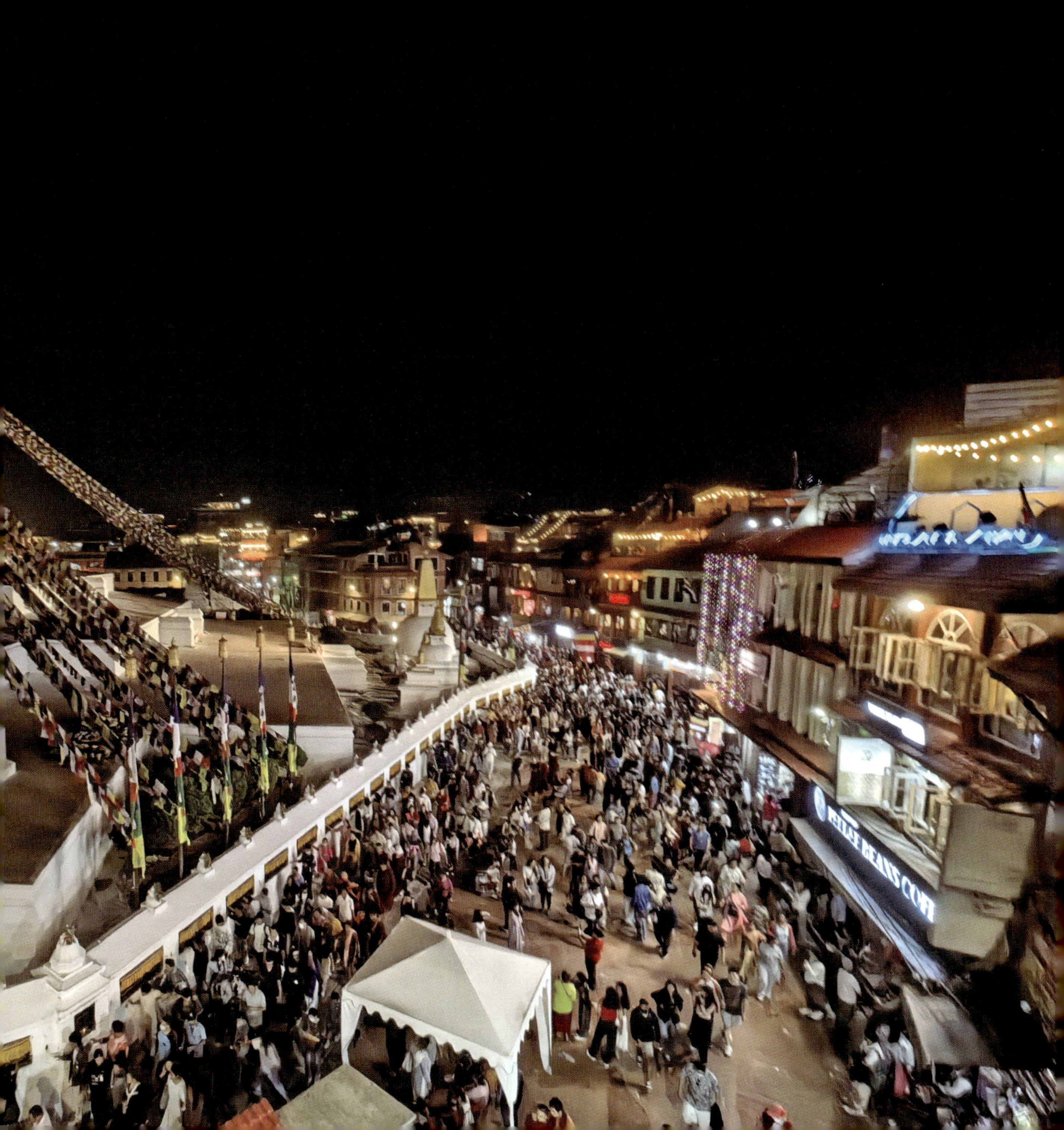

Kathmandu, Nepal – May 25, 2024

GYIRONG TO KATHMANDU
Sojourn south of the Himalayas

Hollywood has its Walk of Fame, with names of entertainment celebrities affixed to the pedestrian walk. For decades since 1960, this star-studded boulevard has become, for fans and tourists alike, a tribute site when visiting Los Angeles, evoking movies they cherished their childhood to adulthood, and even in old age. Today, the Chamber of Commerce of Hollywood can add newly minted stars, with a sponsorship rate of US$75,000 each. Such commercialization of course takes away some shine from the earlier stars.

A couple of decades after the beginning of this popular Hollywood phenomenon, the Kathmandu Guest House (a misnomer as this is a fine classic hotel by any count) started its own Walk of Fame in its center courtyard of the hotel. This is to honor many of its notable guests who are explorers, mountaineers, authors, scholars and even politicians. The list includes such luminaries as Edmund Hillary and Tenzing Norgay, the first summiteers on Everest, Peter Matthiessen, author of the Snow Leopard, George Schaller, the preeminent field biologist the book Snow Leopard described, and other climbing giants who conquered mountain giants, like British Chris Bonnington and Italian Reinhold Messler. Of course, movie greats like Robert Redford and music icon the Beatles cannot be left out.

Tony Wheeler, founder of Lonely Planet, holds a special place, both on the Walk of Fame as well as on a ceramic-tiled wall opposite the reception area of the hotel. He is quoted saying, "KGH is a bottleneck, where a traveler will pass at one time or another when in Nepal"; KGH being short for the Kathmandu Guest House. One tile claims the following, "Writers, anthropologists, philanthropists, mountaineers, artists, social workers and especially Nepal lovers choose KGH to congregate and share their tall tales. International writers use the garden of KGH to write some of the best literary works of their lifetime. Most of the books written about Nepal in the 70's and 80's were written in the KGH garden."

With such notion, I plan to write my best article on Nepal in the KGH garden. Instead, I received a rather grand welcome as my team of nine dust-clad off-roaders arrived in three off-road vehicles at the gate of the hotel. It turns out that Sarah Giri, an internet friend of mine whom I have befriended through the internet but have yet to meet, has not only helped us secure the rooms at a favorable rate, but also informed the owner Sakya brothers of my pedigree of being a bona fide explorer. So be it, a huge complimentary suite was added to the several rooms we needed, and my abode took up half of the top floor of the hotel's main building. As the saying goes, "Your fame travels ahead of your person." Might as well take it with good grace, especially when my introduction was made by no other

Tiled wall at reception / 接待處充滿故事的瓷磚牆
Lonely Planet's Tony Wheeler /
《孤獨星球》創始人托尼・韋勒

than the wife of the late Prime Minister of Nepal, a much-respected politician in this country. His widow, Sarah, has in recent years turned to helping the deaf people of Nepal, a noble cause.

But my grand reception did not end just with a huge suite. Two days later, my team, dressed in the best "attire" from their expedition wardrobe, watched in a grandstanding ceremony in the center garden the inauguration of my name on the Walk of Fame. Not only that, it was placed in the center part of a four-section walkway. I feel humbled and utterly surprised that here in Nepal, they would take exploration so seriously, surpassing at home in Hong Kong or many places I have visited. Later, I found out that a ceramic tile with my picture at the source of the Yangtze had been made and affixed to the wall opposite the reception area of the hotel. Self-flattering as it may sound, I felt I was standing higher than at 5000 meters elevation where the source is situated.

But my story must go back two days earlier to when we crossed the border from Tibet's Gyirong County into Nepal. This is the only designated point for vehicles with special permits, on a per car per day charge, to cross into Nepal, whereas exit can be through the traditional Zhang Mu port to the east. There are eight of us at this point in three cars, with some twenty pieces of luggage needed for our expedition. Customs required us to unload all luggage, big duffels and crates with cooking gear. They were to be hand-carried through customs inspection and immigration, before putting them back in the cars on the other side of the border. Luckily there were Nepalese porters on hand soliciting to do it for us. Ended up hiring over a dozen porters for this herculean labor job. We all breathed a sigh of relief as we walked across the border bridge, seeing that our reloaded cars were also crossing behind us.

Walk of Fame ceremony / 授星儀式

Home work on the street / 街頭作業
Roadside pizza / 路邊比薩

The Nepalese border guards were more interested in our new model Land Rover than checking our luggage. Soon we were on our way. The Nepalese side has no town, just a few houses and shops. But on both sides of the "road" were long lines of brand new electric BYD cars. Even any dirt space on the side of the gorge was turned into a parking lot for more and more BYDs. As we drove on the very rough road, BYDs would pass us one after another, obviously drivers were on rotation delivering these new cars to their destination ahead. But these drivers took no mercy on the new vehicles in the way they sped through extremely tough roads leaving even us in four-wheel-drive in their dust. Later on, I was to find out that hardly any BYDs were on the streets of Kathmandu. These long lines of electric cars must be transiting Nepal into India, for a much larger and insatiable market.

Along the way, we went through numerous checkpoints, some were guarded by police, others soldiers carrying semi- automatic rifles. Usually we produced a poster with my picture showing that I was a guest to lecture at a Nepal university, and no further questions were asked as they waved us through. Otherwise, I have heard it could be a long hassle and negotiation of payment before one can proceed forward. Surprisingly, despite all the online chats regarding driving into Nepal, we met no other cars from China, not on the day of entry, nor hardly any during our entire two-week stay in the country.

As our border crossing took up half a day, we stopped for the night at Dhunche, a midway town between Gyirong and Kathmandu. It allowed us time to de-climatize from the high plateau to the low elevation of the plain. We also changed our palate from that of Chinese cuisine to the more spicy version of a South Asian diet. We took time to have coffee at a Nepalese shop which comes with a smoking pipe of not tobacco, but some stronger potent plants, something we call "weed". As I looked below to the flush green valley, they seemed to dance in front of my eyes. Later when my eyesight had gotten better, I had the opportunity to play a game of street Ping Pong, without the table, against some kids and enjoyed the interaction, short as it was. It dawned on me that young students here in Nepal are just as studious as those we see in China, being driven to do their homework in school as well as after school, even while lying on the floor next to the street.

My entrance into Kathmandu, in thick traffic, was nothing ceremonial. That was, until I got to the Kathmandu Guest House. In fact, I have been to Kathmandu several times before, each time flown in, with some visits under duress and special circumstances. First time in 2008, I visited the Boudha Stupa in the evening and received a call in the morning that my mother had passed away in her sleep peacefully at home, thus cutting short my visit and flying home. The second visit was in 2009 on the way to Bhutan. Riots broke out near the hotel I stayed and I was trapped inside the closed shutter gate of a market while in the middle of buying snacks. The third time, trapped again, in 2015, inside the international airport ready to fly out when a 7.8 magnitude earthquake struck and all flights were canceled, with the airport "open" as all personnel left and we could come or leave at will, no stamps on the passport, the Duty Free was for once truly free, with bottles flying around. A year later in 2016, I joined a panel of the Himalayan Consensus Summit during the Nepal Economic Forum, and witnessed the reconstruction in progress after the earthquake. On this trip, I decided to explore beyond the façade of what a tourist would see of Nepal, thus bringing in my own team and vehicles.

I delivered two lectures while in Kathmandu, to Nepal Engineering College for Postgraduate Studies and Tribhuvan University respectively. The title was "Science Behind Exploration", explaining the application of space science to ground exploration. It makes us appreciate our good fortune in more economically sound regions with much more modern facilities, as well as the challenges and perseverance that face those with fewer resources and assets. With both, however, the quest for knowledge seems very much the same. Our friend, Professor Narayan who took his PhD from Academia Sinica's Kunming Institute of Zoology, has been collaborating with our own CERS field biologists Dr Bill Bleisch and Dr Paul Buzzard for years. He knew far more about Nepal's high country, Himalayan wildlife and ecology than us added together. Narayan would become our lecturer/guide for the following two weeks of sojourn within his country.

It happened to be birth day for Lord Buddha and the Boudha was appropriately flooded, with pilgrims and visitors flocking to the huge courtyard where the famous stupa with two eyes was situated. In the evening when everyone got off work, the traffic near the temple was clogged up. But Narayan wisely led us through one of the many alleyways into the square as we did our circumambulation, or kora, around the stupa. He had also booked ahead of time the upstairs sit-out balcony of an Italian restaurant that allows us to dine while presiding over the crowded stream of pilgrims below us.

There is a UNESCO heritage town on the eastern edge of the Kathmandu valley. Narayan's family, an old family, has lived in this ancient Bhaktapur town for generations. He is, once again, appropriately on hand to introduce us to his hometown. This municipality is now called a city.

Chariot with deity / 載有神祇的戰車
Offering of candles / 獻上燭火供品

Supplicants of deity / 向神祇祈願的信徒
Bhaktapur UNESCO Town /
聯合國認證巴克塔普爾古城

As such this is the smallest city of Nepal, as well as the most densely populated, yet with a most distinguished ancient history and with many of its own unique artisans who carry the old tradition to this day. Our tour of the town ended at night in the neighborhood town of Patan which coincided with a most special religious festival and ritual, the Rato Machindranath Jatra, honoring the deity Machindranath.

Again we were led through some very crowded streets which ended with this giant scaffolding "transformer", for finding no better word to describe my first sighting of it. It had a very long neck, maybe ten meters, extending to its head. It was somewhat like that of a dinosaur, in particular that of the Brachiosaurus. I use "transformer" rather than "dinosaur" because it does not look organic, seated on a huge platform with humongous wooden wheels, the chariot for the deity. There were statues and chambers with images of deities and pictures of sages around them, with many floral decorations. People were crowding up to make offerings, incense and flowers, but orderly and in turn.

We had chanced upon the Chariot Feast of Rato Machindranath. It is a deeply rooted historical and cultural festival celebrated annually in the Patan area of the Kathmandu Valley for over a thousand years as a symbol of prosperity and rain. It claims to be the longest festival in Nepal, *celebrated between April and June to invoke timely rainfall and a bountiful harvest. The exact timing each year is to be determined by astrologers. We must have brought along the lucky stars lining up for us.*

This particular and unique deity is revered by both Hindus and Buddhists, reflecting the vibrant religious expression and harmonious coexistence of these two major religions in the Valley. For Hindus, the deity is associated with the god Shiva, while for Buddhists, he is an incarnation of Bodhisattva Avlokiteshvara, a figure of compassion.

The festival's most iconic feature is the chariot procession, a massive and ornately decorated structure, that is pulled through the streets of Patan by devotees, accompanied by music, dance and religious rituals. The chariot houses the idol/statue of the deity Rato Machindranath, and the procession is believed to bring blessing and good fortune to the community, and in our case for a safe journey ahead to the Himalayas foothill.

Our team members had a chance to offer candles to the deity on the chariot. We shall leave Kathmandu with peace in our mind, despite the physically rough road and hazardous terrain ahead waiting of us.

尼泊爾 加德滿都 二〇二四年五月二十五日

從吉隆到加德滿都 喜馬拉雅南麓漫遊

眾所周知，好萊塢有條「星光大道」，自一九六〇年代起，無數影視巨星的姓名被銘刻在這人行道上。數十年來，這條星光閃耀的街道一直是影迷與遊客的「朝聖之地」，人們在此追憶從童年到暮年伴隨自己成長的經典電影。不過，如今只要支付七萬五千美元的「贊助費」，好萊塢商會就能為新晉名人在「星光大道」上鑲嵌一顆星星——如此商業化的操作，難免讓早期入選的傳奇影星們顯得沒那麼「稀罕」了。

而在好萊塢星光大道風靡全球的數十年後，遠在喜馬拉雅山腳下的尼泊爾加德滿都大酒店也在其中庭打造了一條獨特的「名人大道」，用以紀念曾下榻於此的探險家、登山家、作家、學者和政要。

加德滿都大酒店的這條「名人大道」上，留下了不少熠熠生輝的名字：首次征服珠穆朗瑪峰的英雄組合——艾德蒙・希拉里和丹增・諾蓋；《雪豹》的作者彼得・馬西森以及該書中提到的著名生物學家喬治・夏勒；還有那些征服高山巨人的登山界傳奇人物，如英國的克里斯・博寧頓和義大利的萊因霍爾德・梅斯納爾；電影巨星如勞勃・瑞福以及音樂界的偶像披頭四也沒有缺席。

《孤獨星球》雜誌的創始人托尼・韋勒在這個酒店有特殊的一席之地，他的名字不僅

KGH & Walk of Fame / 加德滿都大酒店名人大道

刻在那條「名人大道」上，還出現在了酒店接待區對面那充滿故事的瓷磚牆上。他曾為酒店留下了這樣一句「金句」：「加德滿都大酒店就像一個咽喉要道，每一個來到尼泊爾的旅人，走走停停，最終都會經過這裡，或在這裡相聚。」

在牆上的另一塊瓷磚上，有這樣一段文字：「作家、人類學家、慈善家、登山家、藝術家、社會工作者，和那些熱愛尼泊爾的人，都選擇在這裡聚集，分享他們的傳奇故事。許多世界知名的作家在

加德滿都大酒店的花園裡完成了他們一生中最重要的作品。七〇年代和八〇年代,關於尼泊爾的大多數書籍都是在這花園裡誕生的。」

話都撂在這了,我想著,那我也得在這花園裡寫出一篇關於尼泊爾的絕世佳作,沾一沾這些名人的光呀。不過讓我受寵若驚的是,佳作未出,酒店卻已經把我當成名人對待了。當我們九人組駛著三輛越野車風塵僕僕地抵達酒店大門時,迎接我們的是一場異常隆重的歡迎儀式。那之後,酒店不僅給我們打了最佳折扣,還免費為我單獨準備了一間佔了主樓頂層一半空間的豪華套房。

原來,是我那素未謀面但神交已久的網友——尼泊爾著名慈善家,已故總理的遺孀,薩拉·吉里女士提前跟酒店的董事薩伽兄弟打了招呼,介紹我為知名的探險家,這才讓我們有此殊榮。薩拉女士近年來致力於幫助尼泊爾的聾啞人,這無疑是一項崇高的事業。俗話說:「聲明先於行者」。既然如此,我也卻之不恭地收下了這分厚待。

然而,這分隆重的禮遇遠不止於一間豪華套房。兩天後,我的隊員們換上了探險行囊中最體面的「盛裝」,也就是我們探險學會的隊服,在花園中央的盛大儀式上,親眼見證了我的名字被鐫刻於酒店的「名人大道」上。不僅如此,我的名牌還霸佔在四段步

CERS tile / 介紹中國探險學會的版面
HM for stepping on / 屬於 HM 的星星,歡迎來踩

道交匯的最中心位置。這般禮遇令我既慚愧、感激,又驚訝。在尼泊爾,人們對探險事業的敬重,竟遠勝於我的故鄉香港,乃至許多我曾造訪之地。更令人意外的是,酒店接待處對面的牆上,不知何時多了一塊瓷磚,上面是我在長江源頭考察時的照片。雖說這般自我彰顯未免有些難為情,但那一刻的飄然之感,確實比置身海拔五千米的源頭更教人暈眩。

我們在尼泊爾的故事還得從兩天前說起。西藏吉隆縣的吉隆口岸是目前唯一允許私家車過境進入尼泊爾的口岸,而且還要按「每車每日」計費。從前流量最大的樟木口岸如今只允許旅遊大巴通行,所以我們選擇了吉隆進,樟木出。

Border crossing into Nepal / 穿越邊境進入尼泊爾

我們一行八人，三輛車，拖著二十多件大行李，還有裝炊具的鋁箱，車後堆得像移動的小山。海關的要求十分嚴苛，所有行李都得卸下來，手動搬過海關檢查，然後才能重新裝回車上。這對我們來說實在有點太超過了。幸好，口岸有一群尼泊爾挑夫，搶著幫我們搬運，我們順勢雇了十幾個伙計來解決這場「人力浩劫」。當我們終於穿過邊境橋，看著重新裝滿行李的越野車緩緩駛來時，大家都長舒了一口氣。

原本我們還擔心，會遭到尼泊爾邊防人員的二次檢查，不過他們似乎對行李興趣寥寥，倒是我們那輛嶄新的路虎車讓他們「愛不釋手」，圍著研究了半天。很快，我們就正式上路了。尼泊爾這邊的邊境沒有什麼像樣的城鎮，只有幾戶人家和小商店。

但是有個比較有意思的景象，在破爛的路兩邊，停滿了嶄新的比亞迪電動車，整整齊齊地排成長隊，甚至連峽谷邊的空地也被改造成臨時停車場，堆得滿滿當當。當我們在顛簸的土路上緩慢行進時，一輛輛比亞迪車從我們身邊呼嘯而過，揚起漫天的塵土。顯然，這種毫不心疼新車的開法，只有那些輪流換班送車的司機幹得出來。那一路狂飆的架勢，讓我們的四驅都相形見絀。

不過真的到了加德滿都市內後，我發現街頭幾乎看不見比亞迪的蹤影。這才反應過來，這些電動車原來只是途經尼泊爾，被運往了印度這個更大、更飢渴的市場。

一路上，我們經過了「無數個」檢查站，有些由警察把守，有些有手持半自動步槍的士兵。每當這時，我就會甩出一張印有我照片的海報，上面說明，我是來尼泊爾的大學講學的特邀嘉賓。

這招幾乎百試不爽，他們看了之後就直接放行，一句多餘的問題都不問。據說，如果沒有這樣的「通行證」，管你是來做生意的商人還是遊客，都得經歷漫長的麻煩程序，甚至還得費心談價、付費，才能繼續上路。有些奇怪的是，儘管網上有很多關於中國遊客在尼泊爾自駕旅行的討論，我們這一路上卻幾乎沒有碰到過其他來自中國的車輛，無論是在入境那天，還是在接下來整整兩週的行程中。

由於光是跨越邊境就花去了半天時間，我們決定第一晚就在位於吉隆與加德滿都之間的通澤鎮修整一下。這般停留，正好給了我們時間適應從高原地區到低海拔的轉變，同時也給了我們的味蕾轉向南亞辛辣滋味的空間。

舟車勞頓，我的視線開始有些模糊。在咖啡館小憩時，意外發現店裡的煙斗裝的不是菸草，而是大麻。俯瞰腳下那一片碧綠，竟感覺整個山谷都在我眼前搖曳起舞。等到視線稍復清明，我和幾個當地小孩在街邊玩了一場「街頭乒乓球」。沒有桌子，沒有場地，只有球拍和球，但樂在其中。街道

Street ping pong match / 路邊乒乓賽

HM getting high / 有點嗨的 HM

的另一旁，尼泊爾的學生和中國的孩子一樣勤奮，身體趴在街邊地板上，腦袋始終埋於課業之中。

這次進入加德滿都的過程，實在談不上任何「儀式感」，我們一路都擠在烏泱泱的車流裡，像參加了一場耐力測試。直到抵達了加德滿都大酒店，才算鬆了口氣。

其實，我之前已經來過加德滿都好幾次，但每次都碰上了一點「特殊狀況」。第一次是在二〇〇八年，前一晚我去了著名的博達哈大佛塔，還沉浸在它莊嚴的氛圍裡，結果隔天一早，我接到了一通電話，得知母親在睡夢中安詳辭世，我只能匆匆結束行程，飛回家奔喪。第二次是在二〇〇九年，我途經加德滿都前往不丹，卻遇上了街頭騷亂。當時，我剛好在市場裡買零食，結果商店鐵門突然拉下，我被困在裡面好一陣子，感覺自己無痛地當了一回人質。第三次是二〇一五年，那場經歷簡直可以拍成災難片——我正準備從國際機場飛離尼泊爾，結果七點八級大地震突然襲來，所有航班瞬間取消。機場雖然開著，但工作人員早已跑光，進出完全隨意，海關蓋章什麼的沒人在乎，免稅店徹底「免稅」，都直接「免費」了！酒瓶亂飛，酒氣沖天，場面混亂得像《啟示錄》。二〇一六年，我第四次來這裡，參加尼泊爾經濟論壇期間的喜馬拉雅共識峰會，目睹了這個國家為災後重建付出的努力。

這一次，我下定決心不再只當個普通旅客，帶上了自己的團隊和車輛，準備深入探索尼泊爾不為人知的一面。

在加德滿都的幾天裡，我分別在尼泊爾工程研究院和特里布文大學進行了兩場演講，

Kathmandu Valley / 加德滿都

主題是「探險背後的科學」，解釋了太空科學在地面探索中的應用。在這個主題與我們現在所處環境的相互映襯下，我也不免反思，我們有多幸運能生活在經濟條件較好的地區，學習先進的科技，享用前沿的設施。那些資源匱乏的地區，需要以多麼非凡的堅韌來克服種種困難，才能走上和我們一樣的平臺。不管環境如何，對知識的渴望和追求是全人類共通的，這是我深受感動之處。

我們的尼泊爾朋友孔陽教授也參與了這次行動。他在中科院昆明動物研究所取得了博士學位，並與我們學會的野外生物學家畢蔚林博士和保羅・巴澤德博士合作多年。孔陽對尼泊爾的高山地區、喜馬拉雅的野生動植物以及生態系統瞭若指掌，知識量可以說碾壓我們所有人。他將在接下來的兩週裡擔任我們的嚮導兼老師，帶領我們深入這片迷人的土地。

我們在加德滿都的第二日適逢佛誕，博達哈大佛塔人山人海，朝聖者與遊客紛至沓來，廣場上的智慧之眼在煙霧中靜靜看著下方的「水洩不通」。傍晚時分，隨著人潮下班，寺廟周邊的交通更是癱瘓。幸好孔陽熟門熟路，領著我們穿過曲折巷弄，避開人潮，完成了轉經儀式。他還事先預訂了廣場邊義大利餐廳的露臺座位，讓我們得以一邊欣賞佛塔，一邊用餐，一邊俯瞰下方熙熙攘攘的洪流。

在加德滿都東緣，坐落著一座聯合國教科文組織認證的古城，巴克塔普爾。孔陽的家族世代居住在這座古老的小城，所以這兒自然算

Procession at Bhaktapur / 巴克塔普爾的巡禮隊伍
UNESCO Bhaktapur / 教科文組織認證的世界遺產

是他的「主場」。這座昔日的自治城邦，如今是尼泊爾面積最小、人口最稠密，也最具歷史底蘊的城市，城中至今仍活躍著許多傳承古老技藝的匠人。

夜晚，我們來到巴格馬蒂河旁的帕坦，恰逢當地「戰車節」，這是一場有關「紅色馬欽德拉納特」神祇的盛大祭祀活動，也叫「紅觀音節」。據說此節日已有上千年歷史，是帕坦最重要的文化傳統之一，每年於四月至六月間舉行，祈願降雨與豐收，具體日期由占星師決定。

穿過擁擠的街道，我們來到一座龐大的神轎前。這座結構高達十米，長頸般的設計讓我聯想到腕龍，但巨型木輪和堅固的平臺讓它更像「變形金剛」。神轎上裝飾著鮮花，供奉著紅色馬欽德拉納特的神像，還有其他擺得滿滿當當看不清面容的小雕像、佛龕和畫像。信徒們排列整齊，獻上供品與香火，場面虔誠且熱烈。

「紅色馬欽德拉納特」是一位獨特的神祇，受到印度教和佛教徒共同敬奉。對印度教徒而言，祂與濕婆神相關，掌管著雨水和莊稼；而佛教徒則將祂視為觀世音菩薩的化身，象徵慈悲。節日的高潮是神轎遊行——信徒們拉著這座有三層樓高的精美神轎，伴隨著音樂和舞蹈，緩緩穿過帕坦的街道。我們也向祂獻上了蠟燭，祈願接下來的旅程平安順遂。

儘管離開加德滿都後，前方等待我們的將是崎嶇不平的道路和充滿挑戰的險峻地形，但今晚，我們會帶著內心的平靜入睡。尤其是之於我而言，第一次有機會稍稍深入當地感受這座城市，加德滿都的夜，從未如此寧靜又迷人。

安納布爾納

ANNAPURNA

Pokhara, Nepal – June 1, 2024

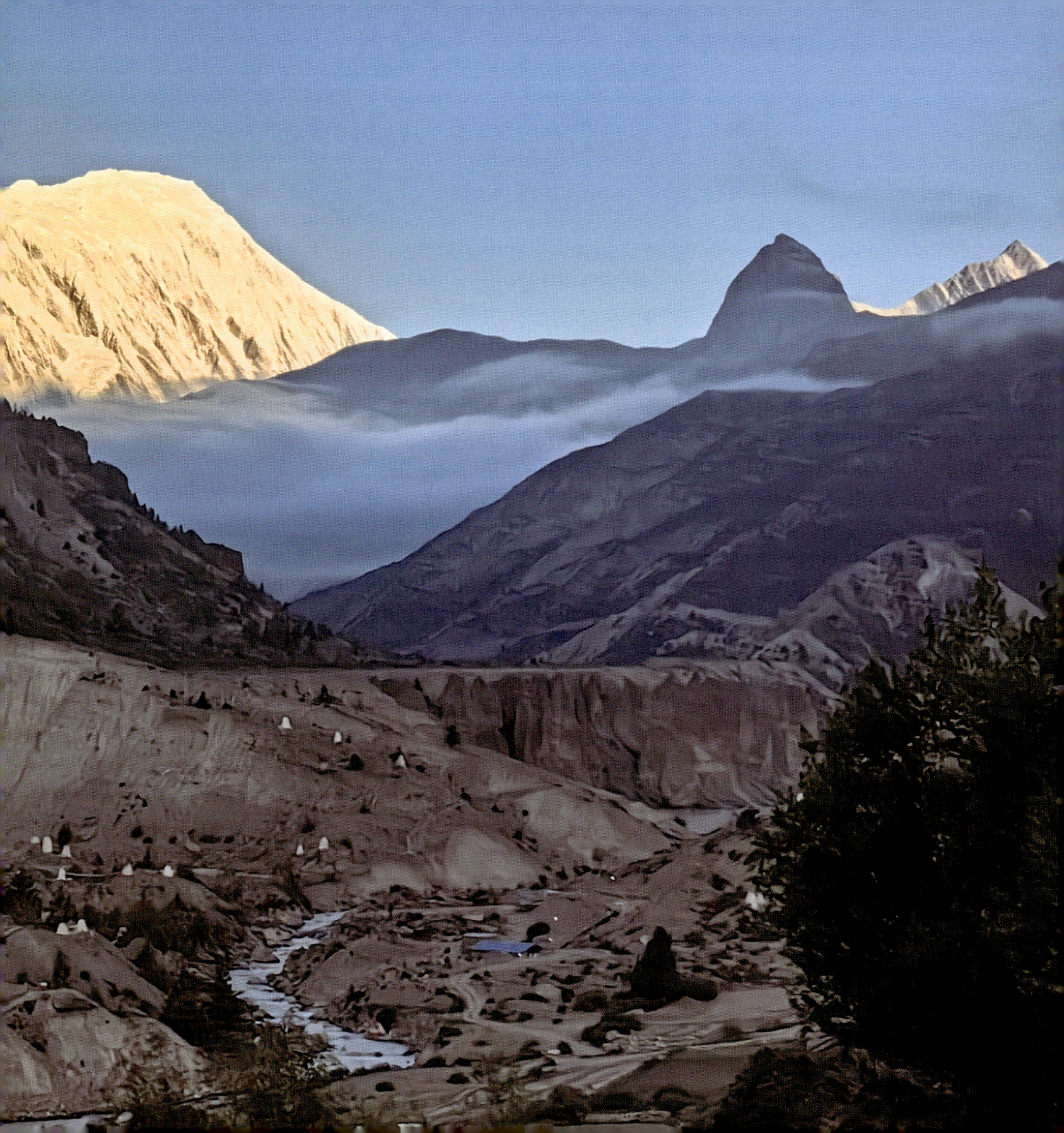

Pokhara, Nepal – June 1, 2024

ANNAPURNA
Deadliest mountain in the world

I first heard of Annapurna, the 10th highest peak in the world at 8091 meters, when I used to hang around UC Berkeley in the early 1970s. It was in the late 1970s that I started camping out in Yosemite, at times during the winter in my VW camper van, reading outdoor adventure and exploration reports. Here in the high Sierra is where many early climbers converged, honing their rock climbing skills among some of the vertical walls the like of El Capitan, now made famous by the award-winning movie Free Solo.

From here, experienced climbers, as well aspiring ones, would descend on the Himalayan foothill and ascend some of the highest peaks in the world. Technically skilled ones may persevere, others succumbed to these mountain giants accepting defeat, still others, maybe the dreamers, would simply perish. One major challenge among these mountain giants is Annapurna. For a long time, it claimed the second highest kill ratio of around 1 in 5, second only to K2's 1 in 4 for those who attempted to summit it. However, with one recent climbing disaster in 2014, a snowstorm struck Annapurna and its surroundings, causing avalanches and killing 43 climbers immediately. Later it was reported that 72 in total perished on the slope on that day. This one climbing disaster catapulted Annapurna to the top death ratio of 27% in metric, surpassing K2.

Glacier of Annapurna / 安納布爾納的冰川

Team on elephants / 象背上的考察隊

One such climbs, perhaps more famous than most, is the 1978 American Women's Himalayan Expedition to Annapurna, led by a UC Berkeley scientist Arlene Blum with 11 female members. Arlene started climbing at an early age and was eager to join some of the major climbing expeditions, but was rejected one time after another due to her being a female. One expedition leader went as far as saying she would be allowed to go only as far as basecamp, to help with the cooking. Such chauvinistic exclusion only gave her more impetus to try harder to reach to the top. She organized and led that 1978 attempt on Annapurna. Despite death of two women climbers in one of her two summit teams, one team did reach the summit on October 15, 1978. One of those two women who reached the top is Vera Komarkova, an exceptionally strong climber. She is a Czech, not an American, albeit with two sherpas that she insisted to take along. Those two are of course men, and there to help break the trail, not to help with cooking.

Since then, the name Annapurna has left a mark in my head. Finally between May and June this year, I have the

Rhinoceros / 犀牛
CERS on safari / CERS 野生動物考察隊

chance to visit the southern Himalayan foothill despite having been on the Tibetan northern side for decades. Two places are high on my list to visit, Annapurna and Mustang, both near the border with China.

We drove west from Kathmandu, first hitting the jungle south where my team of nine would make an overnight stop at a community jungle lodge in order to do a day-time safari to view wildlife. This is where the safari operator Tiger Tops makes its debut in 1971 and became famous for wildlife observations in Nepal. Jim Edwards its founder also advised the then King of Nepal on the set up of the Chitwan National Park, first such park in Nepal that we are visiting. We seated high on a four-wheel drive first, and later rode on elephants. For the entire morning, we observed deer, rhinoceros, crocodile, and plenty of birds as its wetland is a Ramsar site for the protection of migrating birds. However no Bengal tiger crossed our path though our guide assured us that they are around.

The next day, we took the long drive into the mountains heading for Annapurna which has several near 8000-meter peaks, with its highest being crowned 10th in the world. The foothill has many splendid gorges with mist rising, and waterfalls from clear running streams. Tea and coffee stops were most welcome hiatus from the very rough road, which became rougher every hour as we proceeded forward. Finally before night fell and after a full-day drive, we arrived at the Yeti Hotel in the village of Manang. Here from the hotel rooftop, I enjoyed the sunset evening sky, followed by twilight before a galaxy of stars that became my canopy. The next morning a golden sunrise shining on the east face of the snow mountain set the scene for my hearty breakfast.

Our younger team members then set out to hike with a Nepalese guide to the high camp where yak herders are just now busy with collecting the valuable caterpillar fungus, or cordyceps. They would be spending a night and try to document their activities, as well as trying to collect some artifacts from the herders. I would spend a day with Binod Gurung, boss of the Yeti Hotel who is quite an entrepreneur, owning also a tour and trekking company. As it is still low season with few tourists, during the day, he accompanied me in walking through their village while explaining to me the local deity at a shrine temple. The oldest section of the village has many traditional houses built with stones, similar to houses in the lower elevation of the Tibetan plateau. A stone stupa below which can walk through also resonance the larger such stupas in Lhasa. In the Himalaya region, most locals are Buddhist, similar in belief and practice to those living in Tibet.

Afterward, we sat down at his café for tea and a chat. This is when I was in for a nice surprise. Suddenly, my new friend Binod threw out a few words in Cantonese. I balked and looked him in his eyes. He looks exactly Nepalese, maybe with a trait of Tibetan or Sherpa or Gurka slant. Surely he swings his head left and right as he acknowledge any questions I had earlier when we strolled the village alleys. I asked him how he knew Chinese, as it seems not many Chinese, let alone Cantonese, visit this area in Nepal. "As a young man when I was just a teenager, I went to Hong Kong looking for a job," answered Binod.

"I was staying at the room houses of Chungking Mansion in Tsim Sha Tsui with several Nepalese compatriots," he continued. "One day a stringer came along and he was looking for south Asian actors for a film they are making. Three of us young Nepalese were selected and we ended up playing parts as sidekicks led by this Chinese hero Choy Suk, a guerilla army leader," Binod recounted his tale of entering stardom, though in a rather minor role. Soon he went back into his room and brought out a large picture frame with several photos of scene from his film appearance, next to the mustached Choy Suk guerilla leader who is a fictional hero in comic books about the Sino-Japanese War. One picture even had him carrying on his back the injured guerilla leader inside a jungle. With that story, it brought me back to memories of my childhood when I was addicted to the Choy Suk comic.

The following day, my team returned by mid-day from high country with bags of artifacts used by the herders. We said goodbye to Binod and the Yeti Hotel as we retraced the rough road down to the foothill. That evening we stopped at Pokhara, a tourist town by a very nice lake with paddle boats. The lakefront hotel allowed us to take a hiatus as we enjoy a pseudo Chinese cuisine at a dumpling restaurant. I always opt for Chinese food rather than local cuisine due to my palate and stomach is not particularly accommodating to spicy food. But at Pokhara, I regretted my choice of the not-so-authentic Chinese dishes, besides it was also pricier. Likewise, the very ripe lychee fruit I saw on the lakefront trees doesn't taste much like the nectar sweetness of those back home in southern China. From high country to low plain thus ended first half of my visit to Nepal.

Temple of Manang / 馬南村寺廟

尼泊爾 博卡拉 二〇二四年六月一日

安納布爾納

萬仞絕命處，世界第一巔

我第一次聽到「安納布爾納」的大名是在二十世紀七〇年代初，那時我常在加州大學柏克萊分校附近閒逛，那個年代的柏克萊，是美國反文化運動、自由思想和戶外探險文化的中心之一，校園內有許多活躍的登山社團和戶外活動組織，更是極限登山理論與技術討論的重鎮。

安納布爾納是世界第十高峰，海拔八千零九十一米。到了七〇年代後期，我對探險的熱情持續高漲，經常開著我的大眾露營車到處野營，熱愛讓我不畏嚴寒、不懼酷暑。無數個夜晚，我蜷縮在車內，翻著那些關於戶外探險的報告，內心充滿對未知世界的嚮往。

高聳的內華達山脈曾是早期登山者的聖地，他們熱衷於在其垂直的岩壁上磨練自己的攀岩技巧，比如近兩年因獲獎紀錄片《赤手登峰》而聞名於世的「酋長岩」。酋長岩的花崗岩大牆與喜馬拉雅的冰岩混合物地形有著相似的挑戰性，許多由內華達山脈磨練出的攀登者，最終帶著經驗和野心，踏上了遠征世界之巔，喜馬拉雅的征途。

喜歡挑戰的人中總也不乏新手，但能成功登頂的只能是極少一部分頂尖選手，大部分人只能向這些巨峰認輸，甚至有些夢想家的肉體被永遠留在了山上。

在這些致命高峰中，安納布爾納尤為險惡。很長一段時間裡，它的死亡率高達五比一，每五人嘗試登頂，就有一人喪生，僅次於世界第二高峰喬戈里峰的四比一。不過，一場山難徹底改寫了這個數字——二〇一四年，一場暴風雪突襲安納布爾納，引發了雪崩，瞬間奪走了四十三名登山者的生命。後續報導顯示，當天共有七十二人葬身於此。這場災難讓安納布爾納的死亡率飆升至百分之二十七，一舉超越喬戈里峰，成為全球最致命的高峰。

在無數關於這座山峰的險奇故事中，一九七八年那支「美國女子安納普爾納登山隊」尤為矚目。這支隊伍由加州大學柏克萊分校的科學家阿琳·布盧姆率領，十一名隊員清一色都是女性。

阿琳從小就熱愛攀岩，渴望參加大型的登山遠征活動，但因為性別多次被拒。曾有男性領隊冷嘲熱諷地對她說，她只能跟到大本營幫忙做飯。這種性別排斥並沒有擊退她，反而讓她更加堅定，決心用行動證明自己。於是，她親自組織並領導了這次一九七八年的全女子安納布爾納遠征。

Annapurna & glacier / 安納布爾納峰與冰川
Annapurna terrain / 安納布爾納地貌

遠征途中，十一名隊員被分成兩隊。其中一隻隊伍遭遇了不幸，兩名隊員在途中遇難。另一支小隊於一九七八年十月十五日成功登頂，實現了一次突破性的壯舉。登頂者之一是薇拉·科馬爾科娃，一位實力非凡的捷克籍攀登者。她堅持帶上兩位男性夏爾巴

ANNAPURNA

人同行，而他們並不是被派去後勤支援「煮飯」，而是發揮所長負責開路。

自那以後，「安納布爾納」這個名字就深深印在了我的腦海裡。過去幾十年的探索經歷，讓我已經非常熟悉喜馬拉雅北側的西藏地區，今年五月至六月間，我終於有機會造訪它的南麓，而我的目標也很明確：靠近中國邊境的兩個區域，安納布爾納和木斯塘。

從加德滿都出發一路向西，我們來到了巴格瑪蒂省西南地區的叢林地帶。我們的九人小隊在叢林小屋中停留了一晚，準備第二天的野生動物觀察之旅。我們停留之處，正是尼泊爾首家野生動物觀察組織「老虎頂」的發源地，該組織自六十年代起便以專業導覽聞名。創始人吉姆・愛德華茲曾協助尼泊爾王室規畫建立該國首座國家公園，也就是我們即將造訪的奇旺國家公園。

第二天一早，我們先是坐上高底盤的四輪驅動車，隨後又換騎大象，開始了叢林探索。公園內的濕地是受拉姆薩爾公約保護的遷徙鳥類棲息地，一路上，成群的鹿、悠然覓食的犀牛、潛伏在河

Spotted deer / 花鹿
Red-napped ibis / 赤頸鷺
Elephant safari / 大象之旅

邊的鱷魚，以及數不清的鳥類陸續出現，滿目生機。不過，最讓人期待的孟加拉虎並未現身。

翌日，我們駕車一路向山區進發，目標就是安納布爾納自然保護區。這裡有好幾座接近八千米的高峰，其中最高峰在世界上排名第十。山麓地帶處處可見雲霧繚繞的壯麗峽谷，清澈溪流形成的瀑布飛瀉而下。在崎嶇難行的山路間，能在茶館和咖啡站稍作歇息實在令人欣慰，而隨著行程推進，路況每小時都在變得更加顛簸。經過整日車程，終於在夜幕低垂前，我們抵達了馬南村的「雪人旅館」。我站在旅館屋頂，欣賞落日餘暉染紅天際，暮色漸沉後，滿天繁星如穹頂般籠罩四野，彷彿整個銀河成了我的帳篷。

次日清晨，金色的陽光灑在雪山的東坡上，為我豐盛的早餐增添了一分絕美景緻。早餐過後，我們隊伍中年輕的成員們在一位尼泊爾嚮導的帶領下，啟程前往高山營地。那裡的犛牛牧民正在忙於收集珍貴的冬蟲夏草。他們會在那裡過夜，記錄牧民的活動，並收集一些當地牧民的工具和生活用品。

Crocodiles / 鱷魚

Binod with old & new stupa / 比諾德與新舊佛塔

Stone houses of Manang village / 馬南村的石砌民居

而我則和雪人旅館的老闆比諾德・古隆共度了一天。他是一位相當有魄力的企業家，不僅經營著酒店，還擁有一家專門做旅遊和徒步服務的公司。現在正值旅遊淡季，村裡遊客稀少，白天他便陪同我漫步村莊。在神龕寺廟前，比諾德講起了當地的神祇信仰，村落最古老的區域仍然保存著許多石砌傳統民居，與西藏高原低海拔地區的建築風格相似。一座石砌佛塔下方留有通道，其形制與拉薩的大型佛塔遙相呼應。喜馬拉雅山區居民多信奉藏傳佛教，其信仰習俗與西藏同胞如出一轍。

晌午，我們在他那間小咖啡館歇腳喝茶，這時，這位尼泊爾新朋友突然蹦出幾句廣東話，驚得我瞪大了眼睛。我仔仔細細地看著他，明明是典型的尼泊爾面孔，頂多帶著幾分藏族或廓爾喀人的特徵。方才在村裡，他回應我的問題時，還會輕輕左右搖頭，帶著典型的南亞式肢體語言。我忍不住問他：「你怎麼會說中文？而且是粵語？這裡應該沒多少中國人來吧，講粵語的就更少了。」

「年輕時在香港待過。」他咧嘴一笑。「十幾歲跟著老鄉擠在尖沙咀重慶大廈的劏房裡。有天來了個星探，說要選幾個南亞臉，我們三個尼泊爾小夥子就這麼被選中了，去演了電影配角。」

他回房間翻出珍藏的劇照，原來他們參演的是改編自香港經典抗日漫畫《財叔》的電影《財叔之橫掃千軍》，比諾德在裡頭扮演抗日游擊隊長財叔的手下。泛黃的照片裡，留著小鬍子的財叔威風凜凜，而比諾德正背著「負傷的隊長」在叢林裡跋涉。這畫面，頓時勾起了我兒時追更《財叔》連環畫的痴迷勁兒。

隔日正午時分，我的隊員們從高山營地歸來，帶著滿袋牧人使用的器物。我們告別比諾德和雪人旅館，沿著崎嶇山路返回。傍晚時分，我們在觀光小鎮博卡拉落腳，湖畔的划艇在平靜水面上輕輕搖曳。

湖濱旅館讓我們得以稍作休憩，由於我的味蕾和腸胃實在難以適應辛辣的當地飲食，所以向來偏好中餐。不過在博卡拉，一家中式餃子館讓我「踩了大雷」，這家不甚道地的中式菜不僅滋味平庸，價格還格外昂貴。就連湖畔樹上熟透的荔枝，也遠不如中國南方那甘美如蜜的滋味。

從巍峨的高地到這湖畔小鎮，尼泊爾的前半程就這樣在味蕾的失落與視覺的饜足間，悄然作別。

Foothill lake at Pokhara / 博卡拉山麓湖泊

木斯塘的暗哨

MUSTANG

Mustang, Nepal – June 3, 2024

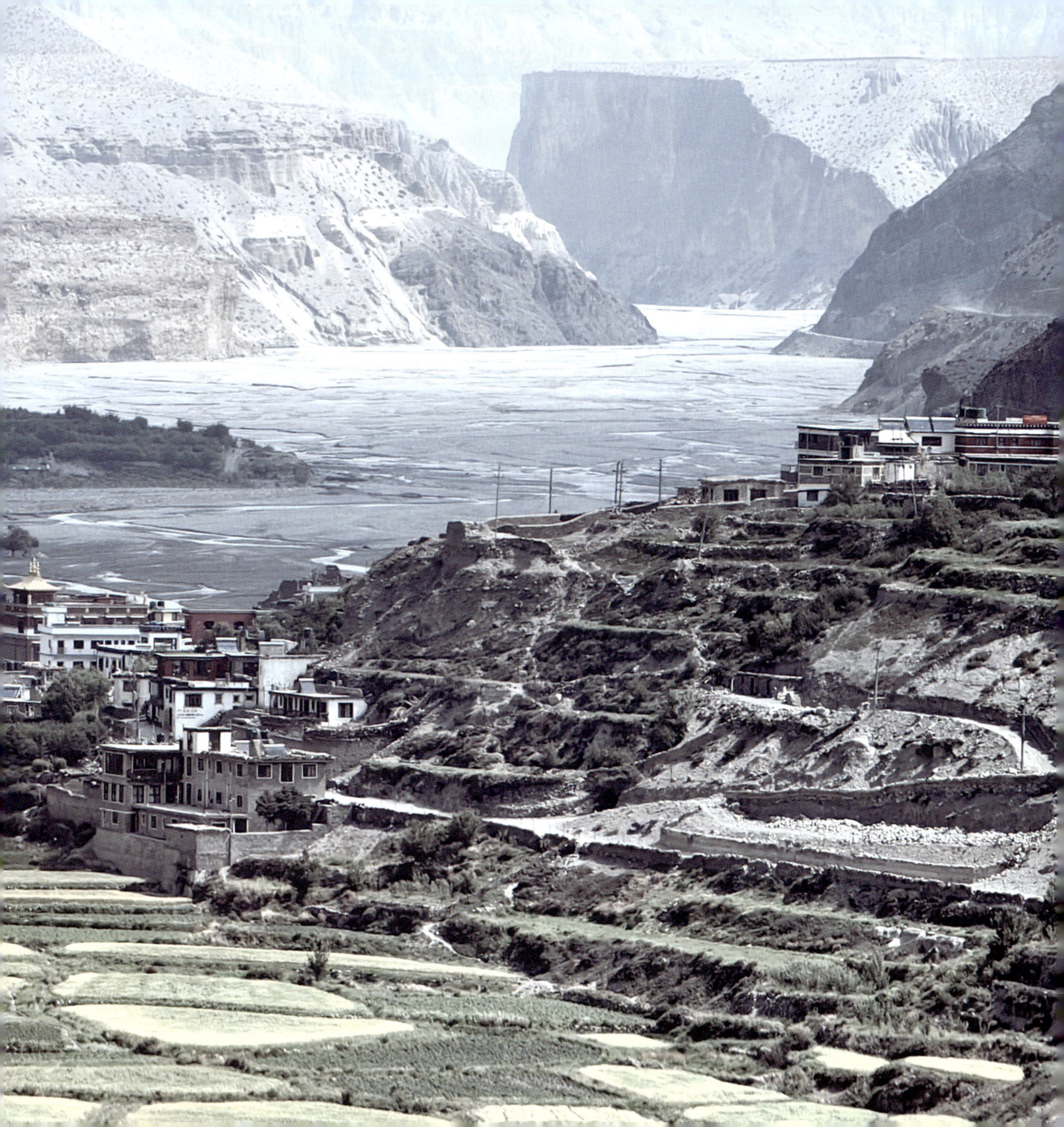

Mustang, Nepal – June 3, 2024

MUSTANG
Guerilla hideout south of the Himalayas

I have wanted to visit Mustang at the border with China's Tibet. It was made famous by the Tibetan insurgent guerilla since the early 1960s. Several books and papers had described that turbulent era in recent Tibetan history. With support from the CIA, incursions were made by exiled Tibetan guerilla groups throughout those years, maybe decades, in harassing the Communist army along its southwestern border. Mustang became a place with enigma to many of us with interest on Tibet, be it about its physical or political geography. It is purportedly where the 17th Karmapa left Tibet in his escapade to India and ultimately to the West. I have met him when he was seven years old during his enthronement at Tsurphu Monastery outside of Lhasa, and later at his secured residence in Dharamsala India. I have even met the Prince of Mustang, now "King", at a culture conservation conference in Germany some twenty-five years ago.

But no, I was told in Kathmandu that Mustang is out of reach. Special permit need be applied well in advance, and permission also quite unlikely given, especially for Chinese nationals. However, our team can get to the border of that region, still nominally high and a part of Lo Mustang. So be it, we would go as far as possible. Along the way, we stopped at a nice hostel in Lete with a spectacular view of Annapurna to our east and a glacier mountain to our west. Dinner however had to be *prepared by our team as the hostel was short-handed during low season. Next morning, early ray casting a shade of gold on the southern flank of Annapurna was a joy to behold during breakfast on the roof deck.*

A fair section of this road is paved, or in the process of being paved. Along the way, we saw many jeeps passed us by, fully loaded with Indians. They were on the way to, or from, Muktinath, a sacred site for both Hindi and Buddhists. At the border army checkpoint to enter upper Mustang, we turned into a smaller road leading up the mountain. Here is a village town at the junction where the YucDonalds Hotel only offers imagined respite for someone addicted to the McD golden arch, yours truly that is.

As we climbed the switch backs going higher, the scenery unveiled below of the wide river gorge with eroded sandstone hills recall terrain of western Tibet not far to the north. The white stupas and Tibetan style monasteries dotted the faraway hills fully complement that this is an extension of the Tibetan plateau. A small village along the way has a few scattered shops selling handicrafts and trinkets, again rather Tibetan in style. Two ladies, a look-alike mother and daughter, worked over a traditional hand-and-foot loom where we bought a few gift items of fabric with motifs.

End of road has many buses and cars parked, with street venders and small

West face of Annapurna / 安納普爾納西壁
Eroded terrain of Mustang / 侵蝕地貌

MUSTANG 183

eateries. This is where the pilgrims would begin their hour-long hike to the sacred site. Young men were quick to hawk their horses for those who wanted to ride to the site. Some elders chose to ride in sedan chairs carried by four collies spreading the weight, and the fees. I was exhausted from my long ride, and opted to stay behind for once, at the only hotel nearby at an elevation of 3700 meters while enjoying the spectacular view below me as if looking down from heaven. But heaven can be brought down to earth as I saw some Indian pilgrims returning from their prayers with bottles of sacred water, bringing home for sharing with their loved ones.

With this thus ended my visit to Nepal as we retraced our way back to Kathmandu, some two days away. But we must make a last stop as we descended the mountain, at Namgyaling Tserok Camp. This is one of 12 Tibetan refugee camps of Nepal, with this one having some forty families and maybe up to 200 individuals. These are families and descendants of Khampa guerilla fighters from

Mother & daughter / 織布的母女

Pilgrim being carried / 被抬著的朝聖者

the 1960s and 70s, with other self-exiled families during the early 1960s following liberation of Tibet in 1950 and land reforms in the late 1950s.

I crossed a long iron suspension bridge over a fast-running cascading stream and entered the village. As I walked along an alley way, I could hear the deep sound of a drum. Following the beat of the drum, I got to a semi-closed door of one of the homes. Quietly taking off my shoes and sliding myself inside a small room, I see in dim light a seated old man in Tibetan monk's clothing. In front of him is a small sutra that he was chanting while beating the hanging drum with rhythm. His deep voice perfectly complemented that of the drum.

Momentarily I feel I am transformed back into the heart of Tibet. The political division as well as the high Himalayan mountains suddenly become no longer a frontier. As that very moment I felt that spirituality can transpire beyond and above what the physical earth and human world can impose upon us.

Tibetan old lady / 藏族老婦人

Tibetan monk praying / 誦經的藏族僧人

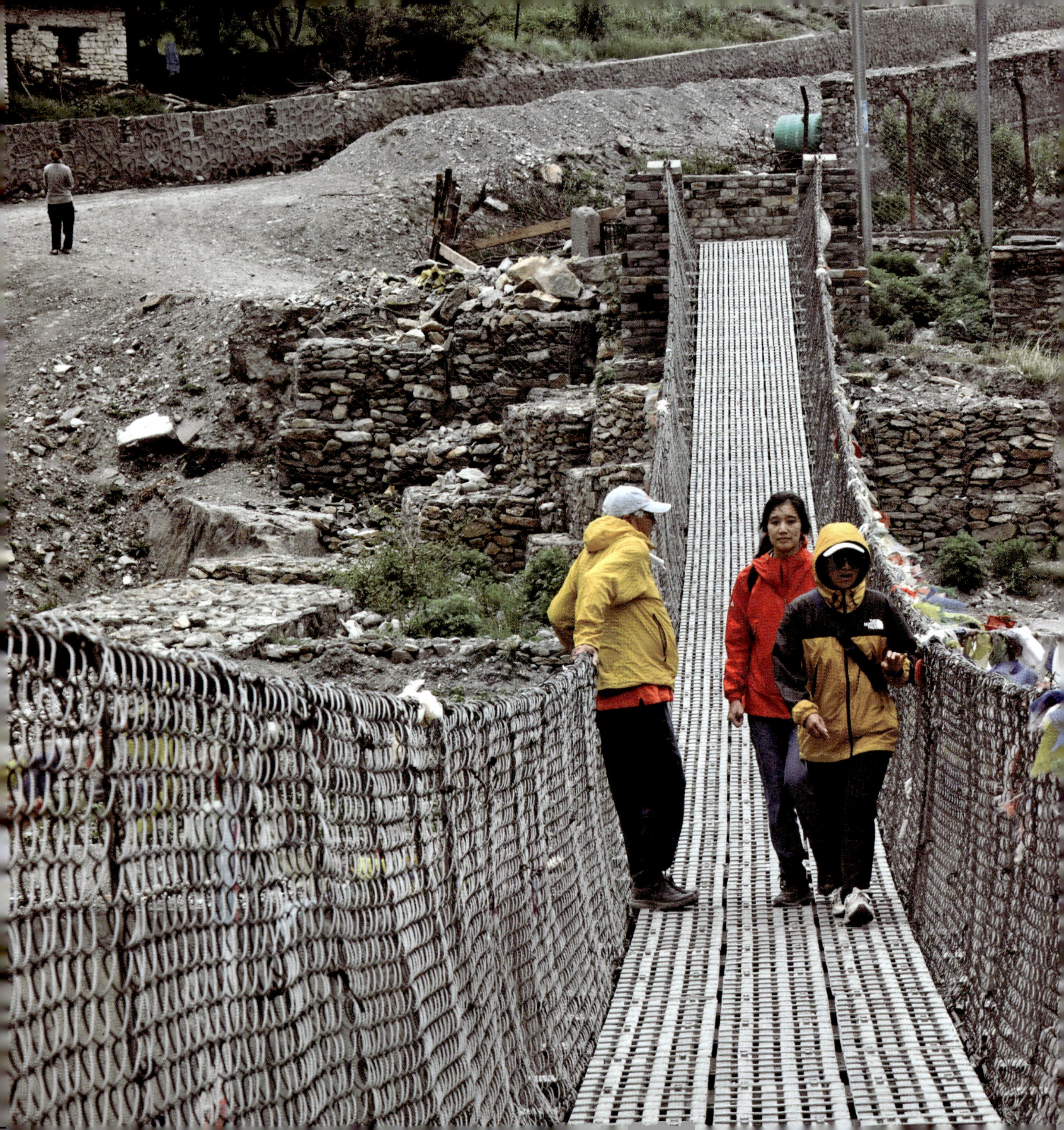

Tibetan refugee children / 藏族難民兒童
Schools for refugee / 難民自建學校
Bridge to refugee village / 橋通藏難民營

MUSTANG 187

尼泊爾 木斯塘 二〇二四年六月三日

木斯塘的暗哨

康人游擊隊的藏身之處

這趟尼泊爾之行中，我一直想造訪這個位於中國西藏邊境的小鎮，木斯塘。自上世紀六〇年代初以來，這裡因藏族準軍事游擊隊「四水六崗」而聞名。那段動盪的歷史有很多書籍和文字紀錄。在美國中央情報局的支持下，流亡在邊境一帶的康人游擊隊多年來越境騷擾解放軍，使這裡成為一片無論是從地形還是政治背景上來講，都迷人又危險的土地。

據說，第十七世噶瑪巴逃往印度時曾經路經此地。我曾在拉薩楚布寺見證過他七歲時的坐床儀式，後來又在印度達蘭薩拉他的住所與他碰過面。我還曾在二十五年前的一個在德國舉行的文化保護會議上遇見過木斯塘的王子，如今的「國王」。

然而，我在加德滿都被告知，木斯塘地區目前需要提前申請特別許可才能進入，而中國籍人士幾乎不可能獲批。不過，我們的團隊可以在木斯塘的邊界稍作考察，那裡仍屬於木斯塘王國，又稱洛王國。於是，我們決定走到能去到的最遠處。

途中，我們在萊特村的一家旅館停留。東望安納普爾納峰，西瞰冰川山脈，視野壯麗。但因正值淡季，旅館人手不足，晚餐只能由我們自己動手烹飪。第二天清晨，安納普爾納南坡被晨光染成金色。我們在旅館的屋頂上邊吃早餐，邊欣賞眼前的美景，整個

Monastery on spur / 山崖寺廟

世界彷彿都靜止了。

這片區域的路況比之前強了不少，大部分已經鋪設好，或者正在鋪設中。我們一路上看到許多滿載印度人的吉普車從身邊駛過，他們來來往往的目的地是一個印度教和佛教徒都視之為「救世之地」的寺廟——穆克蒂納特。

到達通往木斯塘的邊境檢站時，我們轉上了一條更小的山路。這裡有一個村鎮，看到路口的「麰當勞・雪山大飯店」招牌，我不禁莞爾，笑著想，這應該是專門為像我一樣的「麥門信徒」準備的吧！

隨著我們沿著蜿蜒的山路不斷攀升，腳下的景色漸漸展開。寬闊的河谷和被侵蝕的砂岩山丘讓人聯想到不遠處的西藏西部地貌。遠處的白色佛塔和藏式寺院點綴在山巒之間，將這片土地烘托得宛如青藏高原的延伸。途中經過一個小村莊，幾家零星的商店售賣手工藝品和小飾物，風格依然帶有濃厚的藏族色彩。村裡有兩位婦人，看起來像是一對母女，正在用傳統的手腳織布機忙碌著。我們在

那裡買了幾件帶有特色圖案的布藝作為紀念品。

終於到了路的盡頭，那裡停滿了巴士和汽車，街邊擺滿小販攤和簡易餐館。從這裡開始，徒步一小時，便可前往聖地穆克蒂納特寺。年輕男子忙著租售馬匹，供那些想節省體力騎馬前往的人使用。一些年長者則會選擇乘坐由四名挑夫抬著的轎子，挑夫們分攤重量，也分攤酬勞。

我因長時間的旅程疲憊不堪，這次選擇留在附近唯一的一家旅館。這裡海拔三千七百米，站在高處俯瞰下方的壯麗景色，彷彿置身天堂。看到一些印度朝聖者祈禱完畢，帶著裝滿聖水的瓶子返回，準備將這分神聖的祝福帶回家，與摯愛之人分享。那一刻我明白，天堂也能被帶到人間。

就此，我的尼泊爾之行已接近尾聲。我們準備沿著來時的路折返加德滿都，約需兩天時間。不過在途中，我要求在南加藏民營稍作停留。

這是尼泊爾的十二個藏人難民營之一，居住著約四十個家庭，總人口大約兩百人。他們是二十世紀六〇至七〇年代「四水六崗」隊員的家屬與後代，還有一些是二十世紀五〇年代西藏解放及土地改革後，選擇追隨他們的達賴喇嘛流亡至此的藏人家庭。

進入村莊需走過一座長長的鐵製吊橋，橋下是奔湧的激流。沿著村內一條小巷漫步時，我聽到低沉的鼓聲從遠處傳來。循著鼓聲，我來到一扇半掩的門前。輕輕脫下鞋，悄悄滑進一間昏暗的小屋內，只見一位身穿藏傳僧袍的老者端坐其中。他面前放著一本

經書，口中低聲吟誦，手隨節奏敲打著懸掛的法鼓。深沉的嗓音與鼓聲完美交織，莊嚴又寧靜的氛圍於我而言是那般熟悉。

那一瞬間，我彷彿回到了西藏深處。政治的分裂與喜馬拉雅高聳的山脈，都不再是阻隔。我深切地感受到，精神的力量可以穿越世間的一切界限，超越自然與人世加諸於我們的所有限制，達到一種無形而永恆的自由。

Tibetan style architecture / 藏式建築

日本首家度假酒店

FIRST RESORT IN JAPAN circa 1878

Hakone, Japan – September 22, 2024

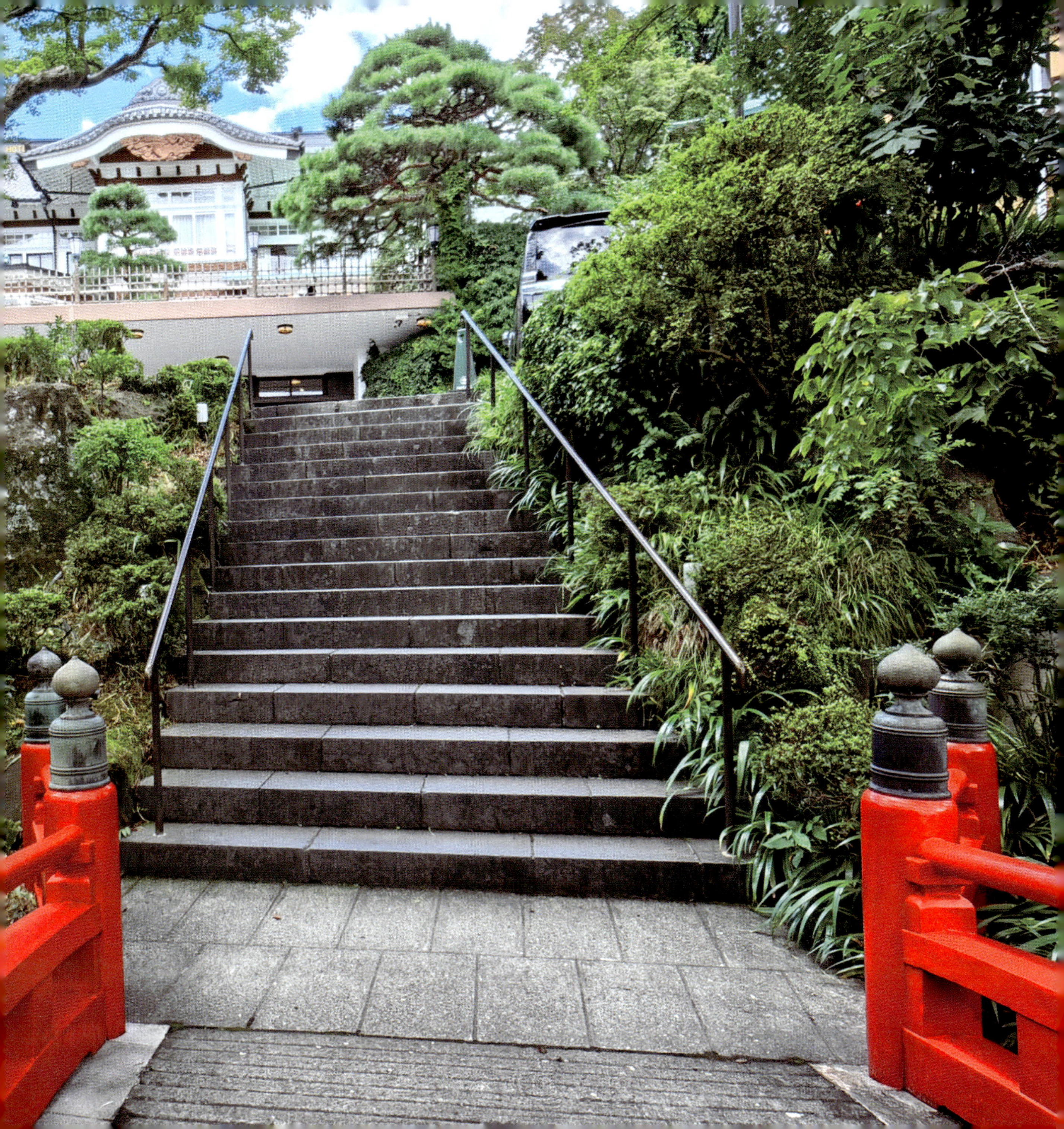

Hakone, Japan – September 22, 2024

FIRST RESORT IN JAPAN circa 1878
Still leading in many ways

Einstein stayed here. Charlie Chaplin played tennis in its court and left a drawing of Mount Fuji on a piece of paper. Archduke Franz Ferdinand von Habsburg of Austria whose death triggered the First World War was a guest. Chiang Kai-shek stayed while visiting his wife Sung Mei-ling's mother in Japan. John Lennon also came with Yoko and her mother, together with his son Sean. Yes, also Helen Keller, the most admirable blind and deaf author, and a civil and women rights-advocate. The list goes on and on, including successive Emperors and princes of Japan.

But my rendezvous with the Fujiya Hotel in Hakone has a rather fortuitous beginning. I am a frequent visitor to Tokyo's used book district of Jimbocho where the neighborhood hosts maybe 150 bookshops, selling just about anything printed from past to present. My haul of books, old maps and photo albums, have gone home with me as overweight luggage. While each item may be special for me, like maps and photos I have used to embellish my writing interest, one book stands out special among other historic publications.

It is bound thick with strings on its edge, like old classic books of the past. But the strings are worn and partly torn, making it precarious to go through the six hundred double-sided pages within.

Each two pages have two inside folded empty pages, such that the ink printed would not penetrate through the thin paper. On its fabric front page is printed the title "We Japanese" in English, not sideways as proper English writing dictates, but top to bottom in alphabetical line-up as classical Japanese would have it. Thumbing through it gave me the desire that I must visit this iconic hotel.

My copy is unique and rare, with three editions bound as one, from 1934, 1937 and 1949, with each additional edition having expanded contents supplemental to the last edition. The owner/manager of the hotel during that era was Kenkichi Yamaguchi, a third-generation successor of the founding owner. He wrote prefaces to all three editions, being included at the front of the book. It offers me a chance to read the changes in attitude and fortitude of a Japanese from the pre-war epoch years, to the war years of supremacy, and subsequently losing the war and being humbled under occupation, when the hotel was secured by the US government until 1956.

After reading select parts of the book, I feel an urge to visit the hotel in person, despite having visited Hakone many years ago to take in the breathtaking view of Mount Fuji. An easy train ride from central Tokyo got me there in less than two hours, connecting to a local bus took me to within twenty meters the steps leading up to the Fujiya Hotel. The same

Einstein at hotel / 愛因斯坦在酒店
Charlie Chaplin in 1932 / 查理・卓別林，一九三二年

FIRST RESORT IN JAPAN circa 1878   195

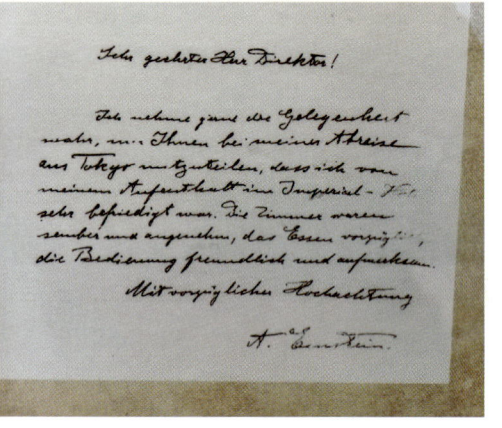

My copy of *"We Japanese"* / 我收藏的合訂本
Einstein's writing / 愛因斯坦手跡

red ornamental bridge that likely bears the footprints of many dignitaries and celebrities is there to welcome me while the doorman gave a nice bow with his hand showing the entrance into the hotel lobby. As the restaurant would not open until 11:30, I opted to visit the museum first.

Today, integrated resorts are coming up all over the world, into jungles and even beyond the Arctic Circle. But few if any can boast to be over a hundred years old. The Fujiya Hotel in Hakone was founded in 1878 and is closing in on 150 years old. The Fujiya comes with many surprising amenities, not just an indoor pool said to be Japan's first one, but a museum describing its long history, with its structures now registered as a tangible cultural property, and designated as historical buildings.

Destination weddings at resorts have been in vogue for a couple decades, but the Fujiya comes with a well-adorned chapel for wedding ceremonies, with a grand piano in the foyer, and inside seating for up to 150 guests. Not that I was ready for a wedding, but that chance purchase of the book prompted my visit and the effort seemed not wasted. Mounted on both walls of a corridor leading to the museum gives a fascinating story of its founders, as well as the inner making of the Fujiya, from the front office, guest facilities, and restaurants, to the kitchen and even the laundry and ironing room.

Wedding ceremony chapel / 婚禮教堂

INDEPENDENCE DAY DINNER

Thursday Fourth, July 1946

Appetizers
Consomme American
Tenderloin Steak Bearnaise
Buttered Green Beans
Corn in Cream
Batonet Potatoes
Peach Sundae
Washington Pie
Dinner Roll. Butter. Jam.
Coffee or Ice Tea

Fujiya Hotel   Miyanoshita

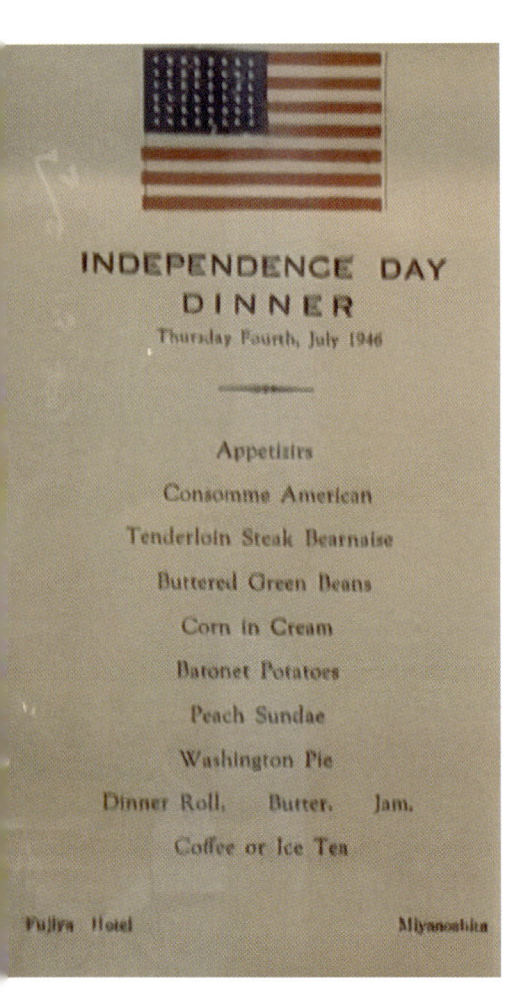

Independence Day menu / 獨立日菜單

What caught my attention was some relics of the hotel's in-house printing press, with old-style type-face blocks printing the daily menu for the several restaurants, and rubber plates that produced the backside page with interesting information and caricatures about Japan. Many of these are extracted from the contents of the book that I had acquired.

One of these special menus is framed and on display, on Thursday Fourth, July 1946 for America's Independence Day Dinner, almost a year after Japan's surrender in WWII and during the time of US occupation of Japan. Dessert included Peach Sundae and "Washington Pie", a rather patronizing selection. At the time, the US flag has only 48 rather than 50 stars to the thirteen bangles. There is also on display a menu from Sunday 15th February 1948, for the Sweet Heart Dinner-Dance with several celebrities autographing over it.

I have at times pondered upon the Japanese psych after the War. I believe in retrospect, they felt they had lost only to the US and considered Allied countries only won with collateral success. Without Pearl Harbor that triggered America into WWII, they probably could have consolidated much of their gain and became a real empire. It is not my imagination that when bowing in front of Americans, they bow lower, at least in their hearts, as Japanese respect strength and force.

But after the War, Japan in turn became a beneficiary as no military spending was allowed, prohibiting them from having a defense, let alone offence, budget. The rebuilding of the country and its economy was left to the Americans. It was at a time when the U.S. was still embracing its moral high-ground posture, despite dropping two atomic bombs on civilian cities demonstrating also that it has a limitless bottom line, when pushed. Japan, with its strong industrial base came back fast and strong economically, ultimately requiring America to again rein it in after the booming 1980s. The same was true with Germany. Today America cannot afford to win a war, let alone losing one. That's why after Korea, Vietnam, Iraq and Afghanistan, America feels no obligation in helping to rebuild any of these countries, calling it a truce, a draw or a retreat with honor, is rather face-saving.

If I am becoming too analytical, blame it on my fine education in America, especially through years as a journalism school major. But my Art double major curriculum soon took over with my interest turning to the Fujiya Hotel Museum. It has a library, though almost all books are in Japanese. The photographs of the most noted guests graced the wall with Chiang Kai-shek leaving behind four words of calligraphy with his signature during his visit in 1927. This was well before Japan plundered much of Manchuria in 1931 and entered Beijing, then Shanghai and beyond in 1937, leading

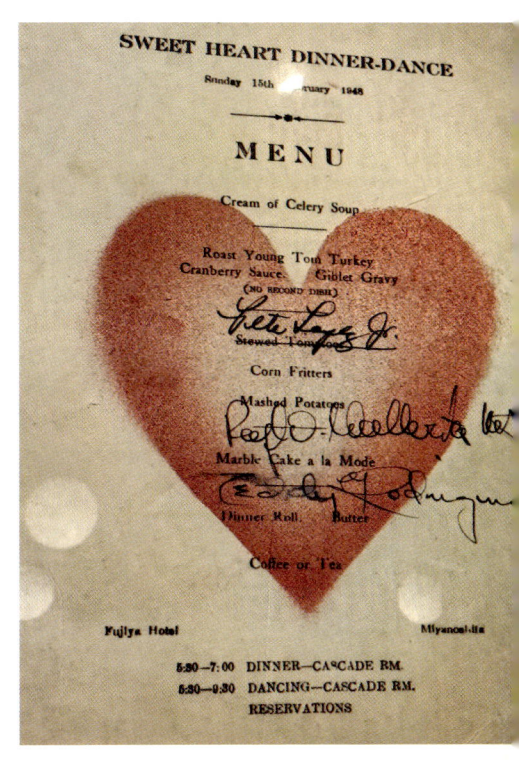

Sweet Heart Dance menu / 甜心舞會菜單

FIRST RESORT IN JAPAN *circa 1878*

John Lennon visit / 約翰・藍儂的到訪

to an all-out war with China. Obviously, the then hotel owner/manager did not consider those battles in China as a war, as in his Preface he called those years as being "pre-war", probably considering December 1941 as the watershed when Japan took on the entire Asia and the American Pacific islands as the battlefield.

On the same wall, I found Charlie Chaplin's 1932 minimalist Mt Fuji more tranquil. A pictorial chronology of the hotel told tales of important milestones of the Fujiya. Some old china and silver wares were on display, and a small room had films on a loop, including the lengthy restoration of the hotel to make it earthquake proof.

By now, it was almost 12:30 and I removed myself to the Restaurant Cascade that serves "simple" Western dishes, bypassing the more expensive eponymous French and ornamental Japanese restaurants. Some young Japanese, perhaps more cost conscious, are seated at the window lounge having tea with a tower of pastries in front.

As I entered this rather large restaurant, only four to five tables were taken. But before I finished my lunch, the place would be totally full, as a big bus brought in a Japanese tour group of men. It seems the Fujiya is a destination and the restaurant seems to be serving up a fixed menu of curry with rice and beer to everyone, maybe thirty or more in this group. My set lunch menu, however, was more substantial besides being more colorful than curry when served. Perhaps as an old tradition, the daily menu is printed with a chop and a date, turning over to a page of information about Japan. Today's description replicated one of the pages in my old book. I must read about the Japanese sandal footwear with drawings, be it appetizing or not.

While I would like to describe more of the customs and history included in this very fine old book, it must be left to readers to find their own copy through our friendly internet market. Most items described took up one page, or at most two to three pages, but rarely. However, the "Magic Silkworm", as credited to be discovered by a Chinese Empress, takes up six pages, the longest of all. Surprisingly, the Ainus indigenous people of northern Japan who has been official target for assimilation for over a century and only received special recognition in 2019, took up three pages. Likewise "The headhunters of Formosa" then still occupied by Japan until the end of the War in 1945 also took up two pages.

Among all the "oddities", actually such a title took up substantial pages in the book, one, though only taking up

Chiang Kai-shek writing / 蔣介石親筆

Charlie Chaplin's drawing / 查理・卓別林的畫作

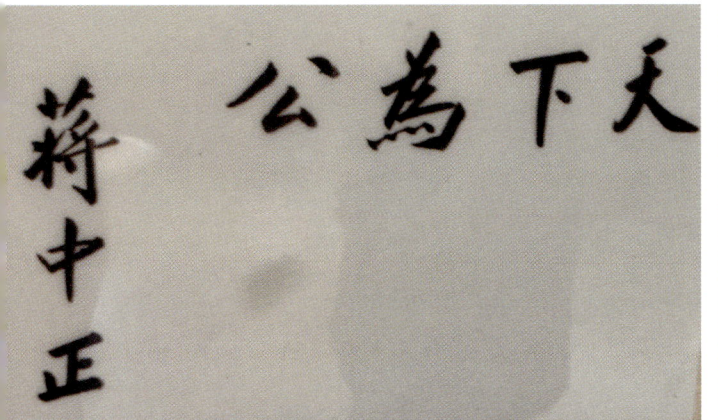

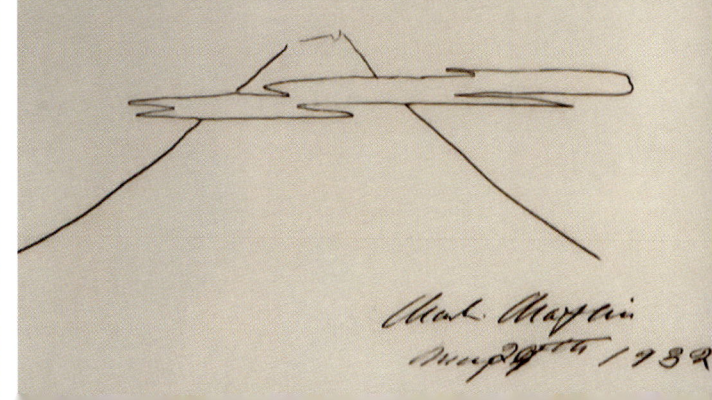

one page, stands out worthy of recounting – "International Mustache Club", with headquarters at the hotel. It was founded by Mr. H.S.K. Yamaguchi, the second Owner/Managing Director of the Fujiya Hotel. One interesting qualification, "men or women with beards or whiskers are welcome to become members, besides those with mustaches." The club's vision is grand: "The object of the club is to do its bit in creating a feeling of good fellowship among its members, and to show that people of different nationalities are good fellows at heart, and that, after all, without distinction of race or creed or color, everyone desires to live in peace and harmony with the rest of mankind." Members, however, must submit an autographed photograph bearing "a mustache, whisker or beard, that is at least two inches in length". Should this be shaved off the membership becomes void. With that as entrance bar, Hitler, Japan's War-time ally, would not qualify as his mustache is an inch too short, whereas its enemy Stalin, like Einstein, could well become a member.

An added note in the book to end the paragraph, "In a communication received from the Bald-headed Men's Club of Japan, the sympathy and get-together spirit of the International Mustache

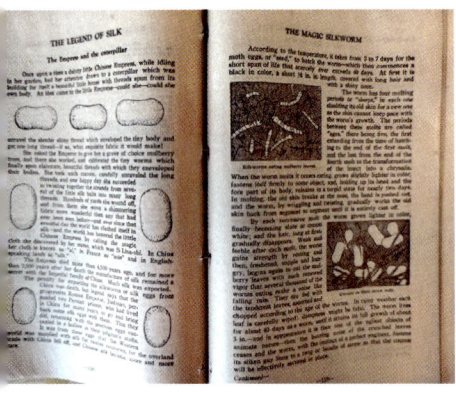

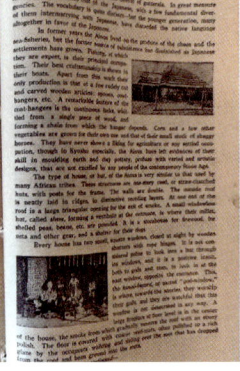

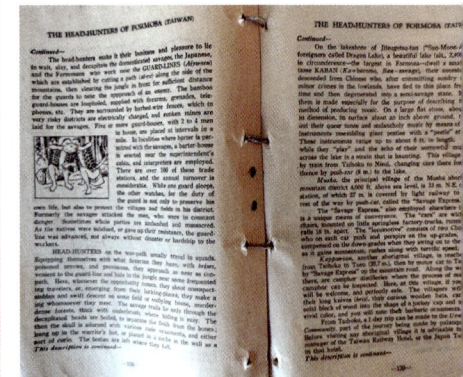

Pages on Silk Worm / 關於嫘祖養蠶的內容

Pages on Ainus / 阿伊努族

On headhunters of Formosa / 台灣獵首部落

Club were solicited, and despite the apparently antagonistic requirement for membership in these clubs, the latter gladly extended its good fellowship to the bald-headed men, even though the hirsute adornments of the members could not be well transferred to the bald domes of the former's members as contributions for their lack of hair." Thus explained on page 152 with twelve photos of mustached men, though without any woman.

I would have loved to spend a night at the Fujiya Hotel, but balked at the current low season price of some US500 per night. Directly across the street is the Fujiya Hostel, missing only one alphabet. It is posted online with 5.0 rating, at only a paltry US50. I will opt to stay there and enjoy all the amenities of the Fujiya Hotel, perhaps without the indoor pool. Sayonara.

Self-printing tools / 油印工具

日本 箱根町 二〇二四年九月二十二日

日本首家度假酒店
百年風華 典範猶存

愛因斯坦曾在此下榻；卓別林在其網球場揮拍對弈，留下親手繪製的富士山素描；遇刺事件引爆第一次世界大戰的奧地利法蘭茲・斐迪南大公亦曾是座上賓；蔣介石訪日探望岳母宋老夫人時在此停留；披頭四的約翰・藍儂帶著岳母、妻子小野洋子與二人的獨子西恩同來；還有最令人敬佩的盲聾作家、平權運動先驅海倫・凱勒；以及歷代日本皇室成員。在這兒，百餘年風雲際會，名流足跡從未間斷。

富士屋酒店，位於日本神奈川縣箱根町宮之下溫泉畔，創業於一八七八年明治時期。我與其邂逅，始於一段意外機緣。

東京神保町古書街聚集著約一百五十家書店，從古至今的印刷品幾乎無所不包，我是這裡的常客。我總帶著超重的行李回家，裡頭塞滿淘來的舊書、老地圖與相冊。這些藏品於我各有意義，譬如為文章增色的地圖與照片。某一日，有一冊古籍在眾書中脫穎而出，抓緊了我的眼球。

這本以線裝訂的厚冊，有六百頁雙面印刷的內頁，書脊處的棉線已然磨損斷裂，翻起來必須十分小心。每兩頁之間都夾著對折的襯紙，以防墨跡滲透單薄的紙張。織物封面上，英文書名《我們日本人》不以橫排呈現，卻仿照日式典籍的豎排傳統，將字母

Helen Keller / 海倫·凱勒

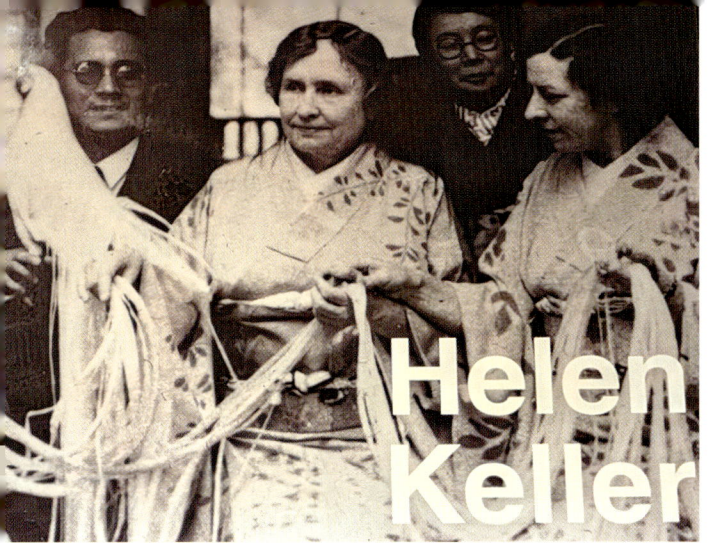

Double pages in-between / 書中的跨頁內容

自上而下排列，十分獨特。首頁的落款顯示，這本書是由富士屋酒店於二十世紀初期編撰並出版的，為了向住在酒店的外國遊客介紹日本的文化、習俗和歷史，幫助他們更好地理解和欣賞這個國家的獨特魅力。指尖撫過泛黃紙頁時，一個念頭油然而生：「我一定要去看看這座傳奇酒店。」

我收藏的這套合訂本堪稱絕無僅有，將一九三四年、一九三七年與一九四九年三個版本合訂為一冊，每版皆在前版基礎上擴充了內容。書中包含了當時酒店的所有者兼經理山口謙吉的序言，他是富士屋酒店創始人家族的第三代傳人。透過這些文字，我得以窺見一位日本人在戰前昂揚、戰時狂熱到戰敗後只能謙卑的精神轉折。當時酒店還曾被美國政府徵用，直至一九五六年才歸還業主。

我雖多年前曾為富士山絕景而造訪過箱根，但讀罷書中章節，仍驅使我帶著強烈的嚮往親臨這座酒店。從東京市中心搭乘火車，便能在不到兩小時內輕鬆抵達箱根，轉乘當地公車後，富士屋酒店的

FIRST RESORT IN JAPAN circa 1878   205

Hotel room section / 酒店住房部

石階距下車處僅二十公尺。那座見證無數名流足跡的朱紅裝飾橋依然如故，門房躬身行禮，優雅地指引我進入大廳。趁餐廳尚未營業的空檔，我決定先參觀博物館。

如今，功能設施齊全的綜合性度假村在全球遍地開花，從熱帶叢林到北極圈內都能見到它們的身影，但很少有酒店能自豪地宣稱擁有超過百年的歷史。而箱根的富士屋酒店，如今已有接近一百五十年的歷史。這裡不僅擁有據傳日本首座室內泳池，更設有記載悠久歷史的博物館。酒店的建築群現已被列為重要的文化財產，並被指定為歷史建築。

在度假村舉行婚禮已風行數十載，但富士屋的禮拜堂尤其別具韻味。門廳擺放著三角鋼琴，廳內可容納一百五十名賓客。雖非為婚禮而來，但那次偶然的淘書確促成了這趟不虛此行的造訪。通往博物館的走廊兩側掛滿了展板，生動地講述了酒店創始人的故事，還有從前台、客房、餐廳到廚房甚至熨衣間的運營細節，這座傳奇酒店的百年風華躍然紙上。

最吸引我注意的是酒店內部印刷所的一些遺存，包括用老式字模印刷的每日菜單，以及用橡膠版製作的菜單背面頁，內容多是一些關於日本的趣聞和漫畫插圖，許多都在我收藏的那本書中出現過。

First indoor pool in hotel / 第一個室內泳池
Printing press room / 印刷室

FIRST RESORT IN JAPAN circa 1878

其中一份特別的菜單被裱框展示，日期是一九四六年七月四日星期四，正值美國獨立日。彼時日本於二戰中投降將近一年，正處於戰後的貧困與重建之中。菜單顯示，晚宴的甜點部分包括「蜜桃聖代」和「華盛頓派」，這樣「經典」的美國選擇顯得有些居高臨下，不過也確實是戰後美國全面控制日本的最好體現。那個時候，美國的國旗還只有四十八顆星。此外，還有一份展示的菜單是一九四八年二月十五日星期日的「甜心晚宴舞會」，上面還有不少名人的簽名。

我時常思索戰後日本人的心理狀態。他們似乎只真心承認敗給美國，而將其他盟國的勝利視為搭了「順風車」。若不是珍珠港事件激怒美國參戰，日本說不定真能鞏固戰果，建立起龐大的帝國。這絕非我的臆測，你可以稍稍留意一下，當日本人向美國人鞠躬時，那彎腰的幅度絕對要比向別國致敬時更深，我想，至少在日本人心底，美國才是他們「唯一」的「大哥」，畢竟這個民族向

Wedding dress with piano / 婚紗與鋼琴

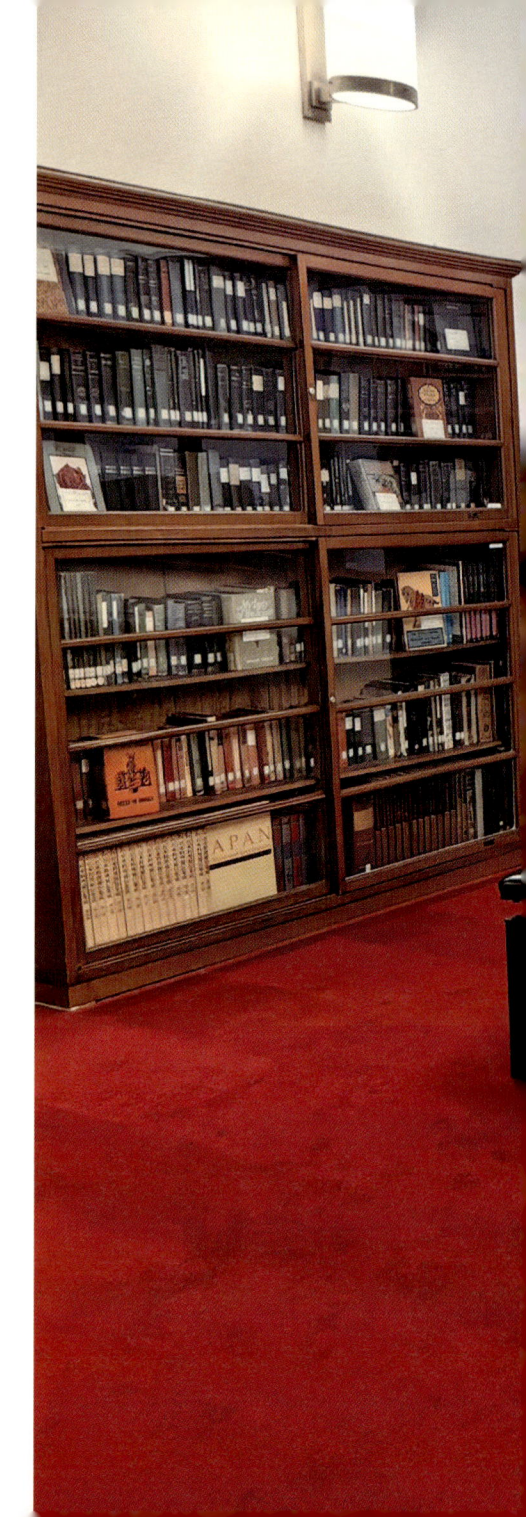

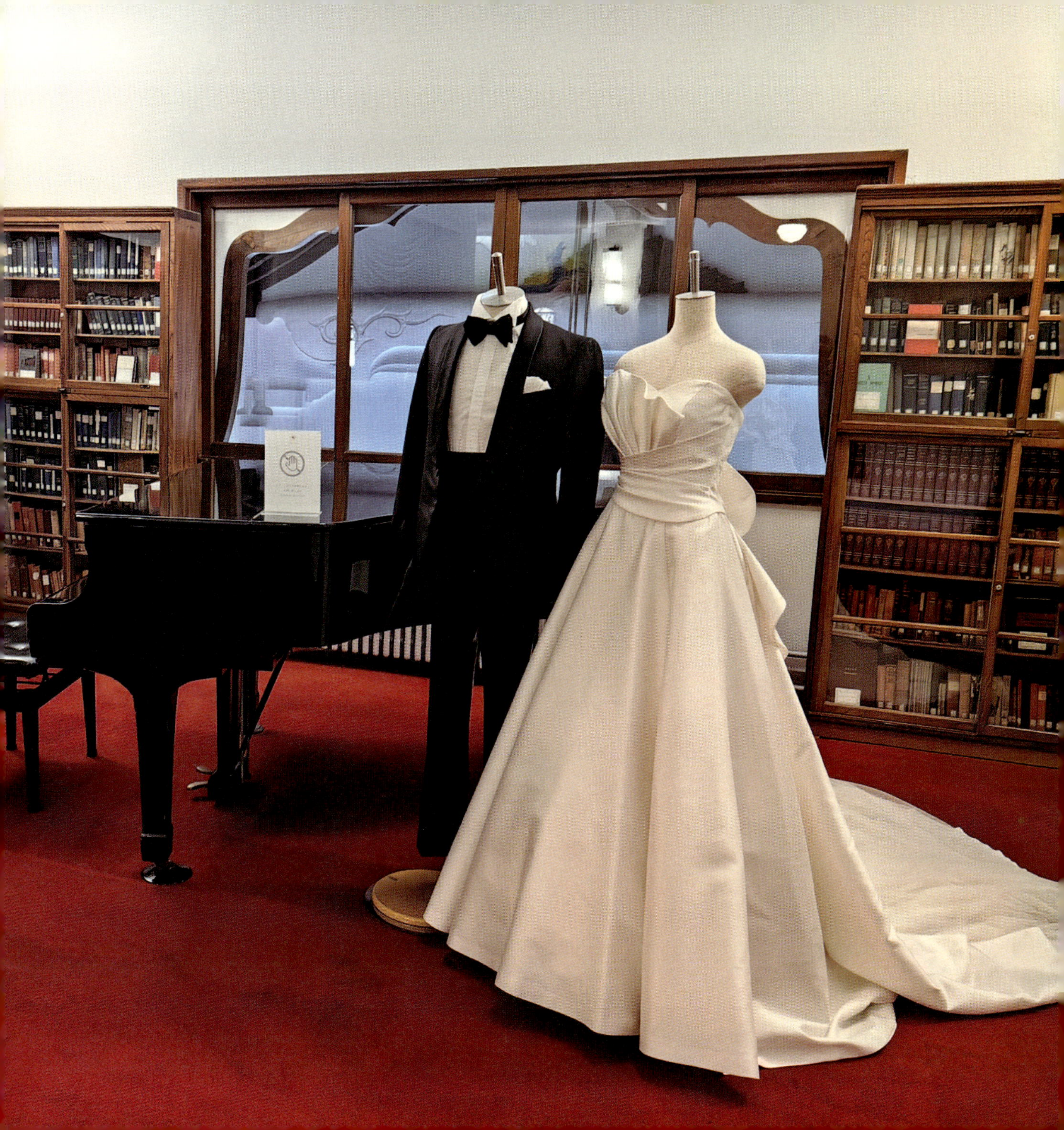

Menu of day / 當日菜單

來只對強權低頭。

諷刺的是，戰敗反而讓日本因禍得福。軍事發展的禁令成為經濟崛起的保護傘，重建重擔全由美國扛起。當時的美國還端著道德領袖的架子，儘管那兩顆投向平民城市的原子彈，早已暴露其底線可以多麼沒有下限。憑藉深厚的工業底子，日本經濟快速復甦，直到一九八〇年代繁榮到需要美國再次出手打壓，德國也拿的是同樣的劇本。如今的美國既贏不起戰爭，更輸不起面子。所以從朝鮮、越南到伊拉克、阿富汗，美國再也懶得裝什麼人道主義戰士、搞戰後重建，所謂「體面撤軍」不過是給自己找台階下。

若嫌這番分析太過尖銳，那得怪我當年受到的美國教育太好，特別是來自新聞學院的訓練。不過我的另一個藝術學位很快把我的注意力拉回了富士屋酒店的博物館。館內藏書雖多是日文，但牆上的照片很有意思：蔣介石一九二七年造訪時留下的四字墨寶，那時距離日本一九三一年侵佔東北、一九三七年進犯華北還早得很。顯然當時的酒店經營者，壓根沒把侵華戰爭當作「戰爭」，他在序言中稱那些年是「戰前」，大概覺得一九四一年珍珠港事件後，跟全亞洲開戰才算動真格。

同面牆上，出自卓別林一九三二年的富士山簡筆畫倒顯得歲月靜好。酒店的老照片訴說著歷史變遷，陳列的瓷器和銀器閃著幽光，

小放映室裡循環播放著抗震改造的紀錄片——所有展品都心照不宣地迴避著某段歷史，就像日本人鞠躬時那「恰到好處」的弧度。

時近正午十二點半，我刻意略過那些價格高昂的法式餐廳與裝潢華麗的和食料理亭，選擇了一家酒店內供應「簡式西餐」的餐廳。幾位年輕的日本客人坐在靠窗的沙發區，面前擺著精緻的三層點心架，看得出他們也是衝著性價比來這裡享用午茶的。

這間挑高寬敞的餐廳起初只有零星幾桌客人。但當我用餐到一半，整間餐廳突然被一車日本觀光客擠滿。這群約三十多人的旅行團成員都是男性，上桌的清一色是咖哩飯配啤酒的固定套餐，顯然，富士屋酒店已成為旅行社的固定打卡點。相較之下，我的午餐不僅分量更豐盛，擺盤配色也比單調的咖哩飯精緻許多。

餐廳至今仍延續著一項傳統：每日菜單都會蓋上當日的日期印章，背面則印著關於日本文化的趣味

Restaurant Cascade / 酒店內的西餐廳

Appetizer / 前菜

小知識。有趣的是，今天這頁插圖我在神保町古書街淘到的那本合訂本中見過，是介紹日本傳統草履的，也不知道他們為什麼把這種東西印在菜單上，好像對促進食慾沒什麼幫助。

雖然我很想更詳細地介紹這本精美古書中描繪的風俗與歷史，但還是留給有興趣的讀者們自己去發掘吧，現在網絡市場這麼發達，找到一本也不難。書中的絕大多數主題介紹都很簡短，通常只佔一頁，例如關於日本的傳統習俗、民間故事、或是各地的奇聞軼事，偶爾會延伸到兩三頁，也並不多見。不過，有關黃帝的元妃「嫘祖養蠶」的故事，卻足足佔了六頁，是全書篇幅最長的一部分。

有關日本北部原住民阿伊努人的記述也佔了三頁，這有點令我意外，畢竟這個民族在過去一個世紀裡一直被官方刻意同化打壓，直到二〇一九年才獲得官方認證。我們學會的其中一個保育對象，「台灣的獵首族」鄒族，也得到了兩頁的篇幅，此書出版時，台灣還在日本統治之下，直到一九四五年戰爭結束。

在這本充滿趣聞的書中，有個僅佔一頁卻令人拍案叫絕的軼事——「國際鬍鬚俱樂部」。這個總部設在富士屋酒店的組織，由第二代老闆山口先生創立，入會條件相當有意思：「不論男女，只要留著鬍子或鬢角都可以加入。」

俱樂部的宗旨聽起來相當崇高：「促進會員間的情誼，證明不同國籍的人本質上都是善良的，無論種族、信仰或膚色為何，人人都渴望與他人和平共處。」不過入會門檻可不簡單，必須提交一張親筆簽名的照片，證明自己擁有「至少兩英吋長的鬍鬚」，

一旦剃掉就自動喪失會員資格。按照這個標準，日本二戰時的盟友希特勒那招牌小鬍子還差一英吋，反倒是對面的史達林、愛因斯坦，比較符合入會標準。

書中還特別加了一段令人莞爾的註記：「日本光頭俱樂部曾來函，希望國際鬍鬚俱樂部能發揮『同袍情誼』。儘管兩個俱樂部的入會條件有點相互矛盾，鬍鬚俱樂部還是大方地接納了這些『寸草不生』的夥伴——雖然會員們茂盛的鬍鬚，終究無法移植到光頭同好們閃閃發亮的頭頂上。」第一百五十二頁如此寫道，並附上了十二位鬍鬚會會員的照片，紀錄中會員未曾有過女性。

我本想在富士屋酒店住上一晚，但看著淡季也要五百元美金的房價，錢包都在瑟瑟發抖。對街的「富士屋旅舍」，評價五顆星，價格卻只要五十元美金。這種性價比，根本就是超商價錢吃米其林。反正名字都差不多，除了游不了那個古董級泳池，其他富士屋酒店的福利我也能享受。這麼想著，我帶著對富士屋酒店「下次一定」的心，住進了對街的「富士屋旅舍」。「莎呦哪啦」！下回見啦！

Tea cafe / 茶咖啡廳
International Mustache Club / 國際鬍鬚俱樂部

FIRST RESORT IN JAPAN circa 1878

照片中央的女孩（上）

GIRL AT CENTER STAGE (Part 1)

Shanghai – November 1, 2024

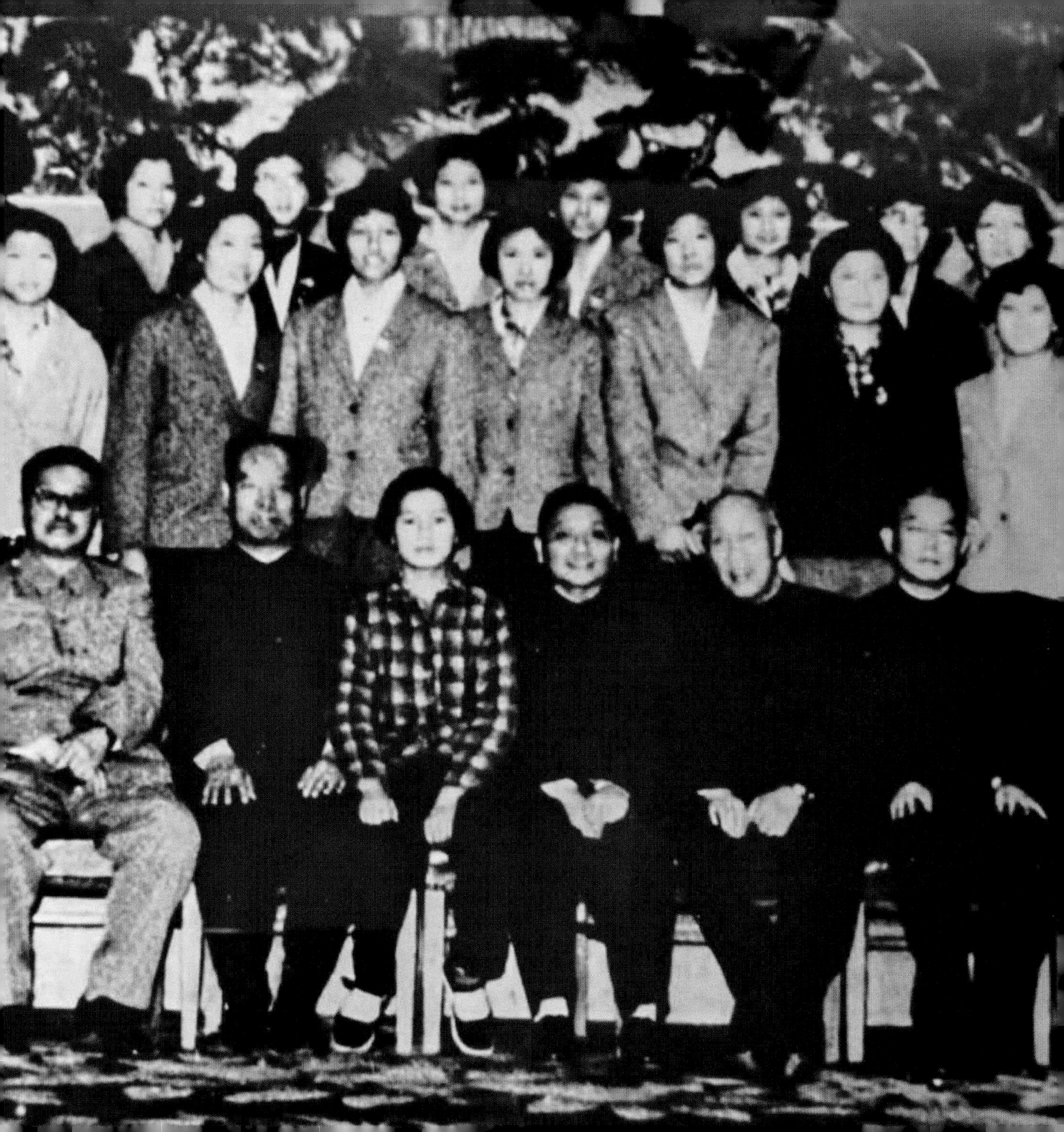

Shanghai – November 1, 2024

GIRL AT CENTER STAGE (Part 1)
And the Hong Kong Connection

"What am I supposed to do but listen," said Cheng Minzhi. "I was barely sixteen at the time. Several leaders waved me over calling me, "Xiao Gui" (Little Devil), to sit in the middle among all of them," Minzhi continued as I asked her about a very special photo, taken in 1961.

The elderly lady now in front of me is eighty, but her eyes sparkle like the sixteen-year-old girl in the picture. Deng Xiaoping was seated to her left, next to Deng was Dong Biwu, one of the twelve founders of the Chinese Communist Party in 1921. To her right was Peng Zhen, former Chairman of China's National Congress and Mayor of Beijing. Next to Pang was He Long, Marshall and Vice-Premier of the PRC, and to He's side was another Vice-Premier Li Fuchun. The remaining seated figures are all of no small stature, including Li Weihan and Li Xiannian, yet allowing the young girl to take up the center stage.

The occasion was a gathering of Chinese table tennis (ping pong) national athletes during the first time China hosted the Championship in 1961, the 26th World Championship. Cheng had just joined the national team as the youngest member ever, thus getting noticed by the Chinese leadership. "I was so impressed, even to this day, that our Central leaders are so genuine, casual and down to earth," said Cheng with her eyes firmly fixed on this photograph on the wall of her home. Since when have we ever seen a line-up of China's leadership with a little girl sitting right in the middle, her legs dangling not reaching the ground?

I first met Cheng Minzhi in February 2024 in Macau when she came to give a lecture at the Macau University of Science and Technology. I was so impressed by her performance, both on stage and at the ping pong table, that I decided to seek her out for an interview in Shanghai. But I am after more than a photo or a former world champion in Ping Pong. The photo I saw earlier this year however was the catalyst, as I realized that this young girl in the photo must be very important and well-connected. I tried to invite Minzhi to my villa hotel on the outskirts of the city but instead, I ended up being invited to her home in downtown Shanghai. It is a multi-storied house, and appropriately a table tennis table sat squarely in the middle once inside the door.

"I am here not so much to talk about you, as there is plenty of information online about you already. But I want to find out about some key figures who have intersected with you in your life," I got straight to the point on why I came all the way to Shanghai. "Please tell me something about your women national team coach Rong Guotun. He was born and raised in Shau

Cheng Minzhi at play / 鄭敏之賽場風采

GIRL AT CENTER STAGE (Part 1)

Cheng lecturing in Macau / 鄭敏之在演講

Kei Wan near my home in Hong Kong," I asked of Minzhi.

Living with his family in a squatter hut on a hillside, Rong cut his fame by becoming the champion ping pong player in the then British colony, winning three titles, single, double and mixed double, in 1957. As a teenager, he left school at 13 and later worked at a pro-China leftist workers union. Such organizations were not unlike other progressive and pro-workers unions like the UAW (United Auto Workers) in the U.S. But being pro-China put a "no-no" tag on it under the British-ruled regime of the time.

Despite winning the championship, he was marginalized by the Hong Kong Sports Federation when they put together a table tennis team to compete overseas. As a result, his friends prompted him to join the provincial team of nearby Guangdong Province in Mainland China, when then China's Sports Association Chairman General He Long offered him an invitation. From there, within a year he rose to become national champion, and soon after representing China at the 25th World Table Tennis Championship in 1959, and won. That trophy was the very first international championship among any sport that China has ever won.

Thereafter, Rong became the coach for China's men's team for a while before being transferred to become head coach for China's women's team where

Minzhi belonged. In 1961, he led China's men's team to the 26th World Championship and won the team title for China, against the strongest Japanese team who had taken that title for eight years in a row. In 1965, he led China's women's team when China swept most top titles, Men's Single, Men's Double, Women's Double, and Team, in the 28th World Championship.

But in 1968, upon being humiliated during the Cultural Revolution, Rong committed suicide, choosing to die with dignity rather than being disgraced in public, especially in front of all his fellow athletes whom he had coached for years. During those days, I was still in high school in Hong Kong and played the game almost daily at school. My father got me a ticket when the World Champion Zhuang Zedong and Silver Medalist Li Furong, came to Hong Kong for an exhibition game in the mid-1960s. At university in the U.S., I once represented the school team. But today, I only keep a table at home and play against a serving machine. In fact, I keep such ping pong tables and serving machines at several of our project sites that I visit often.

"Rong became a coach for the China table tennis team between 1963 and 1964, and he was head coach for our four key women players, aiming for the championship at the 28th World title in 1965. We were focusing on dislodging the Japanese who have dominated the titles for eight years

Rong Guotun playing / 容國團賽場英姿

Rong with trophy / 手捧獎杯的容國團

in a row," Cheng recalled. "His efforts in securing not only his personal champion title, but expanding it to the entire China team should not be underestimated," Cheng said with a tone of praise.

"I remember very well the day in 1965 when Lin Huiqing and I were playing women's double at the world championship in Yugoslavia. We Chinese were by then world-famous for playing with pen-hold, thus all international players targeted us on that during practice. Rong wanted to surprise our competitors, especially the Japanese, so we lined up the two penholders Liang Lijin and Li Henan against the weaker Europeans, whereas we two would play the Japanese with handshake hold. This was very strategic thinking. Rong demanded us that not only to win, but to play with style and up the standard for all to see. It was a very grand goal he laid out for us," recounted Cheng on the moment they took on the world on a world stage.

"We all listened to him very well, not like some arrogant top players. He spoke little, but with a firm and forceful tone. He didn't lean toward his favorite players, and was always right to the point and fair in his comments. He called me as Xiao Yianzi (little swiftlet), and we admired his dedication and professionalism. Never did we need to patronize him with words of praise. He was a grandmaster type of coach. Compared

Cheng & Lin with trophy / 鄭敏之與林慧卿手捧獎杯

to him, I as a national coach feels belittled. Just not having his kind of aura. His eyes show his determination, assuredness and firm conviction. Such is born with and not learned, such minute details cannot be replicated or simulated", Cheng continued to express her impression of Rong.

"Our coach was always calm, never calling out or cheering, providing certain firmness like a ballast that stabilizes the team," Cheng continued. "Before I entered the competition ring, he just gave my hand a firm grip and said, 'Now is time to go all out.'" "I felt at that moment, strength was conveyed to me. We all knew we were not representing ourselves, but an entire nation," Cheng recounted time at the championship game. "At first, I was a bit nervous, could not even feel which side of my paddle was hard and which side soft. But when I saw my opponent the Japanese gold medalist Masako Seki seemed also very nervous and kept shaking her hands, I began to calm down." "When I won, he spoke softly to me, 'You played well,' just that without showing much emotion. That type of maturity like that of a general guiding a battle is very stabilizing to us psychologically, I really miss him," with genuine sadness on her face, Cheng got emotional and even teared up when talking about Rong, saying, "Chinese table tennis wouldn't be where it is without Rong—he played such a big part."

"My double partner Lin Huiqing, also a women World Champion single player, is a better player than myself. She is more mature and stable. I can get upset and irritated when losing, thus affecting my performance," Cheng while determined and confidence about herself, also showed her more humble side as we chatted on.

"You know, in the 1950s China's top players, what we called the Ping Pong Three, Fu Chifong, Chiang Yungning, Rong Guotun, were all from Hong Kong. The other two joined China's national team before Rong."

History swept by, and the Ping Pong Three all passed away young in the 1960s. One consolation is that all three top players from Hong Kong had their honor restored and put on the pedestal of China's Ping Pong greats. Since 1985, China started the "Three Hero Trophy" in table tennis, in recognition of and tribute to these iconic players. This championship is hosted in rotation in Beijing, Shanghai, Guangzhou, Hong Kong and Macau, and has now been organized for over thirty years.

I could not help but make my own comments based on observations and also from experiences I have dealt with, which I try to share with Minzhi. By now, we have become quite personal since she had poured out her feelings and emotions to me, including some very private happenings. Some of my close friends whom I have known for decades during my fifty years of work in China also suffered greatly during that period.

Wu Tianfu, born 1919, was a senior cadre who acted as my main liaison person and have accompanied me on two major expeditions in 1984 and 1985. As a young man in the mid 1930s, he left his comfortable home in Singapore, through Vietnam and arrived in Chongqing. With help from Ye Jianying he managed to get to Yenan, then the red base, and joined the 8th Route Army against the Japanese. He was among the last to evacuate Yenan with Chairman Mao when the advance forces of Nationalist General Hu Zhongnan struck with surmounting army in 1947. After 1949, Hu worked in Beijing with the International Department of the CCP Central Committee, he helped in hosting Vietnam's Ho Chi Minh's multiple visits to China, and even that of Che Guevara of Cuba. During the Cultural Revolution, he was purged and banished to freezing Manchuria and worked in a farm.

Huang Jingpo, once a model county chief of Yenan, and later Governor of Qinghai who helped me a great deal in getting to the new-found Yangtze source in 1985, was also banished to the Northeast during those testing times. After retirement to Beijing, I visited Huang. Despite qualified to use a car and driver for his rank in retirement, he led me from my hotel to his home near Beijing train station by taking a local bus. Such modesty may not be the only litmus test for senior cadres, but certainly tells plenty in this case.

Another friend Leonard Lin, an ace fighter pilot who was overseas Chinese from the Philippines, inflated his age as being older to qualify for flight lessons in Kunming, and later joined the US 14th Air Force in WWII. After the War he continued flying in China for Moon Chin, my friend who founded in Shanghai Central Air Transport Corporation (CATC). Later CATC was moved to Hong Kong upon Shanghai's liberation by the Communist Army. Lin defected with an airplane of CATC in November 1949 to China and became a flight instructor. He ended up feeding pigs in a rural farm outside of Shanghai during the Cultural Revolution. He told me back then the toilets were the cleanest as his job was also to clean all the toilets. Later he was allowed to leave the Mainland to Hong Kong in 1978 with Ten Hong Kong Dollars in his pocket. In fact, such examples are too many to list.

But the past, no matter how significant, has already become history. The wheels of time keep turning, and society continues to advance. In today's China, we have every reason to believe that such events not only shouldn't happen but won't happen again—because this is a new era, and we are moving forward with strength and purpose.

"It seems a common practice all over the world that those with no status or accomplishments to claim are most likely to smear others and try to bring down those with fame and success. By doing so, they feel they ride higher and have accomplished more than those people whom they are targeting," I told Minzhi as related to the Red Guards as well as other minions I have come across. Minzhi listened and gave me a small smile. She said that while the world is indeed complex, people's pursuit of conscience and truth should be eternal.

I ended this part of our interview with a joke. *"You know, we are both Cantonese, you hailing from Zhongshan Shiqi where Sun Yat Sen is from, directly next to Macau. My ancestors are from Zhongshan Nanhai, just nearby to yours. Looks like we Cantonese folks have always had a special vibe—we're all sharp and full of wisdom, aren't we?"*

I told Minzhi a parody and we both laughed.

In the grand story of modern China's rise, there have always been people willing to step forward, pay the price, and ride the waves of change with the pulse of the nation. From Wong Fei-hung's legendary chivalry to Sun Yat-sen's bold revolutionary dreams, and Rong's fearless dedication to Chinese table tennis as both a player and a coach, each of their stories shines like a spark in the tide of history—together, they're the vivid footprints of generations pushing China toward greatness.

上海 二〇二四年十一月一日

照片中央的女孩（上）

她與來自香港的人們

「我那時候還能幹什麼？只能老老實實聽著照做唄！」鄭敏之笑著回憶。「那年我才剛十六歲。幾位領導朝我揮揮手，喊著『小鬼』，讓我過去，坐他們中間。」當我問起那張一九六一年的經典照片時，鄭敏之的目光裡透著幾分俏皮。

眼前的她已經是八十歲的老太太了，可眼神依然亮得像星星，彷彿還是照片裡那個十六歲的少女。在那張照片裡，她的左邊坐著鄧小平，鄧小平旁邊是董必武，一九二一年中國共產黨十二位創始人之一。而她的右邊，則是彭真，時任全國人大常委會委員長兼北京市市長。再往右，是賀龍元帥，國務院副總理，解放軍的傳奇人物，在他旁邊則是另一位副總理李富春。照片中的其他人們，也都是響噹噹的大人物，比如李維漢和李先念。然而，就是在這樣一群重量級人物中，偏偏是這個稚氣未脫的少女，坐在了最顯眼的正中央。

那是一次意義非凡的聚會，一九六一年，第二十六屆世界乒乓球錦標賽首次在中國舉辦。國家隊的運動員們齊聚一堂，迎接這激動人心的時刻。而在這群熱血沸騰的運動員中，有一個格外引人注目的小姑娘，鄭敏之。彼時她剛剛加入國家隊，是當時最年輕的隊員，僅十六歲的年齡，引起了中國領導層的關注。鄭敏之回憶起那段往事，目光緊緊鎖在掛在家中牆上的那張老照片上，輕聲說道：「直到今天，我都能清晰記得

Cheng at Macau Science & Tech Univ / 鄭敏之在澳門科技大學　　　　Cheng with HM in Macau / 我與鄭敏之的澳門初識

領導們的樣子，他們是那麼真誠、隨和、接地氣。」她微微一笑。「你見過國家領導人和一個小姑娘排排坐著合影，而她的腳還搆不到地，晃來晃去的嗎？」

我第一次見到鄭敏之，是在二〇二四年二月的澳門。那時，她應邀在澳門科技大學做講座分享。我坐在台下，深深折服於她的表現。站在臺上，她從容自信，言辭間既幽默又感性，瞬間吸引了所有觀眾。走下講台，乒乓球桌前作指導，她更是技藝精湛、氣場十足，彷彿時間倒流，讓人看到了她初奪冠軍時風采。她的風格讓我下定決心，要深入瞭解她的故事。於是，那張照片成了我的契機。照片中的小女孩，坐在中國領導人之間，顯得既自然又特別，我意識到，她的故事一定非同尋常。起初，我想邀請鄭敏之到我位於上海郊外的別墅酒店聊聊，但沒想到，她反過來邀請我去她位於上海市中心的家中。那是一幢多層老宅，推開門的瞬間，最先映入眼簾的是一張乒乓球桌，正居於門內中央。那一刻，我覺得再沒有什麼能比這布置更適合她的家了。

「我今天來，不是為了只聊您的故事，畢竟網上已經有太多關於您的資訊了。」我開門見山道。「我更希望能瞭解那些與您有過交集的重要人物。比如，能不能和我聊聊您國家隊的教練容國團？他可是出生在香港筲箕灣的人，他家離我家很近的。」

容國團的故事，起始於筲箕灣的南安坊的山坡小屋。他的家，坐落在一個簡陋的木屋區，陡峭的山坡上擠滿了用鐵皮和木板搭建的窩棚。他十三歲便輟學，早早進入社會謀生，後來在親中左派工聯會工作。這樣的組織，在那個時代類似於美國的「汽車工會」，主張維護工人權益。但在英屬香港的殖民統治下，親中立場被視為「危險信號」，他所在的組織理所當然地成為被打壓和邊緣化的對象。然而，這些經歷並沒有阻止容國團追求自己的夢想，乒乓球，成為了他改變命運的鑰匙。

不過，在贏得了香港乒乓球冠軍之後，容國團並沒有受到應有的尊重，反而在香港體育聯合會組建海外代表隊時被冷落和排除在外。失望之餘，在朋友的鼓勵下，他接受了時任中華人民共和國體育動員委員會主任，賀龍元帥的邀請，毅然北上，加入了鄰近的廣東省的乒乓球隊。從此，他的命運被徹底改寫。僅僅一年後，他便一舉成為全國冠軍。隨後，他代表中國出征一九五九年第二十五屆世界乒乓球錦標賽，並奪得男子單打冠軍。這座獎杯，不僅是他個人的巔峰，也是中國體育史上的里程碑——那是中國第一次在國際體育賽事中贏得世界冠軍。

後來，容國團短暫擔任過中國乒乓球男隊的教練，又被調任為女隊的主教練。當時，鄭敏之正是女隊的一員。一九六一年，他率領中國男隊參加第二十六屆世界乒乓球錦標賽，在決賽中擊敗了連續八年稱霸的日本隊，為中國贏得了男團冠軍。一九六五年，

Shau Kei Wan squatter huts / 舊筲箕灣木屋區

他又帶領中國女隊征戰第二十八屆世乒賽。那一次，中國隊幾乎囊括了所有的重要獎項，奪得了男單、男雙和女雙冠軍，創造了歷史性的輝煌。

那段時間，我還在香港讀高中，幾乎每天都會在學校打乒乓球。六〇年代中期，世界冠軍莊則棟和銀牌得主李富榮來香港打表演賽，我父親還特意給我買了張票去觀賽。後來到了美國上大學，我開始代表校隊參加稍微正式一點的比賽。技術雖然算不上很專業，但可以說是充滿熱情。如今，我家裡放著乒乓球桌和發球機，偶爾我會自己練一下。在幾個我經常造訪的學會的中心，我也特意放了乒乓球桌和發球機，有空的時候，打上一局，好像能找回一些當年的熱忱。

「一九六三到一九六四年間，容國團擔任中國乒乓球隊的教練，同時負責我們女隊的四名核心選手，重點目標就是在一九六五年的第二十八屆世乒賽上奪冠，打破日本隊的統治地位。」鄭敏之回憶道。她語氣中充滿著敬佩：「容教練不僅僅是一個冠軍，他的努力將中國乒乓球的榮耀從個人擴展到整個團隊，這是任何人都無法低估的成就。」

「我清楚地記得一九六五年的那一天，我和林慧卿在南斯拉夫世界錦標賽上參加女子雙打比賽。當時，中國選手以直拍打法聞名

Rong with Women's team trophy /
容國團帶領女隊奪冠

於世，因此外國選手在訓練中都會重點針對這一點進行研究。為了出奇制勝，尤其是對付日本選手，容教練決定安排兩位直拍選手梁麗珍和李赫男去對陣實力較弱的歐洲選手，而我和林慧卿則改用橫拍打法迎戰日本隊。這是一個非常有策略的安排。」鄭敏之回憶起那次與世界強手對陣的經歷時說道。「容教練不僅要求我們贏得比賽，還要求我們打出風格、打出水準，讓所有人看到中國隊的實力。他為我們設定的目標格局很大。」

「我們所有人都非常聽他的，他的威信無人能及。不像一些自以為是的『頂尖選手』，他話不多，但每一句都鏗鏘有力。他從不偏袒任何人，對隊員一視同仁，點評非常中肯到位。他總是叫我『小燕子』。我們都非常敬佩他的敬業精神和職業操守。他是那種真正的大師級教練，無需我們用溢美之詞去奉承他。他的存在就是一座豐碑，讓人肅然起敬。跟他相比，我這個國家隊教練，常常覺得自己有太多不足，遠沒有他那種氣場。他的眼神中總是透著一種堅定的、篤定的必勝信念。這種氣質是與生俱來的，無論怎麼學習都無法模仿，那些細微之處無法複製或偽裝。」鄭敏之動情地談起容國團，言語中滿是尊敬。

「我們的教練總是冷靜沉穩，從不在場邊大喊大叫。他就像一塊壓艙石，給整個隊伍帶來一種無形的力量。」鄭敏之繼續說道，「在我上場前，他只是握緊我的手，堅定地對我說：『現在，是該全力一搏的時候了。』就在那一刻，我感受到了一種力量傳遞到我身上。我們都知道，此刻的比賽不是為自己而戰，而是代表整個國家。」

鄭敏之回憶起當時的比賽情景：「剛開始我有些緊張，甚至分不清球拍的正反面。但當我看到對手，日本的金牌選手關正子，也顯得很緊張，不停地搓著手，我反而慢慢冷靜下來。」她繼續說道：「當我贏下比賽後，他只是輕聲對我說了句：『你打得不錯。』沒有過多地表露情緒。但正是這種如同

Cheng & Lin / 鄭敏之與林慧卿

統帥指揮戰役般的成熟和穩重，在心理上給了我們極大的支撐。我真的很想念他。」提到容國團時，鄭敏之的言語總是感性的，帶著滿滿的敬意和懷念，甚至一度落淚：「中國乒乓球的發展不能沒有容國團，他功不可沒。」

「我的雙打搭檔林慧卿，她也是女子單打的世界冠軍，比我更優秀。她更加成熟穩重，而我有時候在輸球時容易急躁，影響發揮。」鄭敏之一邊展現出自信的神態，一邊也流露出謙遜的一面，一如她爽朗又真實的性格。

從鄭敏之的口中聽著容國團一路走來的故事，再回望他來時的路，我不禁想起其他幾位和他一樣屬於「香港歸僑」的運動員，姜永寧和傅其芳，他倆也是來自香港吧！「是的，他們倆和容國團都是在五十年代回來的，他們仨並稱為『乒乓三傑』。傅其芳和姜永寧比容國團更早加入國家隊，那時候，他們一起為中國乒乓球開創了一個輝煌的時代。」

歷史席捲而過，「乒乓三傑」全部英年早逝於六十年代文革時期。一九八五年，中國設立了「三英杯」乒乓球錦標賽，以紀念這三位承載輝煌與悲劇的傳奇人物。自那時起，這項賽事開始在北京、上海、廣州、香港和澳門輪流舉辦，至今已延續三十餘載。他們的榮光，終究沒有被時代埋沒。

訪談至此，我們已經變得相當熟悉，話語間流轉的感受和情緒，讓我也不自覺想起了，在我過去五十年的中國工作經歷中的一些個人經歷和看法，還有一些同「乒乓三傑」一樣，經歷過艱難時期的老朋友。

吳田夫是我相識數十年的摯友，一九一九年出生，是一位高級幹部，也是我在一九八四年和一九八五年兩次重要的美國《國家地理雜誌》探險考察中的主要聯絡人。二十世紀三〇年代中期，他離開了舒適的家鄉新加坡，經由越南輾轉抵達重慶。在葉劍英的幫助下，前往當時的紅色根據地延安，並加入了八路軍，投入抗日戰爭。一九四七年，當國民黨胡宗南將軍率部隊進攻延安時，他是隨毛主席最後撤離延安的人之一。一九四九年之後，吳田夫在北京中共中央對外聯絡部工作，曾多次協助接待越南胡志明訪華，甚至還接待過古巴的切·格瓦拉。然而，在文化大革命期間，他被下放到寒冷的東北，在農場勞動。

我的另一位老友黃靜波，曾是延安的一位模範縣長，後來擔任青海省省長，在一九八五年的考察中

Rong coaching with Cheng on his right / 容國團正在指導鄭敏之

Rong with Women's team / 容國團與國乒女隊

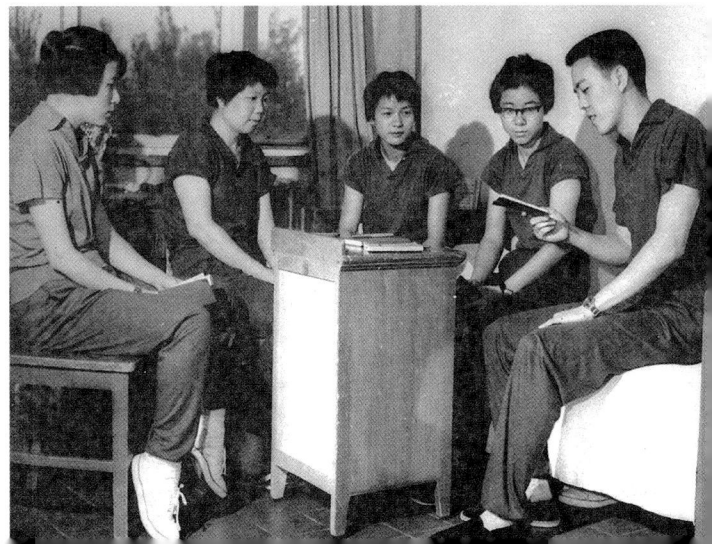

幫助我順利發現長江新源頭。然而在那個充滿考驗的時期，他也曾被下放至東北。他退休後，我曾到北京拜訪他。雖然按級別來說，他享有配車和司機的待遇，但他卻選擇親自帶我從酒店乘公交車前往他位於北京火車站附近的家。這分謙遜或許不能作為衡量高級幹部的唯一標準，但在他身上，卻足以說明很多。

同樣的，還有林雨水先生，他是來自菲律賓的華僑，一位王牌戰鬥機飛行員，曾在二戰中加入美國第十四航空隊。當年昆明的飛行訓練對學員有最低年齡限制，年紀尚小的他為了能夠參加，還謊報了年齡。戰後，他回到中國，為我的朋友陳文寬工作。陳文寬是中央航空公司的創始人之一，這家公司在共產黨解放上海後遷到了香港。一九四九年十一月，林雨水駕駛一架原屬央航的飛機投奔中國大陸，成為了一名飛行教官。然而在文革的那幾年，他卻被下放到上海郊外的農場餵豬。後來他告訴我，當時農場裡最乾淨的地方就是廁所，因為他的工作內容還包括打掃農場裡所有的廁所。直到一九七八年，他才獲准離開大陸前往香港，而彼時，他身上僅僅有十港元。事實上，在那個年代，這樣的故事數不勝數，難以一一列舉。

不過，過去的事終究已成過往。時代在向前，社會在進步，相信這樣的事情在今天的中國絕不該，也定不會再現。

我對敏之說：「你有沒有發現，這世上總有那麼一些人，自己一無所成，卻偏偏喜歡抹黑那些有頭有臉的人。他們見不得別人出名、成功，自己身在泥潭，不爭取自立，卻總想拉別人下馬，站在別人頭上。好像這樣就能顯得自己高人一等，其實只不過是害人害己，自欺欺人。」說到這裡，我不禁聯想到一些人，有的在未曾觸及的歷史裡，

有的則在現實生活中。敏之聽後，笑了一笑，她表示，世界確實是複雜的，但人們對良知和真理的追求應該是永恆的。

對早逝的良師益友的懷念，讓談話的氣氛變得有些低沉，我換了個方向，試圖找回輕鬆的氛圍。我對敏之說：「你知道嗎？我們倆其實還挺有緣分，都是廣東人。你老家跟孫中山是一個地方的，中山石岐，就在澳門旁邊；而我的祖先是佛山南海西樵的，和黃飛鴻同一個村子，離你那兒近得很。這麼看來，咱們廣東人向來有一種特別的精神，全是有識之士呀！」

鄭敏之聽完，淺淺一笑，眼底波瀾無聲。我也笑了，笑意在靜默中流轉，一切已然說盡。

在近代中國的發展史上，總有那麼些人，願意付出代價，緊跟祖國的脈搏，投身於社會發展的大潮中。無論是黃飛鴻那樣的俠義精神，還是孫中山先生倡導的革命理想，又或是容國團在那個年代，作為運動員和教練為中國乒乓作出的努力，都是一代代人推動國家進步的縮影。

From left Chiang, Rong & Fu /
姜永寧、容國團、傅其芳（由左至右）

GIRL AT CENTER STAGE (Part 1)

照片中央的女孩（下）

GIRL AT CENTER STAGE (Part 2)

Shanghai – November 1, 2024

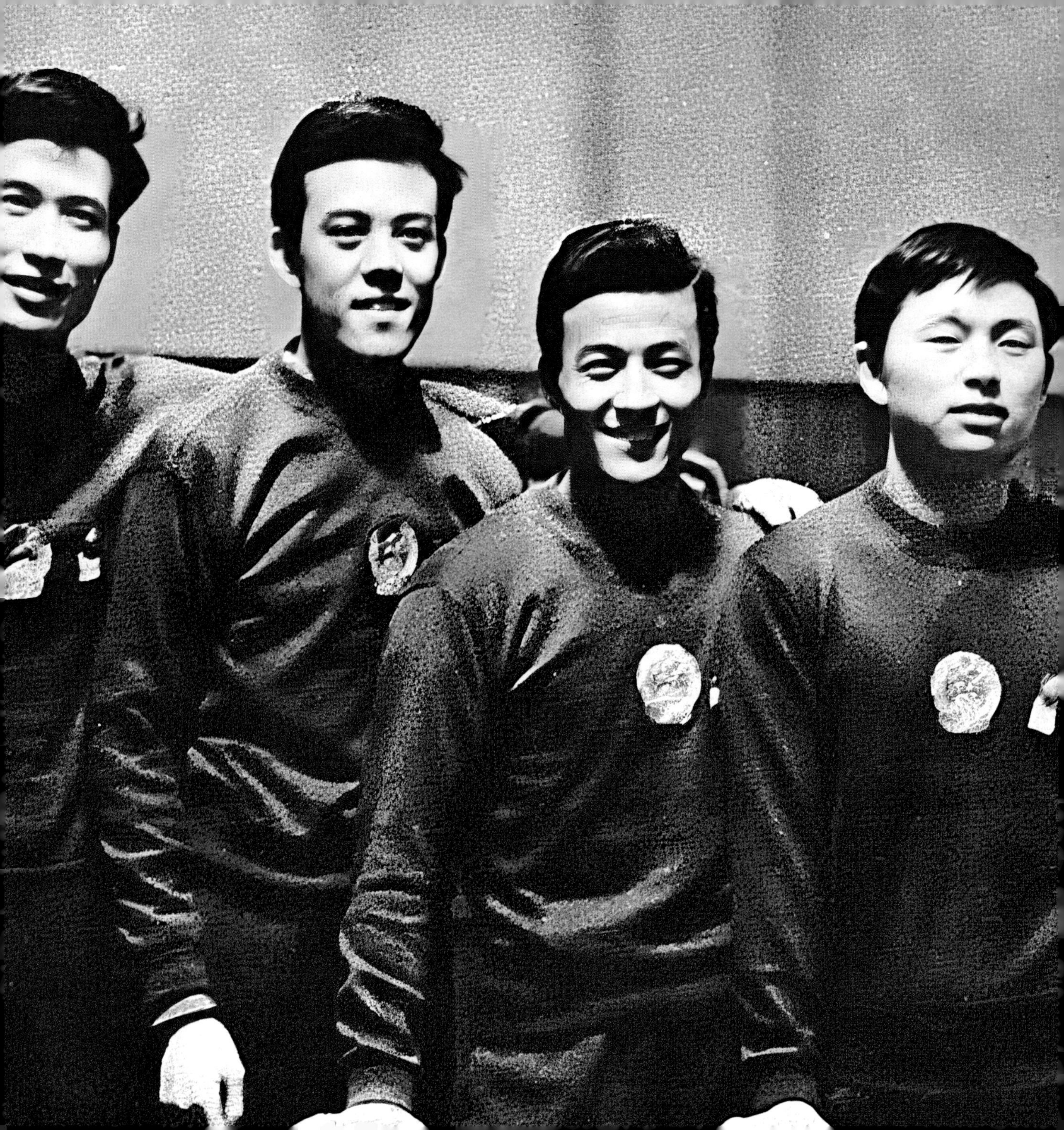

Shanghai – November 1, 2024

GIRL AT CENTER STAGE (Part 2)
Friendship first Competition second

The history of that era got pretty heavy and I wanted to bring our interview to a lighter and happier closing, despite that era of Cultural Revolution excesses was still at its peak. "Let's talk about Ping Pong diplomacy, a period that you have not only witnessed, but were an active participant in," I asked of Minzhi. With another sigh, but of relief, Cheng began her story.

"It was sometime between 1966 to 1970, for around four to five years. All practices stopped, let alone competition which was marginalized as reactionary. We all became lax in the sport. It was Premier Zhou Enlai who called upon us to start again, asking all of us to discuss whether to compete in the 31st World Championship. At that time, it's true that some of us were worn out, and the thought of continuing to play table tennis felt overwhelming. But when Premier Zhou called on us, we, the top players—Zhuang Zedong, Li Furong, Lin Huiqing, Li Henan, and other world champions—found the strength to return to the training ground. Stepping back onto the court wasn't just about playing the game; it meant facing immense pressure from forces beyond the sport itself. Yet Premier Zhou stood by us, resolving every concern and removing every obstacle."

"He paid attention to every detail, our thinking, even our livelihood. He told us 'players must *first learn to be a decent person, be honorable and win hearts.' He also explained why, even during such difficult times, we must remain connected to the world, to have a higher and broader view. I remember well he said 'in world competition, there is only one final winner. But many of the countries participated based on friendship and peace, not that they had a chance to take the championship, such as some smaller or weaker South Asian and African countries. They were there to demonstrate worldly friendship.' I am so thankful to our Premier,"* Cheng continued.

"Premier Zhou also explained why we must go join the international meet in Japan. It is because the Japan Table Tennis Association recognized China, though the government has not yet accepted us. That they must separate the organization from the government. He even sent us to Europe to compete, so as to gain experience in international arena", Cheng seems locked on to crediting Zhou Enlai for their resurfacing, or liberating, back into the table tennis scene.

"In the beginning when we went back into international competition, the Women's team did alright but the Men's team dropped several notches. But within a year, they worked hard and shot back to the top again at the 31st World Championship in 1971 in Nagoya Japan. That's when Zhuang by chance ran into US player Glenn Cowan who got into the wrong bus

World champion Zhuang Zedong / 世界冠軍莊則棟
Li Furong at play / 賽場上的李富榮

GIRL AT CENTER STAGE (Part 2)

carrying the Chinese team. When Zhuang presented Cowan with a silk print scenic portrait, that simple act ushered in what is now called Ping Pong diplomacy. The rest of the history we all knew too well, leading to Kissinger's secret visit followed by President Nixon's state visit in 1972. I was lucky and witnessed this entire process," recounted Cheng in summary.

From here, Cheng went into some specific and rather personal accounts. "I remember very well the day May 1, 1971. For me, it was an epic day in my life. It was in the afternoon and Premier Zhou Enlai received the Ping Pong players from Australia. We Chinese athletes were all invited. During

Zhuang & Cowan in Japan / 莊則棟與科恩在日本

our break, the premier said, 'Cheng Minzhi, I want to play ping pong with you,' thus he led us to a meeting room inside the Great Hall of the People," Cheng said. "Was there a ping pong table inside the Hall?" I asked. "Yes, it is for leaders to relax and exercise during meeting recesses," answered Cheng. "What happened next was a bit shameful to repeat, but I would tell you," she continued. I pushed, "How badly did Zhou Enlai lose to you?"

"He knows how to play, but obviously he has to attend to many more important issues. Just a day before on April 30, he had just hosted the princess from Iran, and our team returned on May 1 from the 31st World Champion. Playing with our premier, I did something I should not have done," Cheng talked on. "Did you intentionally lose to him?" I asked. "It is not that; it's a minute detail. I saw two paddles on the table, one pen hold, the other handshake. I usually play handshake, but I thought it easier if Premier would use that, and I can easily take him on even with pan hold. He did not say anything and took up the handshake paddle. We played for about fifteen minutes. When we stopped, he asked 'Don't you usually play with handshake hold? You are despising me, aren't you?' I was really surprised that given all his busy work, he would notice that I play handshake hold," Cheng revealed with some shame on her face. "You didn't play with your left hand though," I tried to console her.

"At that point, Premier told us all to stay and have dinner at the Great Hall of the People, and to join them at Tian An Men Gate in the evening to celebrate the May Day Parade. He instructed, 'When everyone leaves tonight, the team members must stay as I want to have a photo with you all,' then he took leave. That evening, high above Tian An Men, he called me over and specially introduced me to Chairman Mao. I met many other China's leaders that night. Premier's wife Deng Dajie (big sis) embraced me and said, 'You all are wonderful, small globe shaking big globe.' It wasn't later that I knew the full meaning of what she said, that the tiny ping pong helped spin the world."

Zhou playing Cheng / 周總理與鄭敏之乒乓對決
Cheng met Chairman Mao / 鄭敏之和毛主席

"But that was still in the midst of the Cultural Revolution. Jiang Qing, Mao's wife, was a key revolutionary. Have you had any dealings with her?" I asked prudently. "Yes, she was very much into photography and often asked to make portraits of top athletes. I still have a couple color photos that she took of me," answered Cheng as she showed me two images taken in 1974 when she was wearing a red sports shirt. I thought such a vocation must be considered rather bourgeois for others, but progressive for Jiang who was in a leadership role.

Though our long interview touched on many incidents of international play, one stood out worthy of recounting. It was during the 31st World Championship. Back then, it was customary that secondary players or retired athletes would be recruited to sit among spectators to note down the oppositions' play styles, so as to devise a counter attack during real competition. Without current filming replay to study, they would make notes on a pad to record the opponents' serving and playing techniques, frequencies of certain play, etc. And it was during a game with the North Korean, a comrade in arms of China, that such an incident flared up. "We secretly studied the Korean's play to make sure of winning. Their players were actually quite good at the time," recounted Cheng.

"When Premier Zhou found out about it, it was past eleven at night when *he called for me and a sleeping leader of our team to his office. He scolded us why we did such underground work to our close friends. That in the international arena of exchange, we must be open and transparent. When we went to Korea, their president hosted us with open arms and we should reciprocate. He was so upset that his face turned red. I kept answering quietly 'I don't know, I don't know,'"* Cheng explained. *"In fact, prior to the game at this 31st World Championship, Premier Zhou already advised us to be kind to the Korean team. During those difficult days, we have few friends internationally. He reiterated that the North Korean participated in the game in Japan because of their relationship with China. Above all, he said there were over 600,000 overseas Koreans living in Japan and they would all be eager to watch how their compatriots played. Premier said if the Korean athletes did not do well, it would affect the hearts and complex of the overseas Koreans. He meant that without affecting the big issues, we should allow the Koreans to gain some games. But our leadership took the champion trophies too seriously. In one game we can let go of the Korean, instead we beat them totally. That made Premier Zhou quite unhappy,"* Cheng said near the end.

"Premier Zhou gave an example that I remember clearly. It was Premier Zhou who advocated 'Friendship first, competition second' that became a political slogan of the time. He said, 'You went to America to play against the Americans. Can they beat you? Not possible. We should be more relaxed and play it as an exhibition game.' Later that is why when Nixon visited China, he said 'the biggest winners are the people of both countries,' that is precisely the point," Cheng closed her remarks on that note with one addition, *"At that time, losing to the Japanese would be capped as surrendering to militarism, to the Americans was submitting to imperialism, and to the Soviet Union as bowing to revisionism. Such political hats were flying all over our heads. Today, I have opened my heart to you,"* said Cheng and thus ended our interview.

Such experience of Minzhi with premier Zhou Enlai echoes what I have heard about Chairman Mao, perhaps of China's moda operandi before the Cultural Revolution. It was said that his edict to comrades working on the United Front Office was, "Be like an old Chinese coin, round on the outside and square in the middle." He further noted to those working on foreign policy and its implementation, "With small countries, be tender and generous. With large ones, be tough and hard. (小國從寬, 大國從嚴)" Whether such early mottos are still relevant and adhere to is for others to determine.

Before I took leave, we paired up and played mixed double for almost half an hour at her ping pong table against a serving machine. Her stamina at 80 is still right there without missing a beat. In parting, Minzhi autographed a paddle and gave it to me as a gift. It was a handshake paddle, and a fair play. After all, Minzhi and I both used handshake hold, and the gift represented more than any handshake.

After I left her home and on way back to the hotel, more thoughts came to mind. China has been dominating table tennis in the international scene not just for years, but decades, taking championship in all categories. Perhaps it is time for China's sports leaders to take a higher view and revisit the more elevated and strategic philosophy advocated by Zhou Enlai long ago. If we keep winning by huge margin at a game, soon there will be no competitors to play against. Besides former champions going abroad to coach other teams, perhaps China should also start top-end training program to foster foreign players, such that in time we have a more competitive playing field international, something the world would all look forward to.

Cheng & HM play double / 鄭敏之與 HM 打雙打

上海 二〇二四年十一月一日

照片中央的女孩（下）

友誼第一，比賽第二

上世紀六十年代末，美蘇冷戰持續，中蘇關係惡化，美國意識到，中國已經成為社會主義陣營中一個獨立的力量，開始調整對華政策。中國則迫切需要打破被國際孤立的狀態，提升國際地位。世界形勢風雲變幻，中國的乒乓球界也迎來了新的轉機。「我們來聊聊乒乓外交吧！妳是那段歷史的親歷者，還是核心人物啊！」我對鄭敏之說。

她回憶起那段歲月，臉上還是難掩激動，娓娓道來：「一九六六到一九七〇年間，大概四年的時間，所有的訓練都停了，更別提比賽了。我們都懈怠了。然後，某一天周恩來總理親自出面，召集我們一起討論是否要參加第三十一屆世乒賽。當時確實有些人比較疲憊了，不想再打乒乓球，但是在周總理的號召下，我們這些頂尖選手，包括莊則棟、李富榮、林惠卿和李赫男等一眾世界冠軍，還是都重新回到了訓練場。」

「當時，重回賽場還要面對場外種種因素帶來的壓力，不過，周總理幫我們解決了一切後顧之憂。他對我們的關心是無微不至的，從精神思想到生活細節，他都處處為我們著想。他教育我們：『運動員首先要學會做人，要堂堂正正，才會贏得別人的尊重與信任。』他還耐心地向我們解釋，為什麼即使在那麼困難的時期，我們依然要和世界接軌，尋求更高、更廣闊的視野。我清楚地記得他說：『那麼盛大的世界比賽中，冠軍卻只有一個，所以許多國家參賽，並不是為了奪冠，而是為了友誼與和平。你看，

Zhou toasting Cheng / 周總理向鄭敏之敬酒

那些南亞和非洲的小國家,他們堅持來參賽,純粹是為了向世界傳遞善意與合作精神。』這些話至今都深深印在我的腦海裡,我是發自內心地,真心地感激我們的總理。」鄭敏之深情地回憶道。

「周總理還強調,為什麼我們必須參加那次在日本舉辦的世乒賽。他說,雖然當時日本政府尚未正式承認中國的國際地位,但日本乒乓球協會已經承認並給了我們應有的尊重。這表明,協會和政府是可以分開的,這是一個至關重要的信號。他甚至安排我們前往歐洲參賽,讓我們在國際賽場上磨練自己,積累經驗,為未來鋪路。」鄭敏之的話語中充滿了對周總理的敬佩和感激。她認為,正是周總理的遠見和支持,才讓中國乒乓球得以重振旗鼓,再登國際舞台,也讓她和隊友們找回了屬於自己的使命與榮耀。

「剛開始我們重返國際賽場的時候,女隊還算穩定,但男隊的狀態不太行,實力一下子掉了好幾個

檔次。不過他們也真的是拼了命地練，短短一年內就重回巔峰。到了一九七一年名古屋的第三十一屆世乒賽，男隊強勢登頂，把冠軍拿了回來。」

「那次比賽還發生了一件非常有趣的事。莊則棟碰巧遇到了一位美國選手，格倫・科恩。事情是這樣的，科恩一不小心上錯了我們中國隊的大巴，場面一度有些尷尬。莊則棟當時特別大方，沒有多說什麼，直接送給科恩一幅中國的絲綢山水畫。沒想到，就是這麼一個看似普通的小舉動，竟然成了『乒乓外交』的起點。」

「接下來的故事大家都知道了。季辛吉祕密訪華，然後是尼克森總統一九七二年的正式訪問。想想看，整件事的開端竟然是因為一場乒乓球比賽，還有一個上錯車的美國小夥子！我真的很幸運，能親眼見證這段歷史。」鄭敏之說到這裡，語氣掩不住激動與感慨。

「有件事我一輩子都忘不了。」她說：「我清楚地記得一九七一年五月一日，那對我來說是一個非常特別的日子。那天下午，周總理接待了來訪的澳大利亞乒乓球隊，我們中國的運動員也都被邀請參加。休息的時候，總理忽然對我說：『鄭敏之，我要和妳打一場乒乓球。』說完，他就帶著我們走進了人民大會堂的一間會議室。」

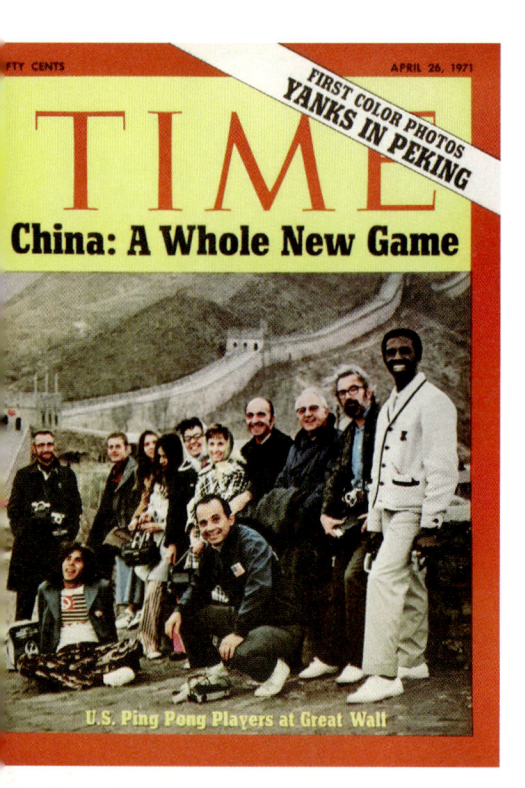

US team in China 1971 / 一九七一年美國乒乓球運動員在長城的合影

我好奇地問：「人民大會堂裡還有乒乓球桌嗎？」鄭敏之笑著回答：「有的，那是領導人在會議間隙用來放鬆和鍛鍊的。接下來發生的事情有點丟臉，但我還是告訴你吧。」她有些不好意思。我忍不住追問：「周總理輸得有多慘呀？」

「其實他會打乒乓球，但大家都知道，他每天要忙太多更重要的事。而且就在前一天，也就是四月三十日，他剛接待了伊朗的公主。我們隊是五月一日當天剛從第三十一屆世乒賽回來。結果那天，我居然做了一件不該做的事。」

「妳是故意輸給他了？」我笑著問。「那倒不是。」鄭敏之有些不好意思地笑了笑：「是一個小細節。當時乒乓桌上放了兩塊球拍，一塊是橫拍，一塊是直拍。我平時是用橫拍的，但我怕周總理拿直拍不好打，我腦子裡就很天真地想，我直拍也能對付周總理，就直接拿了直拍。」

「周總理看出了我的小心思，但他什麼都沒說，也沒揭穿我。他和我對練了大約十五分鐘，休息的時候，他忽然問我：『妳平時不是用橫拍嗎？什麼意思，瞧不起我呀？』」鄭敏之扶額苦笑：「我當時才反應過來，第一感覺是羞愧，同時也非常驚訝。他每天那麼忙，居然還能注意到我平時用的是什麼打法。」

China team in US / 國乒隊訪美

「至少妳沒用左手跟他打，不然可就真是欺負人了！」我笑著調侃道。

「還是那天下午，周總理親切地對我們說：『今晚大家都留下來，一起在人民大會堂吃個飯。晚上還要到天安門城樓上參加五一慶祝活動。』他特意叮囑。『等晚會結束，所有隊員都別走，我想和你們一起拍張照片。』說完，他就匆匆離開去忙其他事了。」

「那天晚上，天安門城樓上燈火通明，人聲鼎沸。周總理在人群中找到我，叫我過去，特意把我介紹給毛主席。他笑著說：『這是我們的國家隊成員！』毛主席點點頭，目光溫和地看著我。我有些緊張，但還是記得禮貌地向他問好。」

「那晚，我還見到了許多國家領導人。周總理的夫人鄧大姐走過來，滿臉笑容地抱住我，對我說：『你們真了不起啊，小球轉大球！』當時我還小，不懂這句話中的深意，但依然深受鼓舞。」

「多年後，我才真正明白鄧大姐那句話的意義。一顆小小的乒乓球，竟然能撬動兩個大國之間的關係，改變整個世界的格局。」

「在那個年代，你見過那麼多大人物，那你接觸過江青嗎？」我小心翼翼地問起。「有，她特別迷戀攝影，還經常要求給我們這些頂尖運動員拍肖像。我這裡還留著幾張她拍的彩照。」她拿出兩張一九七四年的老照片，照片裡的鄭敏之穿著一件鮮紅的運動衫，青春洋溢，目光堅定。

在這場深度訪談中，敏之跟我提到過許多國際大賽的故事，但發生在第三十一屆世界錦標賽期間的一個小插曲，卻是我印象最深刻的一段，值得細細講述。

在那個年代，還沒有如今的影像回放技術。為了研究對手的打法，通常會安排二線選手或退役運動員混在觀眾席裡，觀察記錄對手的比賽風格。他們會拿著筆記本，密密麻麻地寫下對手的發球方式、技術特點，還有某些戰術的頻率，然後用來制定反制策略。而這一次，事情發生在和中國隊「同志兼兄弟」朝鮮隊的比賽中。

「他們那時候的選手水平真的很厲害，為了確保能贏，我們偷偷研究了朝鮮隊的打法。」鄭敏之回憶道。「但這件事後來可惹了大麻煩。」

「周總理知道這事的時候，已經是深夜十一點多了。他馬上把我和正在睡覺的隊領導叫到辦公室。當時真是嚇得我心臟都快跳出來了。」

Zhou greets returning Team China / 周總理接見中國隊

Marshal He Long toasting women's team/ 賀龍元帥與中國女子隊致意

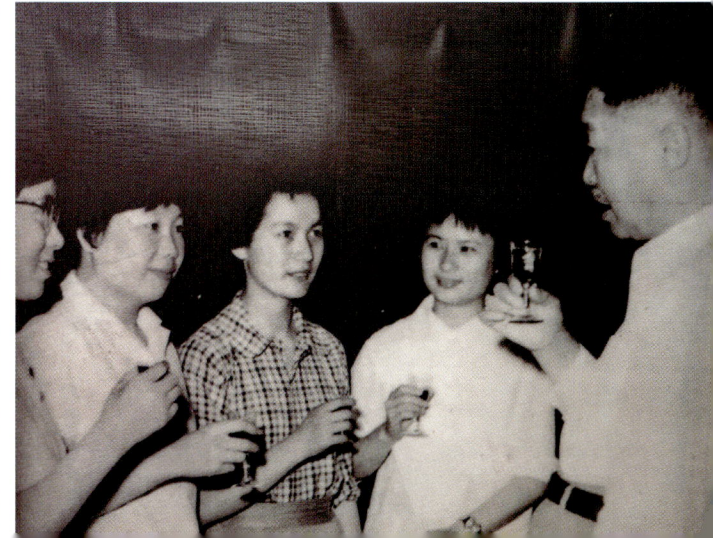

「他一見到我們就問：『為什麼要對這麼親密的朋友搞這種地下工作？』他的語氣特別嚴厲，還說，『在國際交流的場合上，我們應該坦坦蕩蕩！』總理說得很清楚，我們去朝鮮的時候，他們的領導人那麼熱情地接待了我們，現在我們卻背地裡搞這種小動作，太不像話了。」

鄭敏之說到這裡，聲音低了下來：「他氣得臉都紅了，我也不知道該怎麼解釋，只能一直低著頭含糊：『不知道，不知道……』」

「周總理重申，那個年代，我們中國在國際上幾乎沒有朋友。朝鮮參加在日本舉行的比賽，是因為他們與中國的友誼。日本有超過六十萬的旅日韓僑，他們都會熱切期待觀看自己的同胞如何表現。」

「我清楚地記得周總理舉過的一個例子。」她說。「『友誼第一，比賽第二』這句口號，就是周總提出的。他曾對我們說：『你們去美國和美國人打比賽，他們能贏你們嗎？不可能的。所以我們應該放鬆心態，把比賽當成一場友誼表演賽來打。』我想，這也是為什麼後來尼克森訪華時會說：『最大的贏家是兩國人民。』這正是周總理的出發點，是他想要的結果。」

談到當時的國際局勢，我想起了曾經聽到過的一個生動的比喻，頗為形象地描述了那個時代運動員不得不承受的來自賽場外的巨大壓力。當時，輸給日本會被認為是向軍國主義投降，輸給美國則是向帝國主義屈服，而輸給蘇聯會被當作向修正主義低頭。

Zhou hosting at Tien An Men / 天安門城樓上的合照

GIRL AT CENTER STAGE (Part 2)

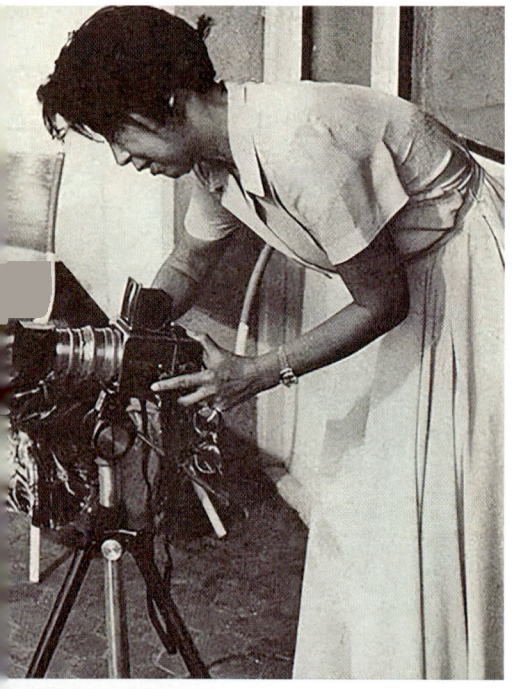

「今天我真是跟你說了很多掏心窩的話啊。」鄭敏之說道，我們的訪談就此結束。

敏之口中的周恩來總理，讓我不禁聯想到過去聽說過的一些關於毛主席的故事，或許反映了曾經中國外交方面的一種行事哲學。據說，毛主席曾對統戰部的同志下過指示：「要像一枚古代的銅錢，外圓內方。」這句話意味深長，既講求對外圓融靈活，又提倡對內堅守原則。

對於負責外交事務的同志，他進一步囑咐：「小國從寬，大國從嚴。對弱小的國家要寬厚仁慈，對大國則要態度強硬。」這準則不僅是對力量與弱點的清醒認知，更是對國際博弈的深刻洞察。至於這些早年的格言和理念，是否在今天仍具意義，是否依然值得被遵循，那就留給後人去評價吧。

臨別前，我和鄭敏之在她家的乒乓球桌上搭檔了一場混雙，對手是一台發球機。我們打了將近半個小時，她已是八十高齡，但體力和反應依然令人驚嘆，每一球都接得穩穩當當，絲毫不見遲滯。分別時，她拿出一塊橫板，在拍面上簽下名字，送給我作為禮物。

在鄭敏之的運動生涯裡，她以橫拍削球打法見長，而我恰好也習

Fashionable Jiang Qing /「時髦」的江青
Cheng as taken by Jiang Qing / 江青鏡頭下的鄭敏之

慣於橫拍握法。這種握法的英文與握手的意思相同，意外地反映出一種靜默而深遠的連接。

就像鄭敏之在那段光輝歲月中，見證的人與人之間架起的橋梁。透過她的描述，我們得以窺見那個時代，優秀的領導人和運動員身上閃耀的「乒乓精神」，那種精神超越了競技本身，蘊含著公平的信念、內在的默契以及跨越疆界的友誼。球桌兩端的對望，無需言語卻真摯深遠。如果那精神能延續在如今的世代，必定能連接更廣闊的世界與人心。

告別敏之的住處，返回酒店的路上，我的思緒愈發清晰。中國乒乓球在國際賽場的霸主地位已延續數十寒暑，各項冠軍盡收囊中。或許當下，中國體育總局該以更高遠的視角，重溫周恩來總理當年倡導的戰略智慧——若總是場場大勝，終將無敵可戰。

派遣退役國手指導外隊當然是一種策略，不過我想，我們還可以啟動一個更高層次的國際培訓計畫，為外國選手提供頂尖的訓練機會。這樣下去，假以時日，必能打造出真正勢均力敵的國際賽場。我相信，到那時，定會出現世界乒壇引頸期盼的盛景，這項運動長久的生命力也將迎來最佳的保障。

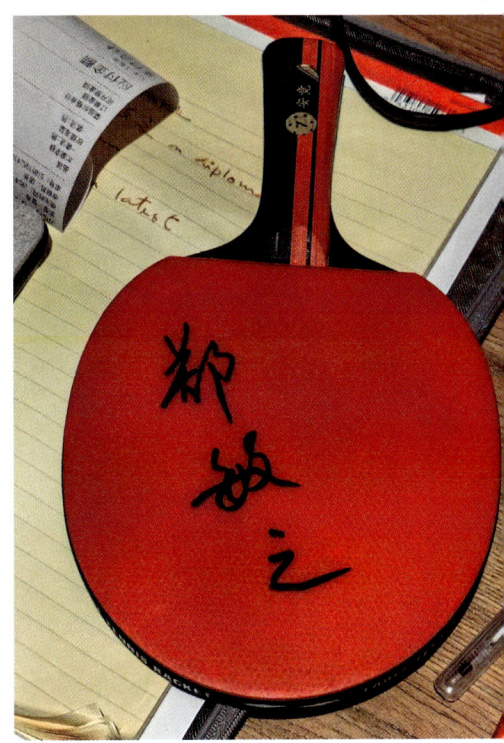

Friendship first Competition second /
友誼第一，比賽第二的海報
Cheng's gift peddle / 鄭敏之球拍禮物

大
自
然
的
未
來

NATURE in future LESS RESERVE

Tokyo – December 2, 2024

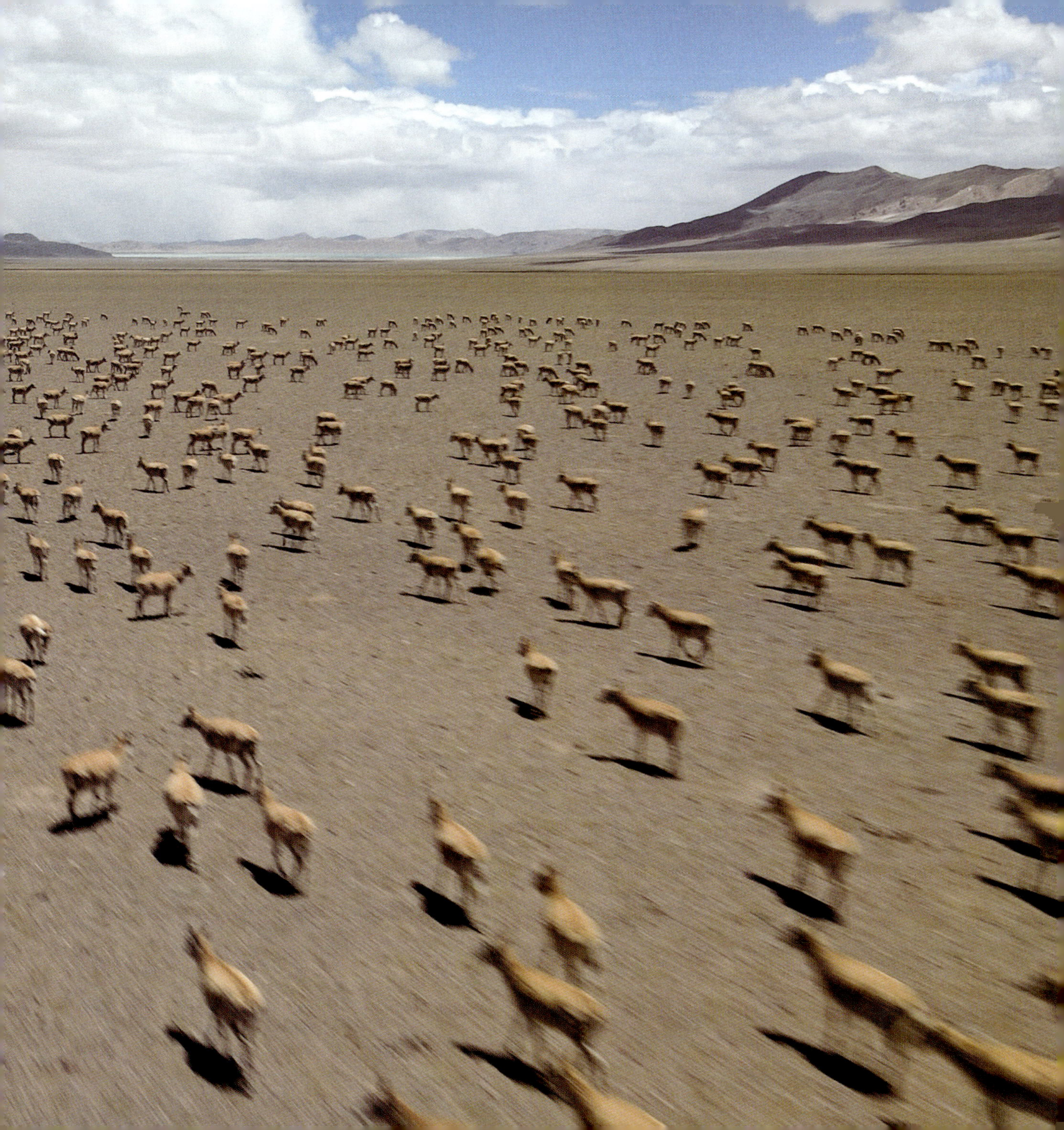

Tokyo – December 2, 2024

NATURE in future LESS RESERVE

Yes, we must have hope, faith and foresight regarding our future generations. Why need nature reserves when all our future children and grandchildren are fed, educated and learned at an early age about caring for our natural world? I can foresee that in time, what was necessarily set up as nature reserves in our generation can be gradually taken down, and be returned to unrestricted grounds for everyone, rather than a paradise for the select few who are one-time protectors of these areas.

I can testify to such slow, then gradual, and now more rapid development within the last five decades of work around many nature reserves and outside of it. On a large scale, I was made Chief Advisor of the Arjin Shan Nature Reserve in 1993, a protected area restricted of entry to just about anyone, with an area of 45,000 square kilometers, larger than Taiwan or Belgium, yet with only some thirty families living within it back in the early 1990s.

When we discovered the first ever known Tibetan Antelope calving ground at the reserve's westernmost extremity in 1998, there was a massacre, wholesale killing as poachers were rampant in gunning down pregnant females, decimating amass this protected species. Our huge and far-reaching international media campaign helped in making the purchase of its product, the high fashion "must-have" shahtoosh, no longer socially acceptable, let alone illegal.

Our media coverage in the likes of CNN, BBC, CNBC, Discovery and National Geographic Channels probably did more in stopping such clandestine trading than the highly publicized policing efforts to such a huge area of the Tibetan plateau. When a lucrative market is there, illegal poaching will continue, as demonstrated by other endangered species trading worldwide.

By the time I last visited the calving ground in 2012, the population of migrating female antelope had multiplied to huge herds. And in 2023 when I did a transact in western Tibet during the migration season, I encountered close-up many herds of females. Even our drone above head received little notice from these herds, grazing while moving as if not bothered. In the past, since I first saw them in 1982, they would go into stampede even from half a kilometers away when we approached them.

Of course, the Tibetan Antelope is only one of many flagship species CERS has worked on over its four decades of existence. We have covered similar situations with the Black-necked Crane, the Wild Yak, Tibetan Wild Ass, Yunnan Snub-nosed Monkey, Musk deer and more. Our recent expedition

Assignment letter for Arjin Shan / 阿爾金山保護區顧問任命信
Poaching massacre / 藏羚羊被盜獵屠殺

NATURE in future LESS RESERVE   259

Northern Tibet campsite / 藏北紮營

to northern Tibet in June further testifies to my theory that wildlife is fast returning to its former numbers, at times in multiple times its former perilous population. Within a short camping stop in Dire, a remote village by the sacred Tangra Yumco, the deepest lake in Tibet, we encountered two Asiatic Bears coming so close to a nomad's camp that two mastiffs had to chase them off. Also a pair of Black-necked Crane hatching by their nest, casually groomed and fed as we watched on. Furthermore, Tibetan Wild Ass, Tibetan Gazelle, Antelope, fox, Blue Sheep were all roaming near the road, sometimes within sight that render a long camera lens useless. It is not unusual that some would cross the road in front of us.

Every winter around February, I would make my "pilgrimage" to Kushiro in eastern Hokkaido, to be among the Red-crowned Crane, Stellar Sea Eagle and White-tailed Eagle. Deer, elk (wapiti) and fox also roamed the bushes and open ground around the pasture land. Some would often come onto the road, like the fox and the deer, and we have to stop and wait for them to move, before continuing with our drive forward. This is another indication of man and wildlife living in close quarters. The swan, taking advantage of an open and natural hot spring I often go to, would be right by my side as I soaked myself in the snowbound spring once belonging to the indigenous Ainu people.

Recently, the University of Hong Kong Wong How Man Centre for Exploration has the honor of hosting conservation icon Jane Goodall to speak at the university. Seeing that the auditorium of over 800 is filled with young students, and over 200 on the waiting list, is a joy. Furthermore, knowing that such generation, known to be with TikTok attention span and instant gratification, would sit through an hour of talk mesmerized by someone who speaks slowly with a hypnotizing voice is very compelling. A good story, especially a real-life story, is always welcome. Goodall's breakthrough work on one species, the chimpanzee, is bringing us all closer to the natural world, despite the fact that the students are from one of the most cosmopolitan cities in the world. Jane, at 90, is still an enigma for our younger generation. That evening, I came across a family of a dozen wild boars right outside my studio home. Nature is indeed among us.

Finally, on the other balance of age, and to further reinforce my newfound belief is someone whom I can proudly consider as my protégé. Chu Wen Wen, a young woman of thirty, started reading my books (I have authored over 30) as assigned by her father to begin learning English at the age of eight. As many of my books published in Taiwan are bilingual, students can use them to learn Chinese or English, if they so prefer. Some five years ago,

Tibetan Gazelle / 藏原羚

Tibetan Wild Ass in north Tibet / 藏北的藏野驢

Wen Wen founded her own non-profit organization in northern Xinjiang to begin a conservation project for the Asiatic Beaver. Though outside of the nature reserve designated to protect this species, she has made huge inroads into expanding the beaver population to a new record. Her efforts not only complemented the work of the reserve, but expanded it much further along the same river system.

Today, her work has expanded to a wildlife rescue Center covering many species of injured wildlife, be it bear, fox, palas cat, deer, antelope, eagles, birds, and of course her beloved beaver. She has millions of young followers and supporters online, and was chosen to represent China's youth born in the 1990s, speaking at the United Nations in New York earlier this year to present her case. Recently while along with me in Hangzhou at Westlake University, she received the great news that she has won the coveted Paulson's Prize, competing against behemoth old NGOs and government agencies.

Rather than inspiring her in my own writing, now she has inspired me to

Full audience at HKU / 滿座的香港大學禮堂
Jane Goodall at HKU / 珍・古德在港大
Best attended lecture / 出席人數最多的講座

Charging Wild Yak / 狂奔的野牦牛

start a new project at the northern frontiers of Hong Kong. Nam Sang Wai is almost adjacent to the world-famous Mai Po Reserve, a Ramsar wetland site to protect migrating birds that spend their winter at this border region of Hong Kong with Shenzhen in China. My hope is to follow Chu Wen Wen's footsteps, so that we too can eventually make a case that we can protect wildlife just as well, if not better, by uncovering more and more areas for our citizens, especially younger generations, to appreciate nature and wildlife living among us. Early winter sightings of the endangered Black-faced Spoonbill in action among hundreds of other seabirds has been very promising. Next is to get them used to our non-intrusive presence, without "blinds" which should gradually become obsolete I believe. Such a façade is like the camouflaged camera lenses, more for show than for function.

But as usual, CERS makes no promise, only delivery, and at times even delivery in stealth. As long as I can quietly observe our future generation enjoying nature freely, I would feel fully gratified. As for our nature reserves, let us hope they would take the cue and gradually remove the borders, allowing everyone to visit at will, if even incrementally. Let us also hope that my prophesy would become a reality, leading others to follow, Amen.

Spoonbill at Nam Sang Wai / 南生圍的黑臉琵鷺
Spoonbill by wetland / 濕地旁的琵鷺

東京 二〇二四年十二月二日

大自然的未來
少一分保留，多一分自由

我們理應對子孫後代懷有希望、信念與遠見。當未來的孩子們從小就被哺育以敬畏自然的心靈，被教導以守護自然的智慧，那麼所謂的「自然保護區」，還有存在的必要嗎？依我所見，在這個時代被迫劃定的「保護區」們終將逐漸消失，重新成為人人可至的尋常天地，而非少數「臨時看護者」獨享的「世外桃源」。

過去半個世紀，我親眼目睹了這場變革從緩慢萌芽到加速推進的過程。最鮮活的例證莫過於阿爾金。一九九三年我擔任這個保護區的首席顧問時，這片比整個臺灣島和比利時還大遼闊的疆域幾乎不允許任何人踏足，當時居住在這片四萬五千平方公里廣袤天地間的，不過三十餘戶人家。

一九九八年，當我們在保護區最西端首次發現藏羚羊產羔地時，目睹的卻是一場血腥屠殺。盜獵者肆無忌憚地槍殺懷孕的母羊，成片屠戮這個在自己的保護區內的瀕危物種。隨後，我們火速發起了席捲全球的輿論媒體戰，最終，購買沙圖什披肩這種「高端時尚必備單品」的行為淪為了非法勾當，更成為文明社會的恥辱印記。

當時，我們透過美國有線電視新聞網、英國廣播公司、財經電視台、探索頻道和國家地理頻道等國際媒體進行了廣泛的宣傳報導，對遏止藏羚羊盜獵產生的實際效果，遠

Using camels in Arjin Shan / 在阿爾金山騎駱駝

Bear attack / 有熊襲擊

比在廣袤的青藏高原上聲勢浩大的巡邏執法隊伍要顯著得多。只要暴利市場存在，非法盜獵就難以根絕，這在全球瀕危物種交易中早已得到驗證。

二〇一二年，我最後一次造訪保護區產羔地時，遷徙的母藏羚羊群數量已蔚為壯觀。二〇二三年，我途經西藏西部，正巧趕上藏羚羊遷徙季節，羊群們的狀態與一九八二年我初遇牠們時形成鮮明對比：那時，只要在五百米外出現人影，整個藏羚羊群就會驚惶奔逃。現在，別提人類了，牠們甚至對頭頂那噪音巨大的無人機都漠不關心，專心地低頭啃食草根，緩步前行。

當然，藏羚羊只是中國探險學會在其四十年歷程中致力保護的眾多瀕危物種之一。黑頸鶴、野犛牛、藏野驢、滇金絲猴、麝鹿等物種也曾面臨類似的危機，而我們也都曾為牠們付出過努力。今年六月，我們在藏北地區的考察進一步印證了我的觀點，那就是野生動物的數量正在迅速恢復，有些甚至是昔日瀕危時期的數倍。

在唐古拉雍木錯旁一個名叫地熱村的偏僻村莊短暫紮營時，我們遇到了兩隻亞洲黑熊，彼時，牠們正緩緩靠近當地牧民的營地，兩隻藏獒發現了牠們，在一聲聲狂吠追逐中，黑熊只能悻悻離開。此外，我們還看到一對黑頸鶴正在巢中孵蛋，悠然地梳理羽毛、相互餵食，我們就在旁邊靜靜地觀賞著，黑頸鶴們也無意避開。一路上，更有藏野驢、藏原羚、藏羚羊、狐狸和岩羊在路邊徘徊，我們的距離近到讓長焦鏡頭都毫無用武之地，甚至時不時地，牠們還會溜達到我們車前，擋出去路，場景自然又生動。

每年冬季，大約二月，我都會前往北海道東部的釧路，進行我的「朝聖之旅」，與丹頂鶴、虎頭海鵰和白尾海鵰共處。各種小鹿和狐狸也經常出現在牧場周圍的灌木叢和空曠地帶。牠們經常會走上馬路，我們不得不停車等待牠們通過，才能繼續前行。天鵝們則最會找地方享受，在原屬於阿伊努人的北海道，有一處我經常光顧的天然溫泉，而那裡的天鵝們是我最忠實的「泡澡夥伴」。

近日，香港大學黃效文探險中心有幸邀請到保育界的傳奇人物珍・古德來校演講。看著可容納八百多人的演講廳座無虛席，候補名

Black-necked Crane by nest / 巢旁的黑頸鶴
Fox on road / 擋在路中間的狐狸
Deer on road / 路上的鹿群

268　大自然的未來

Observing calving / 觀察產仔
Newborn Tibetan Antelope / 新生藏羚羊

Speaking at UN / 在聯合國演講

單更超過兩百人，實在令人欣慰。我很驚喜，在這個短影音當道，人們注意力越來越分散的速食文化年代，這些年輕人竟能全神貫注地聆聽完這場節奏緩慢，娓娓道來的演講。好的故事，尤其是真實的人生故事，永遠具有感染力。珍・古德對黑猩猩的突破性研究和貢獻，不僅讓她成為保育界的傳奇，也讓這些生活在全球最國際化都市之一的學生，感覺離自然世界又近了一點。九十歲的珍，依然是年輕一代心中謎一般存在，她還是那麼有啟發性，智慧與魅力絲毫不減當年。

聽完演講的當晚，我在鶴咀的工作室外撞上了一支「野豬特攻隊」，整整十二頭大家夥兒正組團在我家門口的垃圾堆裡吃宵夜。你看，誰說自然很遙遠？

最後，讓我們來談談另一個年齡層的代表，也是進一步強化我這分「自然應無界」信念的人——一位我可以自豪地稱為我的徒弟的年輕人。初雯雯，一位年僅三十歲的年輕女性。

初雯雯的父親和我是舊識，從她八歲起，她父親便會指定我的書讓她閱讀。我在台灣出版的許多書籍都是中英雙語的，讀者們可以隨心選擇用它們來學習中文或英文，所以初雯雯經常說，她是從我的書裡學習英文的。

大約五年前，雯雯在新疆北部創辦了一個非營利組織，開展了專門保護亞洲河狸的項目。儘管她的項目位於國家規定的保護區之外，但她已經取得了巨大的突破，將河狸的種群數量推向了歷史新高。她的努力不僅補充了保護區的工作，還將這項保育行動沿著同一河流系統大大地擴展了出去。

如今，她的基地已經擴大成了一個野生動物救援中心，保護的動物種類包括熊、狐狸、兔猻、鹿、羚羊、老鷹、鳥類等等，當然還有她最鍾愛的河狸。她在網上的野生動物保護頻道擁有數百萬年輕的追隨者與支持者。今年年初，她被選為中國九〇後青年的代表，前往紐約聯合國總部發表演講。最近，在杭州的西湖大學與我同行期間，她又收到了一個振奮人心的消息，她擊敗了許多大型老牌非政府組織和政府機構，贏得了備受矚目的保爾森可持續發展獎。

現在，與其說我的寫作曾啟發了她，倒不如說是她啟發了我，讓我在位於香港北部邊陲的南生圍開展了一個全新的項目。南生圍緊鄰舉世聞名的「雀鳥天堂」米埔自然保護區，這是一個受國際認可的拉姆薩爾濕地，庇護著往返於香港與深圳邊境越冬的候鳥群。

Chu Wen Wen working on Beaver / 初雯雯的河狸保護項目　　　Eagle & Wen eyeing each other / 老鷹與雯雯對視

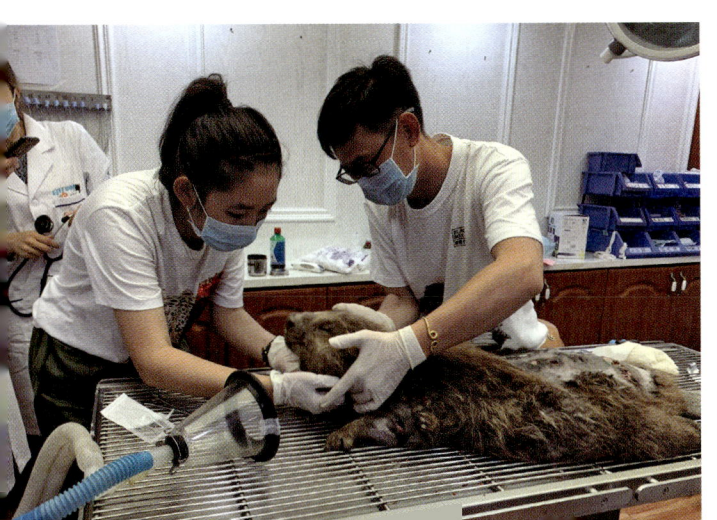

我希望能追隨雯雯的腳步，透過開放更多生態區域供市民，特別是年輕一代，觀察棲息在我們身邊的野生動物，來證明我們同樣能建立有效的保護機制，甚至可能做得更好。今冬，我們已成功觀測到瀕危物種黑臉琵鷺與數百隻海鳥共同棲息的珍貴畫面。

下一步是讓牠們逐漸適應人類無干擾的觀察方式。我相信，那些傳統的「觀鳥屋」終將被淘汰，這些所謂的為了觀察野生動物而設置的專門隱蔽結構，就像迷彩相機套一樣，表演性質遠大於實際功能，只不過是為了體現人類對自然的「控制感」罷了。

一如往常，中國探險學會從不空許承諾，只默默實踐，如潛行般無聲交付。只要能悄然見證我們的下一代自由徜徉於自然，我便心滿意足。

希望我們的「保護區」們終能明白，是時候卸下圍欄，讓熱愛自然的人們隨心所欲地造訪了，哪怕只是緩如苔蘚蔓延，每次只敞開一道縫隙般循序漸進也好。

我更希望，這預見能如春風化雨般，喚醒更多同行者。自然無界，人心亦當如是。願見此日。

Camouflage no more / 偽裝不再必要

一九五五年大陳孤島的船與影

EXODUS OF TWO ISLAND COMMUNITIES IN 1955

Da Chen Dao, Zhejiang – December 17, 2024

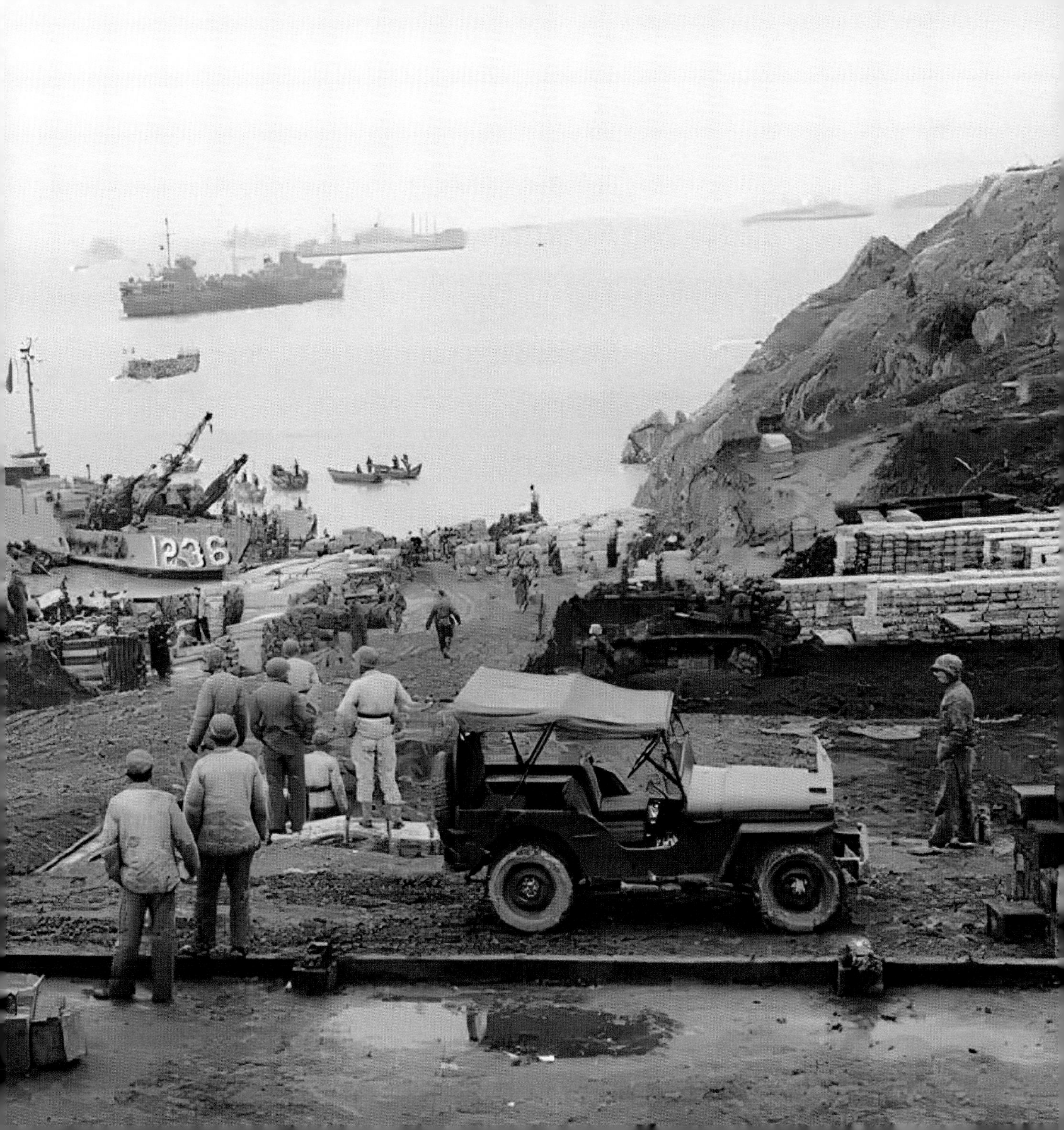
236

Da Chen Dao, Zhejiang – December 17, 2024

EXODUS OF TWO ISLAND COMMUNITIES IN 1955
18,000 civilian human shields saving Chiang Kai-shek's 10,000 troops (Part 1)

"Where are you?" asked Moon on the other side of the phone. "In Tibet," came my usual answer. Once in a while, I would shout back if the connection is not good, "In Xinjiang." Both places I often visited were familiar to Captain Moon Chin, a pilot for CNAC during World War Two. First Moon flew over the Himalayas across the HUMP, crossing from India to China. Then in 1943, he pioneered the first flight across the Karakoram from Xinjiang to Peshawar, now in northern Pakistan, trying to open a second HUMP route in case the Japanese should take upper Burma and close the southern route.

One time, fortune came with such a call when I shouted "I am in Dunhuang, the place along the Silk Road where you have a piece of mural on your wall." "You come, I give that to you," came Moon's reply. So on one of my two regular trips to the US each year, I stopped again at Moon's home in Hillsborough, near the airport in San Francisco. Moon had his mural packed as a gift to me. It is not any mural, but that of a flying Boddhisatva, supposedly from Dunhuang, a piece that he received in 1946 as payment for his garden flat in the French Concession area. That was the year after WWII when Moon purchased dozens of surplus US airplanes and founded Central Air

Moon w/ Dunhuang mural / 陳文寬家中的敦煌壁畫

Transport Corporation (CATC) in Shanghai. He bought, for 180 gold bars, the villa house of Wu Tiecheng, then mayor of Shanghai, and in turn got rid of his other garden flat.

When I stayed with Moon at his home, he told me stories from his childhood in Taishan, Guangdong. On his wall at home is an old picture of his village. I managed to find the abandoned village, and surprised him by showing photos of his house at our next meeting. This discovery came after a long drive from Macao and then onto the back of a motorcycle driven by a villager.

Moon also told me of his many legendary encounters during and after the War. Flying Chiang Kai-shek and many dignitaries before and after the Kuomintang (KMT) retreated to Taiwan. One such episode is about taking his amphibian PBY Catalina to and from the two KMT island strongholds of Da Chen Dao. This last stand of the KMT off the mainland in Zhejiang was given up during the massive retreat in February of 1955, some six years

Civilian evac at beach / 海灘上撤離的平民

after the Nationalist government moved to Taiwan. During the final days of the evacuation, over ten thousand troops and all 18,000 local villagers had to leave the two islands, supported by over a hundred warships of the US 7th Fleet. Old photos of the evacuation resemble a Normandy beach scene, but in reverse, as the exodus of people and troops in exit began.

Moon flew Chiang Ching-kuo, commander son of Chiang Kai-shek, as well as Yu Dawei, Defense Minister, many times back and forth from Taiwan to Da Chen Dao during those heady years leading up to the retreat. It started with maybe one or two flights a week in 1951 to right before the final days at the end of 1954 and early 1955 when he made daily flights there, taking military honchos in and out. Moon even showed me a photo he took of another airplane, a much larger US Navy amphibian PBM bomber/rescue plane, landed in the hidden bay by his side. This was the only time he saw any other plane ever in Da Chen Dao, and likely the last US plane to land in Mainland China until Nixon's visit in 1972. Chiang Kai-shek visited the islands and took a long look at his homeland of Zhejiang in 1954, though he arrived in a warship and not by plane.

On February 8, 1955, the first of three days of evacuation, Moon flew Yu Dawei the Defense Minister there as well, and witnessed first-hand the massive, yet orderly, retreat as it began. On February 10, Moon took his last flight to Dao Chen Dao, taking with him General Sun Liren as the evacuation came to a close. Later records showed that the US had relayed messages through the Soviet Union to China's communist government, asking for a peaceful retreat without their attacking both troops and civilians. I speculate that the "kidnapping" of all civilians, long-time residents of Dao Chen Dao, along with the retreat was a deterrent tactic in safeguarding the KMT troops to have a safe passage to Taiwan, rather than facing the fate of being annihilated like other precedented battles with the Communist.

While an army is supposed to defend the people, in this case, the irony is that the civilians acted as human shields for the army troops, as the PLA were known to value civilian lives. Furthermore, as China just had a truce, or a "negotiated draw", with the US after the Korean War, it obviously did not want to have another unprovoked head-on conflict with the US fleet that masterminded and spearheaded the evacuation with over 130 ships. As with any war conflict, propaganda warfare is essential. Retreat not only rhymes with defeat, but is usually interpreted as such. Thus the Nationalists would pronounce it as a "strategic retreat", in order to beef up defensive and offensive

Exodus in progress / 大撤退進行中

Villagers in landing craft / 登上登陸艇的村民

Evac order underway / 大撤退指令執行中

efforts on other coastal islands. Such an analysis of the Da Chen Dao retreat and evacuation seems to be neglected, for face-saving or other political reasons, by all studies and reports I have come across. Today, those in Taiwan should shower thanks to the Da Chen original residents who have been compromised and resettled into 36 communities throughout Taiwan. Perhaps calling such forced exile as flight to "Free China" when Taiwan was for almost four decades under martial law from 1949 to 1987 also requires some reassessments today.

I had long wanted to pay a visit to these two obscure islands of Da Chen Dao, so that I could surprise Moon once again. Twice I made the effort during the pandemic and both times the ferry was canceled last minute due to stormy weather. Last year in May 2023, Moon passed away at the senior age of 110. But my dream of visiting Da Chen Dao became even stronger and I tried again last month, in early November this year. At the ferry pier in Tai Zhou, again I was disappointed that the ferry was suspended for days due to an approaching late-season typhoon. Stubborn as a bull, zodiac of my birth year, I doubled, tripled and quadrupled my efforts and came again in the middle of December, driving all the way from Hainan to Taizhou yet again. This time, the wind finally settled for me and my team of five successfully crossed by ferry to Dao Chen Dao, less than two hours from Taizhou.

The multiple trials and trepidation reminded me of a theme song I learned in college from the German Three Penny Opera. As the lyric goes for the Useless Song, "If first you don't succeed, then try and try again, and if you don't succeed again then try and try and try…" My obsession was finally met when looking at these two islands where Moon Chin took his daredevil flights, coming in low to avoid radar discovery, and landed in the water of the hidden bay. It was done during much stormier days, both literally and figuratively.

When Shanghai was liberated in 1949, Moon took his CATC to Guangzhou, and subsequently to Hong Kong when the Communists overran Guangdong. In 1951, Moon Chin closed down his Central Air Transport Airlines (CATC) after two of his airplanes defected from Hong Kong to China, together with ten other airplanes belonging to China National Aviation Corporation (CNAC). He moved to Taiwan and founded another new airline, Fu Hsing Air. Two Catalina amphibian planes, also known as PBY, became available when the French canceled their order. Moon went to Baltimore and bought the two planes, flew them to Taiwan and they became the flagships of his newly founded airlines.

Thus began his three decades of flying from Taiwan to many Southeast Asian countries, making covert flights into Burma, Vietnam, and Indonesia, plus multiple ocean rescue missions of US or Taiwanese downed airplanes to pick up survivors in hazardous seas. Many of these missions were contracted by Western Enterprises, a stealth CIA operative during and after the Korean War out of Taiwan, using Da Chen Dao as one of the guerilla training and operation bases. Even the famed KMT General Hu Zhongnan who drove the Communist out of Yenan in 1947, used a pseudo name of Qin Dongchang, and stationed in Dao Chen Dao for two years as commander to reorganize several insurgent guerilla units, some were local renegade gangster-like groups, to penetrate into the Mainland in harassing the newly established PRC.

It seemed fortuitous that our ferry arrived at Xia Da Chen (lower Dao Chen) next to a large rescue ship anchored at the pier. Such a modern rescue ship resonates with the rough sea and hazardous missions Moon had to overcome. The ferry we took was full, taking around 300 or more passengers. Almost all were locals returning after the ferry was canceled a few days ago due again to weather. There were a handful of men with their fishing gear to go sport fishing along the rugged shoreline of the islands. I noticed no tourists during this off-season travel, except the five of us. Winter was approaching fast and service personnels were dispersing vomit bags to passengers, getting ready for the rough seas.

While crossing the ocean, a thought also crossed my mind. It related to my occasional discussion with some of my intellectual friends in Taiwan who were stuck, or had a hang-up, regarding the differentiation and fate between Mainland China and Taiwan. I have always believed that circumstances dictate history, that karma and coincidence trump human planning and endeavors. Having created and managed projects in both Taiwan and Hainan allows me to make the following compared assumptions. Had Sun Yat Sen, founder of the Republic of China, a Cantonese, chose Guangzhou as the capital of the Nationalists rather than Nanjing, history would be written very differently. If such were the case, when the KMT retreated from the Mainland, they would likely be settling in nearby Hainan Island, much the same size as Taiwan, and the Da Chen Dao exodus would never happen. In turn, today it may well be Hainan seeking separation whereas Taiwan would long be a part of the PRC. But history has favored Nanjing and thus Taiwan is where it is today.

Da Chen today / 今天的大陳島

浙江 大陳島 二〇二四年十二月十七日

一九五五年大陳孤島的船與影 人肉盾，掩護撤離

「你現在在哪裡？」每次收到陳文寬機長這樣的問候時，我的回答要麼就是「在西藏！」，要麼就是因為訊號不好，扯著嗓子大聲喊一句「在新疆！」。這兩個地方我都常去，而對於二戰期間曾是中國航空公司飛行員的陳文寬來說，這些地名更是熟悉不過。

當年，陳文寬曾駕駛飛機穿越喜馬拉雅山脈，執行著名的「駝峰航線」任務，從印度飛往中國。隨後在一九四三年，他更是開創了第一條從新疆穿越喀喇崑崙山脈直達現今巴基斯坦北部白沙瓦的航線。這項壯舉是為了開闢第二條「駝峰航線」，以備不時之需。萬一日本攻占緬甸北部，切斷了南部航線，便能另闢途徑。

命運的安排總是出其不意。有一次陳文寬機長的電話打來時，我正在甘肅敦煌：「這是絲綢之路上的一個地方，你家牆上有一幅壁畫就來自這兒！」「你要是到我這來，我就把它送給你。」他語氣輕鬆地回應道。

於是，在我一年兩次的美國例行旅行中，我特地繞道，造訪了他位於舊金山機場附近希爾斯堡的家。他早已將那幅壁畫妥妥地打包好，準備送給我。這可不只是一幅普通的壁畫，而是一幅飛天菩薩像，據說來自敦煌。這件珍品是一九四六年他用位於法租

界的一套花園洋房換來的。

當時，二戰剛結束不久，他趁機購買了數十架美軍留下的飛機，並在上海創立了中央航空運輸公司。同一年，他用一百八十根金條買下了當時上海市長吳鐵城的別墅，然後迅速出手買了另一套洋房，而這幅壁畫正是那筆交易中意外得來的「報酬」。

我住在陳文寬家中時，他講起了自己在廣東台山的童年往事。他家牆上掛著一張老照片，是他故鄉村莊的全景。照片中的景象讓我心生好奇，於是我決定親自尋訪這個村莊。

幾個月後，我從澳門出發，長途跋涉驅車前往，最後還坐上了一位村民的摩托車，才在一片荒煙蔓草中找到那座已被廢棄的村莊。後來當我把那趟旅程中的照片親自遞給他時，他接過來仔細端詳了許久，我能感受到他那瞬間的欣喜和感動，就好像穿越回了那個遙遠的童年。

陳文寬機長曾經向我講述過他在二戰期間、國共內戰、及越戰前後的許多傳奇經歷。無論是在國民黨撤退到台灣之前，還是在他們退守之後，他的飛機都載送過許多政要，包括蔣介石。

其中一段讓人印象深刻的故事，是他駕駛水陸兩用的 PBY 卡特琳

Moon in cockpit of new PBY /
陳文寬在 PBY 駕駛艙內
Moon home village / 陳文寬老家村莊

娜,往返於大陳島這片國民黨「最後的島嶼」兩個據點之間的經歷。這片浙江沿海的島嶼群,曾是國民黨在中國大陸最後的堡壘,直到一九五五年二月的大規模撤退時才被放棄。那時,距離國民政府遷往台灣已經六年了。

大陳島撤退的最後幾天,美國第七艦隊派出上百艘軍艦協助撤離,場面令人動容。超過一萬名國民黨士兵和一萬八千名當地村民,不得不離開這片世代生活的土地。老照片記錄下了當時的情景,彷彿諾曼第登陸的倒影,只不過這次不是前行,而是逃離。

蔣介石的兒子蔣經國是時任大陳島撤退行動的指揮官,在這段動盪不安的歲月裡,陳文寬多次駕駛飛機,載送蔣經國以及國防部長俞大維,往返於台灣和大陳島之間。從一九五一年開始,最初他每週只需要飛行一兩次。但到了一九五四年底和一九五五年初的撤退最後階段,他每天都要飛往大陳島,載送軍方高層進出這片形勢緊張的島嶼。

陳文寬還向我展示了一張他親手拍攝的照片,照片中是一架比他

Chiang Ching-kuo reviewing troops / 蔣經國在檢閱部隊
Moon photo of US Navy PBM / 陳文寬拍攝的美國海軍 PBM 飛艇的照片
Craft flying US flag / 懸掛美國國旗的船隻

的飛機大得多的美國海軍水陸兩用 PBM 轟炸／救援機，停在他身旁隱祕的海灣中。那是他第一次，也是唯一一次在大陳島見到另一架飛機降落。而這架飛機，極有可能是直到一九七二年尼克森訪華之前，最後一架降落在中國大陸的美國飛機。一九五四年，蔣介石曾乘坐軍艦來到這片島嶼。他站在島上，久久地凝視著對岸的故鄉浙江。

一九五五年二月八日，大撤退的第一天，陳文寬駕機載著國防部長俞大維來到大陳島，親眼目睹了這場規模宏大但秩序井然的撤離行動。二月十日，撤退的最後一天，陳文寬載著孫立人將軍離開了島嶼，完成了他在大陳島的最後一次飛行任務。後來的記錄顯示，美國曾透過蘇聯向中共政府傳遞信息，要求對方在撤退過程中保持克制，不要攻擊撤離的軍隊和平民。我推測，國民黨在這次撤離行動中將所有大陳島的平民一併帶走，實際上是一種威懾策略，目的是確保其隊伍能安全撤往台灣，避免像以往與共產黨交戰時那樣被徹底殲滅的命運。

諷刺的是，按理說軍隊的職責是保護人民，但這一次，平民卻成了軍隊的「人肉盾牌」。解放軍一向重視平民的生命安全，而國民黨正是利用了這一點，讓撤退過程得以順利進行。此外，彼時中國剛剛與美國在朝鮮戰爭中達成停戰協議，這場「勉強的平局」令中國不願再與美國艦隊正面衝突，尤其是後者主導並執行了這

Chiang Kai-shek & son 1954 / 蔣介石與兒子 一九五四年

Evac order underway / 大撤退指令執行中

場由超過一百三十艘軍艦參與的撤離行動。

宣傳戰在每場戰鬥中都是不可或缺的一環。「撤退」這個詞，無論是聽起來還是內涵上，都讓人聯想到挫敗和潰散的場景，帶著一種避戰退縮的意味。因此，國民黨將這次行動稱為「戰略性撤退」，意圖為其在其他沿海島嶼的防禦和進攻爭取更多支持。然而，或許是為了某一方能保全顏面，又或許是出於某些不可言說的政治考量，對於大陳島撤退的真實性分析，過去的研究和報告中幾乎都避而不談。

今天，生活在台灣的人們理應向那些大陳島的原住民們表示感謝。他們在這場撤離行動中被迫背井離鄉，並被重新安置在台灣的三十六個社區中。這種流亡曾被稱為「飛向自由的中國」，但我覺得這個說法有待重新審視，畢竟，從一九四九年至一九八七年，台灣在近四十年的時間裡都處於戒嚴統治之下。

大陳島分上下兩島。我早就心心念念地想造訪這兩座鮮為人知的島嶼，一來是為了圓自己的夢，二來也想再次給陳文寬機長一個驚喜。疫情期間我曾兩度嘗試前往，卻都趕上惡劣天氣，渡輪服務在最後一刻取消。

二〇二三年五月，陳文寬機長在一百一十歲高齡時與世長辭，但

我探訪大陳島的願望卻越發強烈。於是，二〇二四年十一月初，我再次啟程。然而，在台州的渡輪碼頭，我又一次失望而歸，因為一場季末颱風迫近，接下來一整週的渡輪服務都被取消。

我生性固執，如同我的生肖牛一般，不撞南牆不回頭。我不甘心，經歷過四次嘗試，到了十二月中旬，我再次驅車從海南一路開到台州。這一次，風浪終於平息，我和我的五人小組成功搭上了前往大陳島的渡輪，從台州出發不到兩小時便可抵達。

這一路上的多次嘗試和波折，讓我想起了大學時期學過的一首歌，德國音樂劇《三便士歌劇》中的一支主題曲。歌詞唱道：「如果你第一次沒成功，那就試著再試一次；如果還是不成功，那就再試、再試、再試……」當我終於站在這兩座島嶼面前，凝視著它們的輪廓，我的執念也終於得以釋放。正是在這裡，陳文寬曾駕駛著他的飛機，為了躲避雷達的追蹤，以極低的高度穿梭，冒著生命危險降落在那隱祕海灣。他的每一次飛行，都帶著無畏的膽識與精準的計算。那是個風雨如晦的時代，天上的風暴肆虐，現實的時局更驚心動魄。

一九四九年上海解放後，陳文寬將他的中央航空運輸公司遷至廣州。隨著共產黨軍隊攻佔廣東，他又將公司轉移到香港。一九五一年，因為他公司的兩架飛機倒戈，從香港飛至中國，加

Evac order underway / 大撤退指令執行中

EXODUS OF TWO ISLAND COMMUNITIES IN 1955

Ferry arrived Da Chen / 渡輪抵達大陳

Rescue & coast guard boats / 救援與海岸警衛船

EXODUS OF TWO ISLAND COMMUNITIES IN 1955

Vacuumed out Da Chen /
撤離後空無一人的大陳

上中國航空公司的其他十架飛機也一同叛逃，陳文寬被迫關閉了中央航空運輸公司。隨後，他前往台灣，創立了另一家航空公司——復興航空。當時，法國取消了一筆對 PBY 卡特琳娜水陸兩用飛機的訂單，陳文寬隨即前往巴爾的摩購買了其中兩架，親自將它們飛回台灣，這兩架飛機也成為他新航空公司的旗艦機型。

自此，陳文寬開啟了從台灣飛往東南亞多國的三十年飛行生涯。他多次執行祕密飛行任務，深入緬甸、越南和印尼，並參與了多次海上營救行動，在危險海域參加針對美國和台灣墜機事故的救援活動。許多這類任務都是受一家叫「西方公司」的企業委託。這是一個在朝鮮戰爭期間設立的，總部位於台灣的美國中央情報局隱祕行動機構。而大陳島則成為游擊訓練與行動基地之一。

胡宗南，這位曾於一九四七年驅逐共產黨出延安的國民黨名將，曾化名「秦東昌」，在大陳島駐紮了兩年。他以指揮官的身分，籌劃並訓練多支游擊隊，滲透中國大陸，對新成立的中華人民共和國展開騷擾與破壞行動。

當我們的渡船抵達「下大陳島」時，恰好靠泊在一艘大型救援船旁。這艘現代化的救援船靜靜停泊在碼頭，不禁讓人聯想到陳文寬機長當年在惡劣海況中完成的那些驚險而艱難的任務。我們乘坐的渡船上擠滿了三百多名乘客，其中大多是幾天前因天氣惡

劣、渡船停航而滯留的當地居民。在這旅遊淡季，船上除了我們五個人，幾乎見不到其他遊客，只有幾個男子帶著釣具，看起來是準備要在大陳島險峻的海岸線上進行垂釣。冬天的寒意逐漸逼近，船員開始分發暈船袋，提醒大家為即將面對的波濤洶湧做好準備。

船在海上起伏時，我的思緒也隨之翻湧，想起了過去與幾位台灣學者朋友之間的討論，他們常常困惑於中國大陸與台灣之間的分裂與命運。我始終認為，時局左右歷史，而因果與機緣往往超越人類的計畫與努力。在台灣與海南兩地參與項目的經歷，讓我對歷史的另一種可能性有了更深的思考。如果中華民國的創建者，廣東人孫中山，當初選擇廣州作為國民政府的首都，而非南京，那麼歷史的進程可能會截然不同。如果國民政府的政治重心位於廣州，那麼他們撤退時，很可能會選擇就近的海南島作為最後的據點，而非台灣，海南島的面積與台灣也相當。若真如此，「大陳島撤退」這一歷史事件根本不會發生，反之，今天苦苦尋求「分離」的或許會是海南島，而台灣早已成為中華人民共和國的一部分。

然而這一切都不是僅憑個人意志能決定的。歷史的齒輪選擇了南京，台灣也因此成為了今天的台灣。

廢墟之上，潮聲歸來

ABANDONED AND RESETTLED

Da Chen Dao, Zhejiang – December 17, 2024

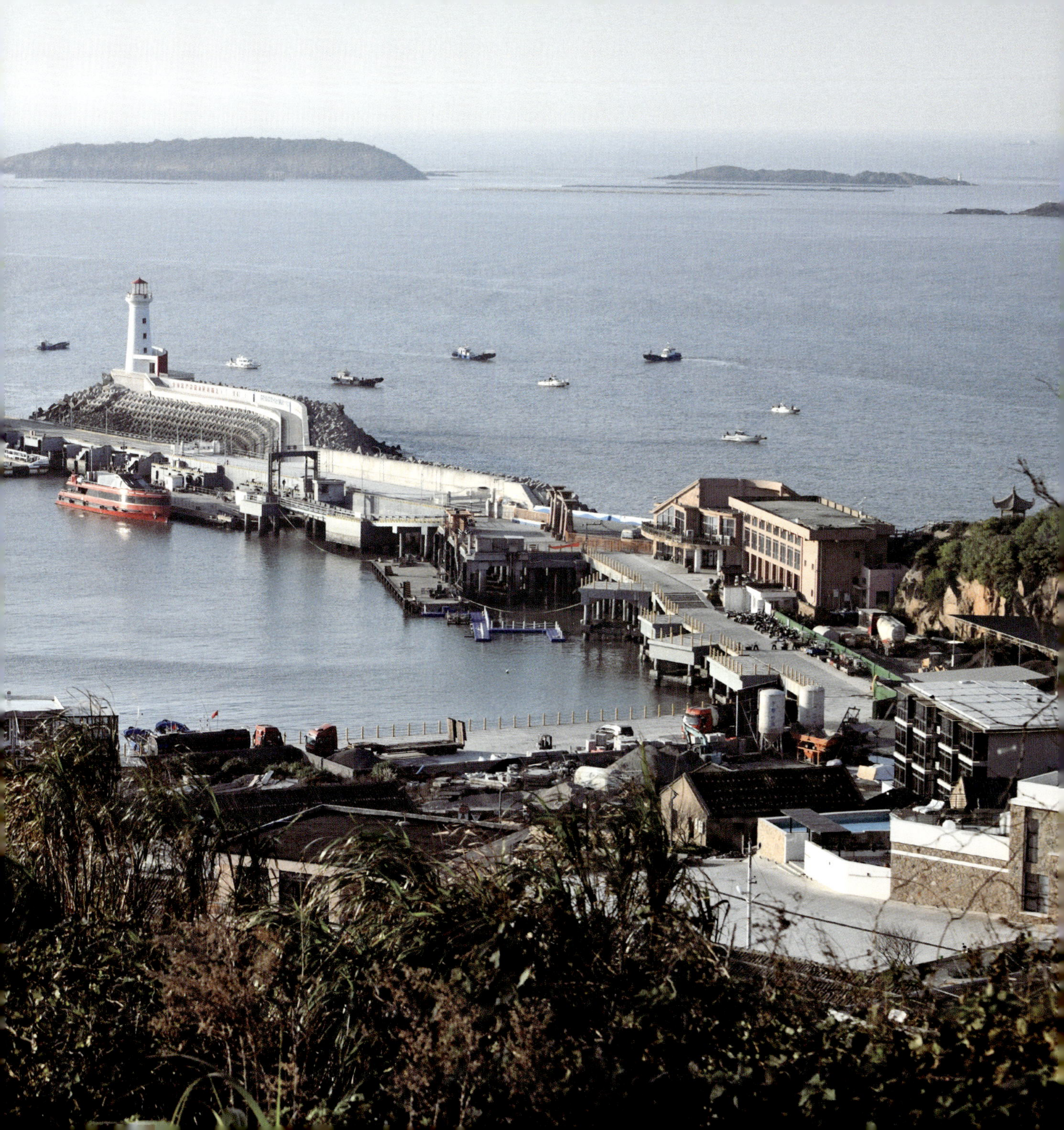

Da Chen Dao, Zhejiang - December 17, 2024

ABANDONED AND RESETTLED
Two island communities of Mainland China
(Part 2)

We were picked up by one of the few cars on the island, by Liu Zhen who was born here in 1963. His parents answered the massive call in the mid-1950s by the Chinese government in mobilizing young people from Zhejiang Province to settle the vacant and bare islands after the Nationalists evacuated everyone. "When I was young, there were many little kids whose parents had answered the government's call and resettled here," said Liu. "We had both elementary and secondary schools then, as many as three classes of students for each form," continued Liu. "But gradually the education standard deteriorated, and everyone started sending their children to school in mainland Zhejiang," he said with a sigh of resentment. "You know, today Zhejiang has top education rankings, even ahead of Beijing and Shanghai," finally I could feel a tint of pride in his voice. "Isn't it funny that now we only have one elementary school, and guess what, our ratio of teachers to students is the highest, seventeen teachers to only twelve students," Liu ended our conversation with a chuckle.

His remark was a stark contrast to a Taoist school I came across as I took some long steps to visit the "Tian Hau Temple", or Maju shrine, on top of a nearby hill. There I observed some fifty

Taoist Tian Hau temple / 天后古廟

young Taoist monks and nuns following their bearded master in learning some melodic prayer chants. Religious attraction seemed to trump tertiary education. Such may also be the case when I saw a newly painted Protestant church at Shan (upper) Da Chen Dao.

The government's call in the mid to late 1950s to resettle the then vacant and vacuumed out Da Chen Dao received answers from many young revolutionaries of the time. Among them was Gao Alian whom we visited with her at her home. Gao turns 80 today and was at the time barely 16 when she left home in 1961, being the fourth group of settlers going to the islands. Without letting her parents know that she had signed up to come to Da Chen Dao, she simply sneaked away. "If they knew, they would never allow me to leave," said Gao. She did not return home for five years, not until she got married and bore her first child. Many young people defied their parents and went as well. Most however did not stay after the first few rough years as their parents came and led them back home.

When the KMT left with their flock of 18,000 local inhabitants, the troops made it a point to knock down all barrack houses and even mined the fields in anticipation of the PLA taking over. So when Gao and other pioneer settlers came to a dilapidated land, they had to rebuild and start cultivating new fields and raised pigs as livestock. The situation was dire and conditions primitive. Nonetheless, she persevered.

I have read somewhere that there were spies sent from Taiwan to the Mainland in the 1960s and asked Gao on the subject. "Yes, indeed. I have personal experience regarding that matter,"

Fish dried in harbor / 漁港晒魚   Interviewing Ms Gao / 高女士講述民兵經歷

answered Gao. "I was recruited into the local militia soon after my arrival, carrying a rifle on patrol of the island," Gao recounted. "Soon after I joined the militia, we found spies had sneaked in and were hiding on the island. Their little boat was sunk and they hide inside a bomb shelter tunnel. At first, we found cigarette butts that were not local, as they had filters. Later we saw their long radio antenna. The discovery was made by only two PLA soldiers, being outnumbered and hard to get the enemy to surrender," Gao told me her spy thriller story.

"The two PLA outside pretended to make numerous whistling sounds as if calling for their squadron to come over. Then they started calling out numbers, pretending that there were many of them. The spies thought they were outnumbered and cornered and thus surrendered, coming out one by one," Gao continued. It turned out they also had dynamites and poison with them, intending to blow up the water tanks and reservoirs, and contaminate the kitchen and the local small theater of the navy. But seeing that there were many new settlers around, they failed in doing so. Gao saw their capture and being marched around for show in the open. In those days, she used to keep her gun by her side when sleeping.

Her story was corroborated by another person I met totally by chance in Shanghai a month ago in November in a hotel. Mr Liang Zuoqing, a senior gentleman I met at breakfast inadvertently started chatting, and I recounted that I just failed in getting to Da Chen Dao due to weather. "Oh, I was a captain in a PLA navy ship for years plying between Taizhou and Da Chen in the 1960s", said Liang. I won't give that a miss and followed with questions later on through our chats. He even published a poem regarding Da Chen Dao in the People's Daily in Shanghai at the time, recounting the romance of swimming in the beach while answering his country's call of duty to serve. His role, as expressed in this poem includes supplying the military and civilian to even guarding fishing fleet at sea.

Liang's comrade in arms Wang Xiaochun shared with me a more detailed account of the spying incident. The time was in 1963, the forward PLA position at the coast intercepted and decoded some Taiwanese radio signals and suspected agents has penetrated the islands, thus ordering patrol and search throughout the islands. A PLA officer, together with a messenger soldier, made two rounds around the island. They found a cigarette butt, foreign to Mainland type, by the beach and got alarmed. The soldier saw an antenna above the tree line and they closed in on their find and successfully caught the three spies.

It turned out these three agents even got around to the army theater before they found out they had mistakenly landed at Da Chen rather than another nearby smaller island. When cornered, one spy suggested firing and shooting their way out, but was convinced by a second spy that he had once been prisoner of the Communist and was treated well, thus all three agreed to surrender. It was said they got to drink and feast when brought to shore, and even dare asked to smoke the best cigarette brand "Da Qian Men". As recounted by the PLA officer Sun Jigang, "the messenger soldier was either too excited or paranoia that he could not hold firm his rifle, yet when he eventually got discharged from the army, he received a Third Class honor, whereas I was reprimanded for not being alerted enough and allowed the spies to sneak into Da Chen."

When the Nationalist stayed in Da Chen Dao from 1949 to 1955, they built many defense bunkers and gunneries. They had planned to use this as a base for a long period and intended it as a base for return to the Mainland. We visited a house that Chiang Ching-kuo used as his quarters during those years. For that sustainable plan, the Nationalist government even issued special currency for

Da Chen. The money then used in Taiwan would have red stamped letters added as being for special circulation within the islands. As not too many such currencies were distributed, today a fifty-cents note is worth over NTD 50,000 (USD 1,500) to collectors.

During the run-up to the final days of the evacuation, Chiang Ching-kuo stayed for ten days at Da Chen Dao. With him was a senior army war correspondent Liu Yifu who recorded those last days in pictures and writing. His book on the retreat and evacuation was published later that year in 1955 and Chiang gave it the title "Soon Will Return", parroting General MacArthur's famous utterance of "I shall return", when defeated and driven out of the Philippines by the Japanese.

Chiang Ching-kuo was last flown into Da Chen Dao by Moon Chin, together with Liu and yet another brief acquaintance I met in the 1990s at the YMCA in Hong Kong. Surprisingly this US army officer, a former adversary of the communist, was just returning from Mainland China as guest of the government. Jack Young Di-Ze, not the Jack Young (1915-2018) my old pilot friend who also flew the HUMP and lived to 103, but Colonel Jack Young (1910-2000) who was an explorer before becoming an army officer, both for the US Army and later as advisor to the Nationalist.

Chiang inspecting islands / 蔣經國視察大陳島留念
Chiang at army camp / 蔣經國在軍營
Chiang with Jack Young / 蔣經國與楊帝澤合影

Motoring around Da Chen / 騎車環遊大陳島

Jack was born and raised in Hawaii until he was three and returned to China. As a young adult, he roamed the hills of western China, escorted the Roosevelt brothers (sons of President Theordore Roosevelt) and successfully bagged two giant pandas as specimens to the US. He was also a key member who handled much of the logistics of the Harvard Mountaineering Club assault on Mount Gongga (7856m) in 1932, sending two members to become the first successful climb of this highest mountain giant in Sichuan. Having led innumerous exploration trips in my career, I fully understand the importance of such behind-the-scene work can make or break an expedition.

In Jack's book "Drink Water Think of the Source", he recounted his days with Chiang Ching-kuo at Da Chen Dao and illustrated his time there with some rare pictures. As the evacuation went to a peak, Jack was taking many photos to record the moment and was warned by Liu Yifu that such activities may be considered "secret". Jack snapped back that such images may become very useful when they should return to the islands. During the last three days from February 8 to 10 which Liu called as D-day, over forty reporters, both foreign and Chinese, were shipped into the islands to record the picturesque event. Today, one can find some of these images online as well. Both Jack and Liu are very meticulous and each one's book mentioned an exacting number of locals being evacuated, 18,416 for Jack and 17,132

Few boats in bay / 海灣中的船隻

Fighter jets on show / 展出中的戰鬥機

for Liu, respectively. I choose to round up the numbers as 18,000, though abstract but symbolic.

In the 1990s, some former Da Chen residents returned to visit or to pay respect to ancestor graves on the hill. Other Taiwanese may come to find out about a place made famous in Taiwan. Today, only occasional tourists come during the summer seasons, staying at the many homestay hostels now built around the island. We stayed at Lan Tin, the most modern of these hostels next to an unused lighthouse, costing RMB 500 per room during low season.

I soon checked out an electric bike for RMB 50 and explored the island. The northern bay was somewhat sheltered. There were plenty of newly constructed fish farms with huge nets submerged below the ocean for the cultivation of the expensive "Huang Yu", or Yellow Fish. But such valuable fish was once sold for a pittance as Liu recounted to us. The contrast was to the extreme. In the early days, when such fish were plenty, they went for RMB 0.8 per Jin, or half kilo. By the 1980s, it was still only fifteen cents sold to the collectives. The private sales may reach fifty cents but ran the risk if caught by the government; the fish would be confiscated.

Today, such fish is rare and hard to come by in the wild. In one case on

Hu Zhongnan's headquarters / 胡宗南的指揮部
Warships on display / 舊軍艦

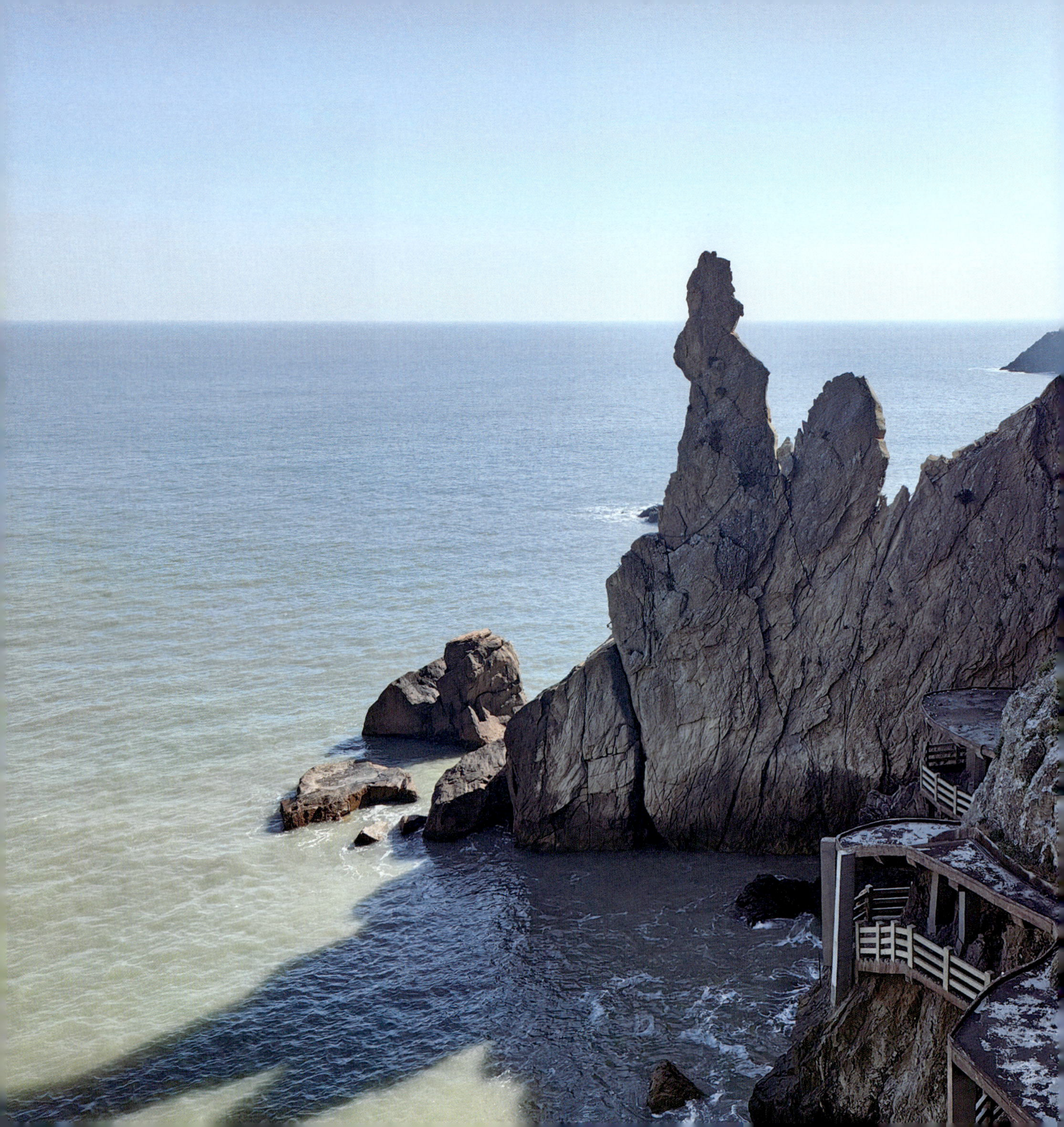

Path hugging cliff / 沿懸崖蜿蜒的小徑
Cliff of upper Da Chen / 大陳島的懸崖峭壁

ABANDONED AND RESETTLED

record in 2022 from nearby Ningbo port when a boat returned from sea with a huge catch of 2450 kilos, it was sold as one lot for RMB 9.57 million, a windfall for the boat owner. Here at Da Chen Dao, the smaller Yellow Fish weighing around three taels would sell for up to RMB 50-60 per half kilo. Those half-kilo ones would go for RMB 80-90, and bigger ones closer to one kilo RMB 300-500 depending on the season. We managed to buy three small ones at 1.8 kilos at a discounted rate of RMB 380 right at a pier when a fishing boat came back to port in the morning. Today, artificial cultivation of fish farms now fills the coastal area and few fishing boats actually go out to sea.

On the second day, I took a local ferry and went the 15-minute ride over to Upper Da Chen Dao, the larger of the two islands yet with fewer inhabitants. There were many bunkers and tunnels as it used to be the headquarters of the troops guarding the islands. Near to the site where Hu Zhongnan used as his base, today there is an old armory on display. Nearby at the hidden bay are put on land several retired PLA warships and gunboats. At an adjacent park, other PLA tanks, troop carriers, gunnery

Da Chen 50 cents now NT50000 /
大陳島的五十分紙幣，如今價值新台幣五萬元

and even a line-up of China's older air force fighter jets are on show. It included variants of the MIG-15, 19 and even later models.

Beyond all the history and stories that I have gathered at Da Chen Dao, perhaps my hour-long stroll along the rugged north coast cliff of the big island is the most tranquil. A long corridor path hugging the perpendicular cliff has been constructed in recent years. It allows visitors, though few, to observe the serenity of the coast as surfs and tides are pounding below my feet. The natural scenery of the two islands will persist for millenniums, as the stories of the last few decades become obliterated and fade under the pounding sound of the waves.

As the wind was fast picking up on the day of my departure, I started wondering if the ferry would arrive at the island at all. It did. Finally, I boarded the fast ferry at 2pm and began my trip back to Taizhou. The waves had been picking up with white foam over the surf. The sea was rough as the boat cut through the waves, splashing seawater even to the upper deck where we had taken up a cabin. I felt like calling Moon Chin again, surprising him that I had finally made it to Da Chen. It was not to be, but I still wanted to write down my experience, especially after my fourth try and succeeded in getting here.

On the ferry, I was told that this would be the last ferry for the next few days, as the wind had picked up dramatically and the islands would again be isolated for the upcoming days. But for those residents isolated in Taiwan's thirty-six Da Chen communities, they may be isolated forever whether the wind is blowing or not.

浙江 大陳島 二〇二四年十二月十七日

廢墟之上，潮聲歸來
被拋棄的大陳島和它重生的傳奇

我們乘上了島上為數不多的汽車，車主叫柳震，一個一九六三年生，土生土長的「大陳人」。他告訴我們，他的父母是在一九五〇年代中期響應政府號召來到這裡的。國民黨撤離後，大陳島人去島空，一片荒涼。為了讓這裡重新恢復生機，政府當年動員了許多浙江省的年輕人來這裡開荒定居。

「我小的時候，島上的孩子特別多，都是父母響應政府號召移民帶過來的。」柳震回憶道。「那時候我們有小學、有中學，每個年級足足能分成三個班。」他頓了頓，語氣變得有些感慨。「可是後來，學校的教學水準越來越差，大家不得不把孩子送回內陸，浙江省內去上學。」說到這裡，他忍不住嘆了口氣，帶著些許無奈。「不過你知道嗎？現在浙江的教育水平在全國是最頂尖的，甚至超過了北京和上海。」當他談到這一點時，語氣中還是透著一絲驕傲。「現在我們島上只剩下一所小學，說起來挺奇怪的，十七個老師，只有十二個學生！」

談話在柳震輕鬆的語氣中結束，下車後，我沿著一條石階小路一路攀登，來到了一座古老的「天后廟」，也叫媽祖廟。這裡的景象與柳震描述的人煙稀少的小學形成了鮮明對比。廟裡，一群年輕的道士和尼姑，大約有五十人，正跟隨一位滿臉鬍鬚的師父，專注地學習祈禱誦經，那聲音流進我的耳中，讓我身心舒暢，也印象深刻。我想，或

許在這片土地上，宗教的影響力已經超越了教育本身。我的這種感覺，在我看到「上大陳島」上那座剛剛粉刷一新的基督教教堂時，變得更加明確。

從一九五〇年代中期開始，在政府的號召下，許多年輕的革命者陸續來到了空無一人的大陳島上開拓定居，其中就包括我們拜訪的高阿蓮女士。如今已八十歲的她，回憶起那段青春歲月，依然感慨萬分。一九六一年，當她作為第四批開拓者登上大陳島時，年僅十六歲。她沒有告訴父母，悄悄報了名，一個人偷偷溜到了大陳島上。「如果他們知道，一定不會讓我去的。」高阿蓮笑著說。直到五年後，她結婚生子，才第一次回家探親。當時，像高阿蓮這樣的年輕人不在少數，許多人都背著父母冒險前行。然而，那時的生活條件十分艱苦，島上的環境對這些年輕人來說是一場巨大的考驗。許多父母後來親自來到島上，把孩子帶回了家，讓他們放棄這場冒險。

回溯到國民黨撤退的那一年，他們帶走了島上所有的居民，總計一萬八千人。不僅如此，他們還特意摧毀了所有的營房，甚至在田地裡下了地雷，試圖給接管的解放軍製造困難。因此，當高阿蓮和其他先鋒移民登上島嶼時，迎接他們的是一片破敗荒涼的土地。他們需要從零開始，重建家園。他們修建房屋，開墾荒地，養豬種田，努力讓這片土地恢復生機。那時的生活困苦不堪，環

Christian church / 基督教教堂

Lighthouse & ship guarding Da Chen / 燈塔與船隻守護著大陳

境也極其原始，但高阿蓮並沒有放棄。在艱難的條件下，她咬緊牙關，堅持了下來，成為重建大陳島的一代先鋒。

我曾聽說，一九六〇年代，台灣曾派遣間諜潛入中國大陸。於是我向高阿蓮求證。她聽後點了點頭，神情中帶著一絲嚴肅：「確實有這種事，而且我還親身經歷過。」

「剛上島沒多久，我就加入了當地的民兵隊。」高阿蓮說。「當時，我們每個人都配了一支步槍，我的任務是巡邏。有一次，有人發現間諜偷偷潛入了島上，藏在一個防空洞裡。他們的船沉了，只能躲在那裡。」

「最開始，我們發現了一些奇怪的菸蒂，那些菸有過濾嘴，跟我們平時抽的菸完全不一樣。一開始我們還不知道是怎麼回事，直到後來，又看到了一根長長的無線電天線，才確定有人藏在洞裡。」

「當時現場只有兩名解放軍士兵，而間諜人數明顯更多，硬碰硬肯定不行。」高阿蓮的語氣漸漸激動起來。「這兩個士兵非常機智，他們假裝自己不是單獨行動，站在洞外不停地吹口哨，製造出很多人在周圍活動的假象。接著，他們還開始報數，比如五號準備！六號就位！間諜聽到後，以為自己已經被大批人馬包圍，無處可逃，就自己一個接一個地走出來投降了。」

「你知道嗎？」高阿蓮壓低聲音繼續說。「這些間諜身上還帶著炸藥和毒藥，他們的目標是炸毀島上的水庫和水箱，污染海軍的廚房，甚至還想破壞我們的小型海軍劇場。他們原本計畫把這片島嶼徹底摧毀，但因為島上新定居的人越來越多，他們根本沒有機會，也不敢下手。」

說到這裡，她語氣稍微放鬆了一些：「我親眼看到那些間諜被逮捕後，被押著在島上公開示眾。」她說：「那段時間我睡覺的時候，槍就放在枕頭旁邊，一刻不敢鬆懈。」

高阿蓮所述，與一個月前我在上海的奇妙偶遇中收穫的故事，意外地相互印證了。那是二〇二四年十一月的一天，我正在一家酒店的餐廳吃早餐，無意間和一位老先生攀談起來。他介紹自己名叫梁佐清，當時我只覺得他是一位普通的退休老人，直到他提到：「我曾經是解放軍海軍的艦長，在上世紀六十年代，我的船常年往返於台州和大陳島之間。」

聽到這裡，我立刻來了興趣，於是繼續追問。不出所料，梁先生還真有不少故事。他告訴我，那段時間，他的任務除了為島上的軍民提供補給，還要護衛出海的漁船，甚至有時要執行攔截敵方間諜的小型行動。他還提到，他曾在《人民日報》上海版發表過一首詩，回憶自己在大陳島的歲月，詩中描寫了在海灘游泳、執行任務以及對國家召喚的深切回應，帶著一種軍人的浪漫情懷。

「不過，那些年可不全是浪漫。」梁先生話鋒一轉。「就拿一九六三年的那次間諜事件來說吧，我的戰友王孝椿清楚得很，他當時就在現場。」

梁先生的話把我帶到了另一個故事的開端。根據他的戰友王孝椿先生的回憶，一九六三年，前沿解放軍陣地攔截並破譯了台灣發送過來的無線電信號，根據內容判斷，可能有間諜已經潛入大陳島。上級立刻下達了命令，要求進行全島巡邏和搜查。

解放軍軍官孫志剛和他的通信兵奉命開始行動。兩人對島上進行了兩次巡查，並在海灘邊發現了一個奇怪的菸蒂。那菸明顯不是本地的，居然有過濾嘴，這在當時的大陸非常少見。他們立刻提高了警惕，開始在周圍仔細搜尋。不久之後，通信兵注意到樹梢上方出現了一根長長的天線。這明顯不是當地的東西。兩人隨即靠近，最終在防空洞附近抓到了三名間諜。

這三名間諜的故事竟然還有些荒誕。他們原本的目標是一個更小的島嶼，但因為導航出錯，誤闖了大陳島。他們甚至膽大到潛入了軍隊的劇場，還沒來得及完成任何破壞行動，就因為蹤跡敗露而被發現。當時，三人還在防空洞裡爭論對策。一人主張開槍突圍，但另一人卻勸住了他：「我以前當過共產黨的俘虜，他們對待俘虜還算不錯，比死掉強，還是投降吧。」最終，三人選擇了放下武器，走出來投降。更令人意外的是，這些間諜被押回岸上後，還大言不慚地要吃要喝，甚至厚著臉皮要求抽當時最好的香菸「大前門」，弄得當地人哭笑不得。

這次行動背後還有些耐人尋味的細節。根據參與行動的解放軍軍官孫志剛的回憶：「通信兵年紀輕，當時可能太過緊張，竟然手抖得步槍都握不穩。但後來他自己編得好，被授予了三等功。而我

Jack with Chiang at Da Chen /
楊帝澤與蔣經國在大陳島

Nationalist flag on Mt Gongga /
國民黨旗在四川貢嘎山

Jack visiting Mainland since 1981 /
楊帝澤訪問中國大陸一九八一年

Lan Tin hotel with old bunker / 瀾庭旅舍與舊戰壕
Da Chen travel mode / 大陳島的交通方式

呢，反倒因為警惕性不夠，讓間諜成功登島，被上級狠狠批評了一頓。」

一九四九年至一九五五年，國民黨控制大陳島的時間裡，他們建造了許多防禦工事和炮台，計畫將這裡作為長期的軍事基地，更期待以此為跳板，實現「反攻大陸」的目標。我們參觀了一座房子，據說是蔣經國當年在島上的住所。為了支撐這項長期計畫，國民黨政府甚至為大陳島發行了專用貨幣。當時，台灣流通的紙幣上會加蓋紅色字樣，標明僅限於大陳地區使用。由於發行量極少，如今，這些特殊貨幣成了收藏家眼中的珍品。一張五十分的紙幣，如今價值超過新台幣五萬元（約合一千五百美元）。

在撤退的最後關頭，蔣經國曾在大陳島停留了十天，與他同行的是一位資深軍事記者劉毅夫。劉用文字和照片完整地記錄下了撤退前最後的日子。一九五五年，也就是撤退的同一年，他出版了這本書，書名由蔣經國親自題為《就要回來》。這個名字借用了麥克阿瑟將軍在二戰期間被日軍從菲律賓擊退後那句著名的話「我會回來」以此表達國民黨對重返大陸的決心。

蔣經國最後一次前往大陳島，是由著名華裔飛行員陳文寬接送的，與他同行的還有劉毅夫以及另一位在一九九〇年代我曾短暫結識的美國軍官。令人驚訝的是，這位曾與共產黨為敵的美國軍

官，當時竟然剛作為中共政府的座上賓，從中國大陸訪問回來。他的名字是傑克楊，楊帝澤。但他並非我的另一位同名飛行員老友傑克楊，楊積，後者曾在駝峰航線服役，並活到了一百零三歲。我提到的這位楊帝澤上校於二〇〇〇年去世，是一位探險家，後來成為美國陸軍軍官，並曾擔任過國民黨的顧問。

楊帝澤出生於夏威夷，在那裡度過了童年，直到三歲時隨家人返回中國。成年後，他活躍於中國西部的大山之間，護送過美國總統狄奧多·羅斯福的兩個兒子，還獵殺過兩隻大熊貓，後作為標本送往美國，成為轟動一時的事件。一九三二年，他參與了哈佛登山俱樂部組織的遠征行動，目標是海拔七千八百五十六米的四川貢嘎山，他作為核心成員負責後勤支援，保障了整個行動的順利。正是他的努力，幫助遠征隊兩名成員首次成功登頂這座四川的最高峰，創下歷史壯舉。作為一名長期參與探險的人，我能深刻理解，這種幕後的籌備與支持，正是決定探險成敗的關鍵所在。

在他滿是珍貴照片的著作《飲水思源》中，楊帝澤回憶了他與蔣經國一起駐守大陳島的日子。當年那個大撤退的關鍵時刻，他一直在不停忙著拍照紀錄，想要盡可能全面地保存這段歷史。然而劉毅夫卻警告他，這樣可能會對「機密」造成威脅。楊帝澤毫不猶豫地回應說：「等我們重返這些島嶼時，這些照片絕對會派上用場。」

一九五五年二月八日至十日的三天，是撤退的最後階段，被劉毅夫稱為「決戰日」。在這期間，超過四十名中外記者被送上大陳島，一同記錄這場既壯觀又充滿戲劇性的撤離行動。如今，這些記者，包括楊帝澤拍攝的部分照片仍然可以在網絡上找到，它們成為那段歷史的珍貴見證。

楊帝澤和劉毅夫都是極其嚴謹的記錄者。對於撤離的總人數，他們給出了不同的數字。楊記錄了一

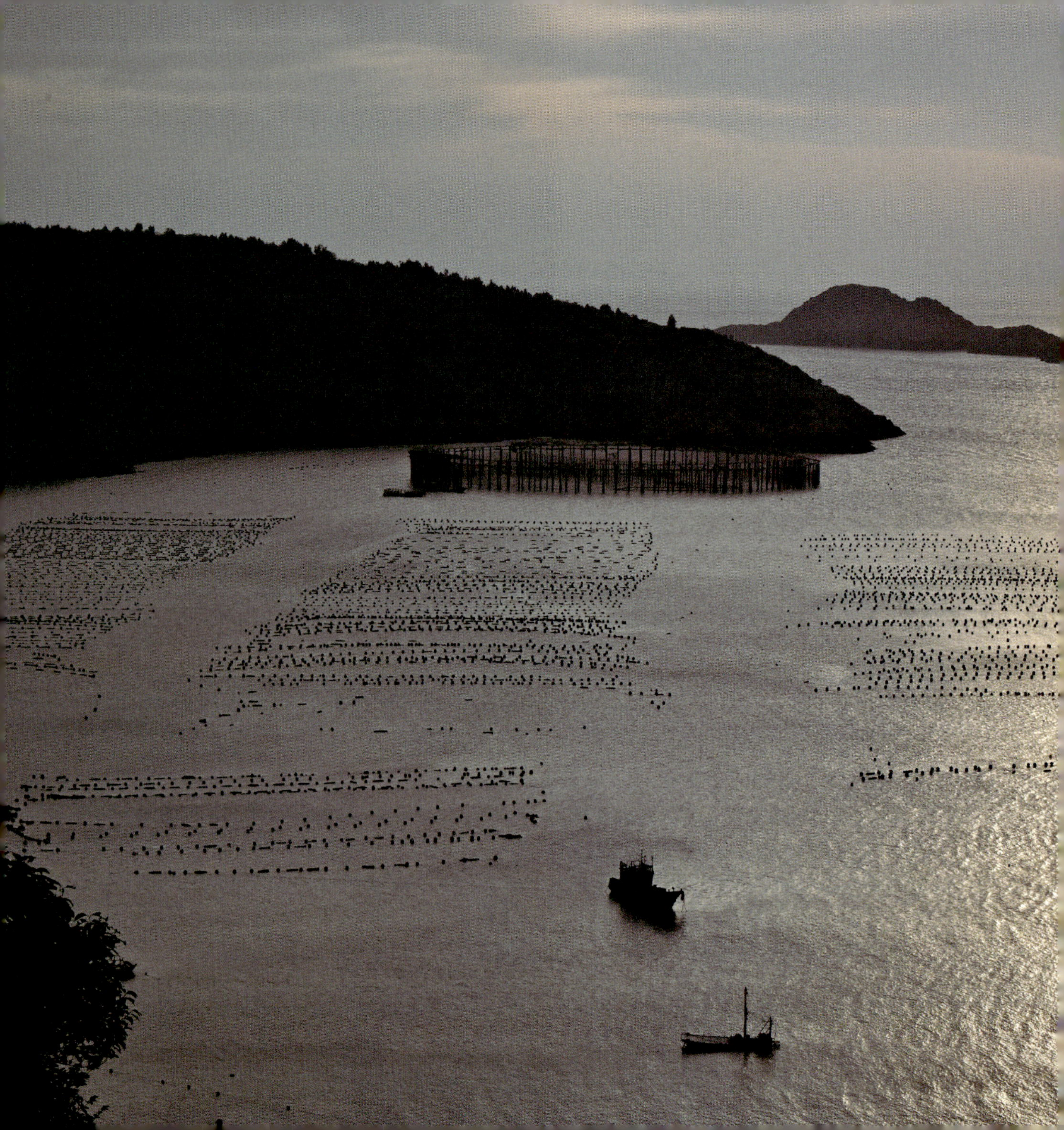

萬八千四百一十六人，而劉的記錄則是一萬七千一百三十二人。他們的差異或許來自統計方式的不同，但無論如何，這些數字的背後是成千上萬島民的命運。在我看來，這些具體數字固然重要，但我會選擇用「一萬八千」這樣一個象徵性的數字來概括這場大規模撤離。它抽象而簡潔，卻足以喚起我們對那段歷史的敬意。

一九九〇年代開始，有一些大陳島的老居民陸續回到島上，探親訪友，或到山上祭拜祖墳。還有一些台灣遊客慕名而來，想親眼看看這片承載了特殊歷史的土地。如今，島上的遊客稀少，僅夏季略為熱鬧。他們多數住在新建的民宿裡，而我們選擇了瀾庭，一座緊鄰廢棄燈塔的現代化旅舍。房間舒適，淡季每晚只需五百元。我租了一輛電動車，五十元一天，迎著海風，探索這座小島。

Da Chen coastal fish farm / 沿海漁場

Yellow fish on dish / 盤中黃魚
Da Chen harbor / 大陳內港

北灣的海面安靜而平和，是一片天然的避風港。岸邊密密麻麻排列著新建的漁場，巨大的漁網深深地浸在海水裡，養殖著價格不菲的「黃魚」。然而這名貴的黃魚曾經卻價格極其低廉。司機柳震解釋道，當年黃魚泛濫，每斤只值八分錢。即使到了一九八〇年代，集體收購價也不過一毛五分錢，私人販賣偶爾能賣到五毛，但這麼做要冒著被政府查扣的風險，一旦被抓，魚全數沒收。

而今天，黃魚的命運完全不同了。野生黃魚幾乎絕跡，價值高得驚人。二〇二二年，寧波港曾有一艘漁船滿載而歸，帶回兩千四百五十公斤黃魚，整批魚以九百五十七萬元拍出，堪稱天降橫財。現在大陳島上，即便是三兩重的小黃魚，每斤也能賣到五十到六十元；半斤的黃魚價格漲到八十到九十元，而接近一公斤的黃魚，則能賣到三百到五百元，價格隨季節上下浮動。我們運氣不錯，在碼頭趁著一艘漁船清晨歸港時，用三百八十元買下了三條黃魚，總重一點八公斤，算得上意外收穫。 如今，島上的海岸線已被密集的漁場填滿，很少再見真正出海捕撈的漁船。站在北灣邊，遠處的海平面漸漸模糊，只有漁場的浮標，隨著微浪輕輕起伏。

第二天，我搭上當地的渡船，花了十五分鐘，來到了「上大陳島」。上大陳島比下大陳島面積上要大一些，但居住人口卻相對較少。這裡曾是駐守部隊的總指揮部，因此島上隨處可見碉堡和

隧道的遺跡。在胡宗南當年的指揮基地附近，如今還保留著一座舊軍火庫，供人參觀。隱蔽的海灣邊，幾艘退役的解放軍軍艦和炮艇靜靜地停放在岸上。附近的公園裡，還陳列著解放軍使用過的坦克、運兵車、炮台，甚至還有一整排中國早期的空軍戰鬥機。展品中包括不同型號的米格戰機，從米格-15到米格-19，還有後期研發出的新型號。

然而，對我來說，最難忘的不是這些鋼鐵巨獸的身影，而是沿著上大陳島北岸懸崖，那一小時的漫步。島上近年修建了一條貼著垂直懸崖蜿蜒而行的長廊步道，遊人雖少，但走在這裡，彷彿置身於天地之間。腳下潮汐翻湧，浪花拍打著岩石，發出低沉而連綿的聲音，與頭頂的寧靜形成鮮明對比。

站在步道上，向遠處望去，海岸線隨著地勢起伏延展，空氣中彌漫著海鹽的清新氣息。這一刻，所有的歷史故事都彷彿退居幕後，只剩下大自然的永恆。兩座島嶼的自然景色不會隨時間消逝，它們將在千年後依舊矗立，而那些曾經的崢嶸歲月，最終會隨著海浪的撞擊聲，漸漸被沖刷、掩埋，化為遙遠的記憶。

離開大陳的那一天，風起雲湧，海面變得愈加狂暴。我站在碼頭，心裡隱隱擔憂，渡船是否能如約而至。好在下午兩點，渡輪劃破海霧，抵達了岸邊。我踏上船，回望這片被歲月和潮汐雕刻的孤島，正逐漸遠去。

海浪拍擊船身激起的白沫像碎裂的水晶，快艇在波濤中上下顛簸，海水甚至濺上了我們所在的上層甲板。風聲呼嘯，彷彿在挽留，又像在低語著一段不願被遺忘的故事。

我坐在艙內，感受著船身的顫動，忽然想給陳文寬機長打電話，告訴他，我終於來到了大陳島。然

而這個念頭只是一閃而過，我知道，有些話，已經不必說出口，有些故事，應該寫下來。歷經四次嘗試，我才終於踏上這片土地。每一步，都像在穿越過去的影像，每一次呼吸，都像在傾聽海浪的記憶。

船上的人告訴我，這可能是接下來幾天的最後一班渡船。風勢越來越大，我看向窗外，激烈翻湧的海浪像在提醒我，這片海域的故事遠未結束。然而，對那些遠居台灣三十六村的大陳居民來說，風浪隔絕的不僅僅是這片海面，而是他們與故土之間遙不可及的距離。

當船駛向更遼闊的大海，我再一次回望島嶼。那裡的懸崖依舊陡峭，潮聲依舊深沉。海域的潮汐可以拍碎一切，卻永遠無法抹去人們對故土的深情。而那些故事，無論多遙遠，終將如同浪花般，屢屢歸來。

Rugged Da Chen coast / 崎嶇壯觀的大陳島海岸

ABANDONED AND RESETTLED

Postscript

With age calling, energy wanes though curiosity and mental ambitions may still abound. As other faculties of the body gradually deteriorate, it may sound grim and anticlimactic, all downhill. But not quite so. Our accumulated experience and knowledge are now more mature and acute, learning to foresee and connect things that in the past may be just linear and single dimensional, but now have become multidimensional and interconnected. It allows me to make analogy in what in the past seems isolated places and incidents.

In some aspects, I am becoming more philosophical, even abstract in looking at the world and life around me. My failing eyesight and diminishing hearing tend to move me closer to arriving at such generalization. At the end, it is more elevating, allowing me to rise and become loftier in view, or descending lower in depth. Both allow me to stretch the boundaries of my physical and spiritual existence.

May my life-long partner of curiosity walk with me into new unknown territories.

後記

時光如漸老的舟，載著褪色的軀殼緩緩靠岸，而精神卻仍似少年時揚帆的模樣。那些消逝的氣力，凋零的感官，原以為是生命謝幕的前奏，其實於我而言是另一重境界的開場。

數十載沉澱的經驗與智識，讓我如今能在浮光掠影中，看見更深層的共鳴。昔年只見一事一物的表象，而今卻能在尋常中見奇崛，在無關處察關聯。往昔如線性的溪流，如今已匯成縱橫交錯的江河，每一道漣漪都和彼此微妙地呼應。

我漸漸習慣以哲人的眼觀世，以詩人的心體物。視野模糊了，反而看清更多本質；耳力衰退了，卻能聽見更深的迴響。這般境界，非關得失，而是生命給予我最珍貴的禮贈──讓思想既能翱翔九霄，又可潛遊深淵，在有限的血肉之軀裡，開拓無垠的天地。

但願這與生俱來的好奇心，這永恆的旅伴，能繼續引領我探勘未知的疆域，直至時間的盡頭。

依揚想亮 出版書目

城市輕文學

《忘記書》——————————————————劉鋆 等著
《高原台北青藏盆地：邱醫生的處方箋》——————邱仁輝 著
《4腳+2腿：Bravo與我的20條散步路線》————Gayle Wang 著
《Textures Murmuring... 娜娜的手機照片碎碎唸》————Natasha Liao 著
《行書：且行且書且成書》————————————劉鋆 著
《東說西說東西說》——————————————張永霖 著
《上帝旅行社》————————————————法拉 著
《當偶像遇上明星》————————————劉銘／李淑楨 著
《李繼開第七號文集：這樣的顏色叫做灰》——————李繼開 著
《窗內有藍天：從三合院小女孩到監獄志工》—————李淑楨 著
《比蝴蝶飛更遠—武漢效應的43種生活》——張艾嘉 雷光夏 潘源良 等著
《隧道96小時—邱醫生的明日傳奇》—————————邱仁輝 著
《一閃一閃亮晶晶：第一屆台灣獨立書店獎》
————————————————財團法人樹梅文化藝術基金會著
《大悲事務所》————————————————日青禾櫟著
《做一件一輩子想起來會笑的事：邱醫生「馬背上醫生」三十年全紀錄》
————————————————————————邱仁輝 著

任性人

《5.4的幸運》—————————————————孫采華 著
《亞洲不安之旅》————————————————飯田祐子 著
《李繼開第四號詩集：吃土豆的人》—————————李繼開 著
《一起住在這裡真好》——————————————薛慧瑩 著
《山海經：黃效文與探險學會》———————————劉鋆 著
《文化志向》——————————————————黃效文 著
《自然緣份》——————————————————黃效文 著
《男子漢 更年期 欲言又止》——————————Micro Hu 著
《文化所思》——————————————————黃效文 著
《自然所想》——————————————————黃效文 著
《畫說寶春姐的雜貨店》—————————————徐銘宏 著
《齊物逍遙 2018》————————————————黃效文 著
《Life as an explorer – First decade 1974 – 1983》———黃效文 著
《齊物逍遙 2019》————————————————黃效文 著
《齊物逍遙 2020-2021》——————————————黃效文 著
《在妳認識世界之前—先認識老爸的33個故事》————胡昭安 著
《異鄉之用》——————————————————馬尼尼為 著
《齊物逍遙 2022》————————————————黃效文 著
《齊物逍遙 2023》————————————————黃效文 著
《齊物逍遙 2024 I》———————————————黃效文 著
《齊物逍遙 2024 II》———————————————黃效文 著

津津有味

《鰻魚為王》———————————————劉鋆 著 陳沛珛 繪者

國家圖書館出版品預行編目 (CIP) 資料

齊物逍遙 . 2025 = Enlightened sojourn/ 黃效文著 . -- 初版 . -- 新北市 : 依揚想亮人文事業有限公司, 2025.09
面 ; 公分
中英對照
ISBN 978-626-96174-9-4 (精裝)
1.CST: 遊記 2.CST: 世界地理
719　　　　　　　　　　　　　　　　　114010161

齊物逍遙 2025

作者・黃效文 | 攝影・黃效文 | 發行人・劉鋆 | 美術編輯・Rene、鍾京燕 | 責任編輯・廖又蓉 | 翻譯・呂怡達 | 法律顧問・達文西個資暨高科技法律事務所 | 出版社・依揚想亮人文事業有限公司 | 經銷商・聯合發行股份有限公司 | 地址・新北市新店區寶橋路 235 巷 6 弄 6 號 2 樓 | 電話・02 2917 8022 | 印刷・禹利電子分色有限公司 | 初版一刷・2025 年 9 月 (精裝) | 定價 1500 元 | ISBN・978-626-96174-9-4 | 版權所有　翻印必究 | Print in Taiwan